Coleridge's Verse

COLERIDGE'S VERSE

A Selection

edited by

William Empson and David Pirie

SCHOCKEN BOOKS · NEW YORK

Published in U.S.A. in 1973
by Schocken Books Inc.
200 Madison Avenue, New York, N.Y. 10016

Introduction copyright © 1972 by William Empson
Textual notes copyright © 1972 by David Pirie

Library of Congress Catalog Card No. 72–88261

Printed in Great Britain

Acknowledgements

The substance of my Introduction here, together with some material about Donne making changes in his love-poems (published in *Just So Much Honour*, ed. J. P. Fiore, Pennsylvania State University Press), constituted the Waynflete Lectures for 1972, sponsored by Magdalen College Oxford.

I forgot to say that *Ellenore* and *Alonzo the Brave*, two absurd poems that Coleridge probably hoped to emulate when he started *The Ancient Mariner*, are available in *The Literary Ballad*, edited by Anne Henry Ehrenpreis (Arnold, 1966).

W.E.

I should like to acknowledge the kindness of The Trustees of the Wordsworth Library at Dove Cottage, Grasmere, for allowing me to consult manuscript material.

D.P.

Contents

[9]

Illustrations

Introduction

I

Coleridge wrote only a few very good poems; not surprisingly, considering how hard the conditions are that his first decisive successes, and his resulting theory, made him need to fulfil. A poem had to be spontaneous, interesting, and profound; an unexpected general truth, of universal concern, had to be illustrated by a direct and urgent experience of the author. This would do for a conversation poem; in a romantic poem, the process should also make the reader feel at home with a remote superstition through his intimate experience of a familiar 'fact of mind'. It is a daunting formula, and perhaps a life of less grinding unhappiness would have produced fewer triumphs, rather than more. He did sometimes, however, especially when young, use poetry just for earnest declamation, and to our current taste the results are usually bad. In this edition, when selections only are given from a poem (headed '*From* so-and-so'), that is not so much to save space as because the poem is judged to lack unity, and the excerpts are often chosen to illustrate a habitual thought of the poet, or the way he was getting ready to write *The Ancient Mariner*; but I think Mr. Pirie has succeeded in combining these requirements with the more important rule of only printing good poetry.

Coleridge from his youth was a leader of the Romantics, which might involve being asked to be a leader in anything (I think Sir Herbert Read's *True Voice of Feeling* gives the most illuminating account of the movement). Maybe because of this duty, or just because he was accustomed to immense success as a talker at parties, where he could gauge the reaction of the audience, or (later) because reviewers had attacked him unjustly, Coleridge was very uneasy about print, and kept altering the text to meet the real or supposed demands of his public. This makes him hard to edit, to an interesting degree. Of course a grand text, for example the Oxford Collected Edition (1912, ed. E. H. Coleridge), sets out to give all the variants; and indeed nearly everything we print here can be found in that, though you would need to look for some of it pertinaciously. But the editor of a selected text, if he is not to shirk his work, needs to decide *why* Coleridge made each of the changes, and whether his purpose was a merely transitory one; if it was, and if the effect of the change is even slightly inferior, the editor should print the original text. Such a decision about motive is often hard to take, so that the editor had better give his reasons, but it certainly can be taken sometimes – there is no metaphysical reason, as is wrongly supposed by W. K. Wimsatt in *The Intentional Fallacy* (1946; now in *The Verbal Icon*), for treating the intentions of an author as inherently unknowable. If you accept his theory you have blinded yourself, so presumably you have to print the last text approved by the author; but editors do not always treat themselves so harshly – we are allowed the 1805 text of *The Prelude*, and one or two lyrics by Blake which he had spoiled or crossed out. For that matter, Mr. C. R. Woodring reports (*Politics in the Poetry of Coleridge*, 1961) that under the dangerous but constitutionally limited police terror of Pitt it was an effective legal protection, as well as a familiar joke, to print in the errata: 'For *murder* read *defence of the king*' and suchlike; I gather that editors have not treated falling into this trap as their sworn duty, but have confessed that they understood the author's intention. This is not to say that an editor should be free to print what he considers the *best* version; he owes a loyalty to the author, or rather, to the person the author was when he wrote the poem. If the author made changes afterwards under duress, to avoid persecution maybe, or to avoid hurting the feelings of somebody now dead, the original

[*14*]

text should plainly be restored; but sometimes, with the passage of years, the author has fallen out of sympathy with this work, or has rejected the beliefs which it expresses, so that by his changes he is in effect trying to write a different poem. It could be laid down, to avoid using the word 'intention', that the editor should print the poem as it was at the fullest and most characteristic stage of its development; but he is unlikely to pick this out if he does not think about the author. A rather similar impasse occurs in Dynamics – in fact, I expect this case is the model which the theorists are emulating. The 'physical forces' are eliminated from the equations by being absorbed into the Equals sign, on the basic assumption that cause equals effect; and maybe they are only a delusion derived from feelings in our muscles; but nobody could learn Dynamics without thinking about forces. Authors themselves hardly ever regard their intentions as unknowable, but they sometimes realize they should take care, as when Max Beerbohm wrote, on revising *Zuleika Dobson*: 'I tried to remember how angry I would have been when I wrote it, if an elderly pedant had made corrections' – the tone of the book needed to be just right, and even small changes might spoil it. (Of course revision might produce a new poem, and both poems might be worth selecting; but this is rare, even in Yeats; perhaps because revision is inherently a half-hearted way to set about a new poem.) An editor then should be prepared to rescue the poem from the later thoughts of the poet; and hence, even in accepting the standard text, he needs to have decided that no such case has arisen. I would not mind agreeing, as a verbal formula, that the intention of an author can always only be guessed at, so long as it is also agreed that the guess, after collating the relevant information, should always be made. Of course a later age, on fuller information, may ascribe a different intention to him.

II

The *Sonnet* to Schiller assumes, as part of its panache, that the reader has accepted the Romantic position already; by now, that position may need a word of defence. Not *any* extravagance of emotion is being praised but the kind which purges and renews, because it prepares you to resist tyranny; the political claim often does not get attention but is always in the air. And *The Robbers* was denied a licence for performance in London till 1799, supposedly because it denounced the *ancien régime* and the tyranny of the Inquisition. The *goblins* stand for the covential literary devices of Gothic horror; Coleridge seems always to have assumed that they are allowable, though it is better to be so exalted as not to need them.

The *Young Ass* appeared in a newspaper the year it was written (1794), but with cuts and variants, thus giving a mild opportunity for practice in gauging the author's intention. He cut *scoundrel monarch* because it might get him arrested and the paper would not print it; but one cannot quite say that he cut *mice with pussy's whiskers sport in love* because it might get him laughed at. With or without such cuts, he would be laughed at; Gilray indeed was soon cartooning him as the ass of the English Jacobins (though not till 1799, just after he stopped being a Jacobin), and Byron, obvious as ever, followed this up with the horse-laugh:

He brays, the Laureate of the long-eared kind.

In effect, Coleridge was inviting such a reaction. But pussy's whiskers were another matter; the passage amounted to a joke against a political scheme to which he was still intensely attached. He would be accustomed to hearing that Pantisocracy was absurd because it trusted men not to behave like brutes, and would enjoy making the answer that, as the alternative procedure was already known to be fatal, one had better show a bit of pluck. (Pantisocracy differed from Democracy, I judge from the derivation, in believing that even an aristocrat might be trusted, after conversion and repentance.) Thus he would feel that, among friends, to recognize the absurdity of the scheme only praised its highmindedness and intellectual rigour; but to print such a joke might encourage the coarse public to jeer. This frame of mind is rather frequent among authors, and regularly misunderstood by commentators; but Coleridge, who started life with a great taste for innocent fun, was especially liable to get tripped up and put to shame by it. Hence, when he made this alteration, he would want the original text to be put back as soon as it could do no harm. On the other hand, a version in a letter to Southey mentions 'Banti', a singer then famous in England, which at the time would assure the reader that the King of England was the scoundrel in view; but for the modern reader it would only be an obstacle.

The Eolian Harp (1795), so a trusting reader might now deduce, will be another joke against something that Coleridge revered, and an even more searching one; it will say: 'An artist who yields himself ungrudgingly to the immediate influences of Nature, or the fashions of his society, must be expected to emit random noises like this horrid toy.' Fortunately the letters and notebooks of Coleridge give us a great deal of background information, and they show him to have gone on admiring this harp long after he had lost the democratic and humane convictions which he had associated with it. The poem is the first of his great conversation pieces, and was written (August 1795) before he came under the influence of Wordsworth. Here Coleridge is in the garden with his bride; for his *Dejection* he is indoors, but no less exposed to the screaming of the machine on the roof, which intensifies his despair. A brief note written long afterwards finds a new ground for praising it (he does not seem to have been keen on music otherwise):

> Eolian harp motive for opening the sash, and at once lets in music and sweet air; purifies and delights . . . (2937)

It is a comfort to know that they could open their tiny windows.

Coleridge twice added further heretical or profound thoughts for his bride to have reproved, in 1803 and 1817; they may be regarded as pantheist, but are vague. More interest attaches to the lines he suppressed in 1803; they say (after 'Such a soft floating witchery of sound'):

As twilight Elfins make, when they at eve
Voyage on gentle gales from Fairy-Land,
Where Melodies round honey-dropping flowers,
Footless and wild, like birds of Paradise,
Nor pause, nor perch, hovering on untam'd wing!

By 1803 Coleridge had become keen to dissociate himself from this tenet. By 1817 he could put the lines back, and print *The Destiny of Nations* too, because he felt sure no one would suspect him of really believing in it. However, lines 32–6 are the ones which must be supposed to call out the reproof in l. 37; they appear at every reprinting, and are very subtly phrased. To say that the World-spirit may induce thought in 'all of *animated* nature' may be startling or obvious, according to its interpretation. Does it exclude the Fairy Peaseblossom, and how is an animal expected to show that the spirit has induced it to think? This poem is very much more beautiful than the Jackass one, but it risks mockery with the same intransigence. However, it has grand party manners, and few readers would have realized that anything challenging had been said, had not the piety of the bride given the alarm.

Religious Musings and *The Destiny of Nations* are hard for us to take seriously, but Charles Lamb when they were new thought the *Musings* the greatest religious poetry since Milton, and many readers at the time would feel them to grapple with a central problem. The beliefs they express ought to interest a reader of *The Ancient Mariner*, because what they are saying (with merely polite expressions of uncertainty) is that spirits like those in *The Ancient Mariner* really exist, so that all the incidents of that poem might really happen. In the same way, *A Vision* shows Yeats to have believed that all the incidents in his two Byzantium poems might really happen (so that to explain them away as Symbolism is misleading). Coleridge had arrived at this position because he needed to believe in a God who was not wicked. As a schoolboy he had readily combined wonder and admiration at the writings of mystics with becoming convinced by Voltaire that the God of the Churches was morally indefensible. It is hard to believe that there was any change in his convictions when he met Southey in June 1794, and was 'converted'. He was a Unitarian and a radical already, but had thought nothing could be done about it; Southey could obviously do something, and to co-operate with him was a thrilling duty. Almost at once, however, Southey found he could step into a family living if he entered the Church, and could then 'bore from within'. Coleridge was deciding to abandon all attempts to get a B.A., his passport into the learned professions, because even that would involve signing the Thirty-Nine Articles. Already in July he is writing:

> For God's sake, Southey! enter not into the church. . . . The following is a Fact – A friend of Hucks' after long struggle between Principle and *Interest* (as it is improperly called) accepted a place under Government – he took the Oaths – shuddered – went home and threw himself in an Agony out of a two pair of stairs!

He sounds rather like Sam Weller here, but he is showing better judgement than his worldly friend. It was true to say, in the eventual letter breaking off their relations (in November 1795 – too late) 'you were diverted from being a Priest, only by the Weight of infamy which you perceived coming towards you, like a Rush of Waters!' (Surely, after what Southey had printed already, he could not have got away with it.) This weight of earnestness for true religion in the young Coleridge is a thing we are liable to neglect.

As he was scrupulous not to encourage the prevalent atheism, he did not make his objections to Anglicanism clear; except that he was anxious, as he wrote to Estlin, to protect

[*19*]

'the great article of all religion, the moral attributes of God' (July 1802). The Lisbon earthquake of 1755 was still reverberating in the public mind. Preachers had told the survivors that God had punished them for their sins by killing the people they loved, and Voltaire denounced the preachers so resoundingly, making so plain that they had an evil conception of God, that the clergy of all sects ever since have been a bit wary of this method of suasion. Even so, if God was the direct cause of natural disasters, it seemed hard to call him good, even after he had been cleared of malice; and one might feel that the God of Newton was worse – fulfilling mathematical laws with infinitely pedantic exactitude, indifferent to their effects on mankind. The recent first-fruits of chemistry and biology had encouraged a hope of release from Newton, because in these studies things seem to have their own local *ad hoc* laws – they are self-operating or even self-correcting, rather than obedient to a universal law. In a way, Erasmus Darwin already recognized this in his stiffly playful works of popular science, using heroic couplets and the 'machinery' of the *Rape of the Lock*; so that the young Coleridge was not being unreasonable, only naive, if he assumed that Darwin believed what he was always saying. He had called Darwin 'the first literary character in Europe', and was frankly shocked, on meeting him (Letter 99, January 1796), to find that he had no religious beliefs at all. Coleridge of course did not dare complain at his not believing in his sylphs and gnomes. At what date he discovered that these spirits of earth, air, fire and water were derived from Paracelsus, whose speculations had led to real medical progress, is hard to get clear, but he would anyway know that there was a non-literary support for them. The creatures, as everyone had felt (consider *The Midsummer Night's Dream*) would often act capriciously and sometimes mischievously, but one could find ways to deal with them, and at least they provided a sort of shrubbery between ourselves and God, who was thus no longer always to blame; Coleridge even argued in *The Destiny of Nations*, though never again, that their rough be-

[20]

haviour had helped to force men into progress from savagery.

It has only recently been understood that Coleridge was merely following a current intellectual trend. *The Active Universe* by H. W. Piper (1963) gives a valuable documentation of the background, as known to both Wordsworth and Coleridge, saying for example:

> The belief that inanimate objects were in a literal sense alive came nearest to establishing itself as scientific orthodoxy during the years of Wordsworth's most active poetic life (p. 115).

The doctrine was not merely Pantheism, the immanence of God in Nature, which had been familiar to Pope; but Animism, the condensation of the universal spirit into local centres of experience – for example, the Spirit of the Moor in Emily Brontë. Modern readers are familiar with such talk in poetry but regard it as admittedly nonsense ('imagery') or at best a device for hinting at some truth which it leaves obscure ('symbolism'). Such was not the point of view of Byron, when he wrote to his publisher promising there would be no metaphysics in Canto 4, and explaining that Shelley had been dosing him with Wordsworth when he wrote Canto 3. Byron thinks of the belief (whether he would call it scientific or religious) as definite and specific, a thing that rode him for a time, but now he has bucked it off.

Coleridge regarded it as ancient wisdom; he maintained that the Renaissance neoplatonists actually had transmitted the esoteric doctrine of Plato, as they claimed to have done, and that modern science urgently needed to recover it. (He seems to have gone on believing in the secret transmission after he had abandoned all the rest.) Wordsworth, as Mr. Piper shows, while holding the same doctrine about spirits in Nature, considered it new and progressive; he had found it standard among the English fellow-travellers in revolutionary Paris, though apparently not among the French political leaders. Thus the reason why Wordsworth and Coleridge were so surprised and delighted by one another when they first made contact (sending off at once to Bristol for the works of Erasmus Darwin), was that they had arrived at the same beliefs from such different directions.

In *The Destiny of Nations* the belief is discussed repeatedly at length, and all these fairy passages had already appeared in Book II of Southey's epic *Joan of Arc* (1796; not in later editions). They are believed to date from the first half of 1795. Coleridge expanded this material from time to time, after quarrelling with Southey, so as to make a separate poem about Joan's visions of liberty; but in early 1797 Lamb advised him to stop, and the additions were not published till *Sybilline Leaves* came out in 1817. *Religious Musings* was printed in 1796, and addresses the spirits in the last paragraph; the poem was much worked over, but the Oxford edition's apparatus shows hardly any changes in this paragraph. It is a handsome set piece, probably dashed off in the first flush of inspiration, during the second half of 1795. The interest of the scholarly dating, which I merely report, is that it shows him never to have written verse which made a frank expression of belief in spirits after his meeting with Eramus Darwin, in January 1796. Of course, he felt certain Darwin was wrong (the man was actually an atheist) but his report suggests that Darwin laughed at him in a wounding manner; and he would become aware that his public might do the same.

Religious Musings had a second printing in 1797, and Coleridge added a snooty footnote to the first line of its last paragraph; he was becoming uneasy about the matter:

This paragraph is intelligible to those who, like the Author, believe and feel the sublime system of Berkley; and the doctrine of the final happiness of all men.

The Author himself had only just taken possession of Berkeley (that perhaps is why he spells him wrong), so this footnote could imply that he had not understood the paragraph himself when he wrote it. In later printings the footnote got attached to other lines, and ended up at the first line of the preceding paragraph, a brief magnificent bit of rhetoric about the vision of God. But of course it belongs to the final paragraph, where Coleridge tells the spirits that perhaps he will join them, though not immediately after his human death, for a later stage in his immortal career; this belief had been held more firmly by the Laplander in *The Destiny of Nations*, who expected to join the dance of spirits in the Aurora Borealis. So perhaps the corpses in *The Ancient Mariner* actually were occupied by ghosts, but ghosts of mature vintage, not of the recently dead crew. Lamb in his critical letters, I should explain, was always firmly in favour of these spirits, regarded as poetry and 'fancy'; what he objected to was making Joan a theoretical democrat, keen on the American Revolution, and an innkeeper's daughter.

This Lime-Tree Bower (written June 1797) calls the land-scape 'a living thing That acts upon the mind', but Coleridge cut that out from editions after 1817, when he had hardened into orthodoxy even further, so that it only appears in the notes of the Oxford text. He retained the next few lines, but I think only because he could rely on the reader not to guess what he had meant when they were written:

> Struck with joy's deepest calm, and gazing round
> On the wide view may gaze till all doth seem
> Less gross than bodily; a living thing
> That acts upon the mind, and with such hues
> As clothe th' Almighty Spirit, when he makes
> Spirits perceive his presence.

When he wrote it, he meant that the spirits of Nature see God fairly often, but only in the passive way that we men see spirits – that is, when they choose to become visible. When Coleridge removed the *living thing* clause (1828) he also altered *clothe* to 'veil', presumably meaning that God does not exhibit himself through Nature at all (but then, why reprint the poem?) We are now expected to make the word *spirits* mean 'men', or rather the poet himself, in the situation described; but this would be a strained idiom for anybody, and surely impossible for the young Coleridge, with his glittering eyes almost catching spirits in every corner of the wide landscape.

Just for once, I can call on a bit of contemporary critical evidence here, though it is not decisive. Lamb in a letter to Coleridge about the poems (14th August 1800), while grumbling a bit, says he would have praised this poem –

> if you had not run into that unintelligible abstraction-fit about the manner of the Deity's making spirits perceive his presence.

If Lamb had taken the word *spirits* here to mean men, he would not have called the idea abstract, because he would have called it blasphemous (he too was a Unitarian). But Coleridge did, I need to admit, inherit an unctuous trick of calling men spirits. The sister of Lamb while insane killed their mother, and Lamb wrote informing his old school-friend and asking for 'a religious letter' (17th September '96). Coleridge responded eagerly, and to good effect, because by 24th October the despondent Lamb had become vigorously indignant. It was blasphemous to tell him he was being made a partaker of the divine Nature, he said, even though it did happen to be in the Bible (II. Peter. I. iv. 'Late and pseudo-petrine, and this phrase sticks out like a boulder left by a glacier' an authority writes to me, so Lamb showed judgement here; but so did Coleridge, as he wanted to recommend the Hermetic ecstasies and took advantage of their cropping up in an Epistle). Also Coleridge had encouraged Lamb to publish something; he is accused of saying:

> It is by the Press that God hath given finite spirits, both evil and good, a portion as it were of His Omnipresence.

'I suppose you mean *simply* bad and good men', answered the exasperated sufferer; and here, you see, he treats it as merely a parsonical idiom; but still, he understands it very well.

Coleridge in writing this absurd sentence, we may be sure, only thought of human white middleclass English-writing males; but he did not aim at excluding any qualified creature, and really would have been glad to print in *The Watchman* a letter dictated by Ariel or Prometheus, let alone a Negress on a plantation. And he knew from his Bible, as well as feeling himself, that for a living man to see God is almost impossibly dangerous. When he wrote the line in the poem, I conclude, he only thought of God as appearing to nature-spirits.

Critics agree that this poem is influenced by a poem of Wordsworth, *Lines left on a Seat in a Yew-tree*, especially from the odd repetition 'gaze till you gaze', which seems to become a formula for a process of hypnotizing oneself. Anybody can get dizzy by gazing at a flat but choppy sea in bright sunlight, because the eye connects the random flashes further and further apart; and the poem of Coleridge seems to recognize this familiar case, though he claims the same result from open country. The man described in Wordsworth's poem died on this seat, in despair from his failure among men and yet, after the double-gaze procedure, in ecstacy from the beauty of the view (it was over a lake):

> Nor, that time,
> Would he forget those beings, to whose minds,
> Warm from the labours of benevolence,
> The world, and man himself, appeared a scene
> Of kindred loveliness; then he would sigh
> With mournful joy, to think that others felt
> What he must never feel. . . .

Maybe Wordsworth was thinking of a few middle-aged women he had known, but Coleridge would feel sure that no human creatures could be in view. The dying man is happy to wonder at the spirits of Nature, and it seems to him particularly wonderful that they feel about us the way he does about them – even Manchester, presumably, they would gloat over with admiration, just as he does over this absolute solitude which is their home. Coleridge would be sure, I think, to read the passage in this interesting way, and Wordsworth either intended it so or had done earlier (the poem was begun early and often rewritten). By the time they were in close contact, they had already become prone to express the belief in evasive language.

The Foster-mother's Tale relies on the familiar sentiments about the Noble Savage, while giving no assurance about them. Some recent literary historians have treated this line of thought as ignorant self-indulgence, but it is already present in the basic travel records of the maritime expansion, which Coleridge had been reading in bulk. Quite a number of white malcontents or misfits, feeling themselves wronged, actually did go and live among the wronged natives, and some of them brought up children there. The fragment does at least show that Coleridge was accustomed to think of real crimes, against men rather than albatrosses, as part of the maritime expansion and the subsequent slave trade.

The parody *Sonnet* is one of three, all published anonymously in the *Monthly Magazine* for November 1797, when the writing of the *Mariner* had just begun. All of them now seem jokes by Coleridge against his own early poems, though only the one we print was so acknowledged. The other two caused an exhausting amount of fuss and bad temper among Coleridge's disagreeable friends; and even Lamb became involved, because (as he explained afterwards) he believed lies told him by Charles Lloyd. He sent Coleridge a terrible letter of theological problems to discuss in Germany, where he was going just then, starting with 'Whether God loves a lying Angel better than a true Man?' Coleridge as soon as he returned recovered the friendship of Lamb and Southey with a firmness and competence that he would never show in any other aspect of his life. It is important I think to realize how much frank warning he had from his dearest friends against the religiosity into which he eventually fell. Also, this trivial quarrel probably had important effects, even if it did not really prevent Cole-

ridge from finishing *Christabel*. Surely, when Lamb wrote
Southey grumbling at his review of *The Ancient Mariner*, say
he ought to have picked on the good bits, and yet agreeing
that he had picked on a 'meaningless miracle' – surely they
ought to have asked their friend what the meaning was? I
expect they would have done, but for this depressing affair. And
yet Coleridge when he wrote his jokes had not seen himself as
at all aggressive; merely as a mouse playing in love with pussy's
whiskers.

III

The chief difficulty in arriving at the right text for *The Ancient
Mariner*, a splendid poem which was much mangled by its
author for reasons of conscience, is that though he made
harmful changes where he had fallen out of sympathy with its
basic ideas he kept on improving it in detail, even to the first
posthumous edition (1834). One needs therefore to form an
eclectic text, always considering the motives of the author in
his successive changes, and only rejecting those which conflict
with the basic impulse and conception of the poem. I cannot
find that any critic saw what this was, at the climax anyhow,
before my co-editor Mr. Pirie, who deserves great credit for
his work on the Hand-Of-Glory verses. Starting from there, I
recover from the variants a consistent story, and this at least
restores the dramatic point, a traditional thing for a ballad to
have.

The poem regards guilt as a mystery, but does not ask 'What
is the Origin of Evil?'; perhaps rather 'Granting that there are
real grounds for feeling guilty, why are our actual feelings of
guilt so bemused and so harmful?' Coleridge when he wrote
the poem already recognized he was liable to attacks of un-
reasonable fear and shame (he seems clear about this in the
retrospective Note 2398) – though perhaps not that such
feelings regularly made him behave worse. What interested
him was that most people had such feelings, not that his own
were peculiar. The poem is magnificently externalized or

[27]

unselfconscious, and this of course is how it wins the children who should be most accessible to its moral. It is about adventure and discovery; it celebrates and epitomizes the maritime expansion of the Western Europeans. This had been the first effect of our almost sudden conquest of the sciences, and also it was the most important historical event for a long time. Coleridge was quite ready to take a patriotic pride in such heroes, and I am not sure whether he realized that the poem contains no indication that they sailed from England. For that matter, the word *kirk* does not mean that they were Scots (as a student in Bristol once anxiously waylaid me to ask) but that Coleridge was imitating the Border Ballads. The *wolf* near the home port might almost survive so late in England but is more likely to be on the Continent; and the *biscuit-worms* are taken from the actual account of the voyage of Magellan, when he and his crew made the first entry from the South Atlantic into the Pacific, and nearly starved to death there. Coleridge is not trying to rob Magellan of his priority, but somehow to generalize from it. No doubt he was proud to be a post-Renaissance Western European, after his very extensive reading in the ships' captains' reports.

Yet all such triumphant advances entail great dangers and much wrong. They might even go beyond what God had intended; Coleridge would realize that the torments of his Mariner carry an echo of the inquiring Faustus and the original eaters of the Tree of Knowledge. But he would consider these standard themes unimportant compared to the real grounds for guilt, lurking close at home. From the sixteenth century, English propaganda against the Spaniards had accused them of ill-treating the American Indians, so that our home public had never really been deceived about colonialism; but a decisive indignation against the Slave Trade (an incidental consequence of the expansion) had recently been building up in Bristol. Coleridge had incurred some personal danger by denouncing it, in lectures and journalism, the year before writing the poem, so he could hardly have prevented his first readers from finding

[28]

some hint of it hidden away there. Indeed, a ballad by Southey on 'The Sailor who had served in the Slave Trade', and was found bemoaning his guilt in a cowshed outside Bristol, makes quite an impressive parallel to the *Mariner*, though Southey disliked the poem and was merely versifying a newspaper report.

Horror of the Slave Trade does I think echo into the *Mariner* at one point, early on, and this helps to keep the poem from mere whimsicality; however, it cannot be part of the story – the explorers cannot foresee the remote consequences of their struggle. Life-in-Death, among other things, is the bad girl sailors meet in port, so naturally the Mariner can recognize her. What is mysterious, as Mr. Derek Roper pointed out in his edition of the 1805 *Lyrical Ballads*, is that, before the lady gets close enough, he recognizes the *ship*: 'Alas (thought I, and my heart beat loud). . . . Are those *her* sails? . . .' He is having a premonition of the Slavers, which would feel out of place if it came later, but here, at the first appearance of any magical object in the poem, it helps to throw the reader into the right atmosphere. Wordsworth said forty years later that Cruikshank, an estate agent in the village, had told the poets a dream of 'a skeleton ship, with figures in it'; but Wordsworth had become rather fond of explaining, when some detail in a poem seemed a bit romantic, that one of the neighbours had thought of it in a dream. The first readers of the poem would be accustomed to seeing 'a naked hulk', the great beams of a wooden ship, bent by steaming them, and fixed into place like ribs, but not covered with planks; derelict ships would be common objects, along the coast near Bristol (I saw barges like that as a child myself, on the Humber). But also, Coleridge had printed in his periodical *The Watchman* during the previous year (March 1796), in a denunciation of the Slave Trade, 'Would you choose the hot iron' (and so forth)

crammed into the hold of a ship with so many fellow-victims, that the heat and stench arising from your diseased bodies rot the very planks?

[29]

This idea that the planks rot off is not treated as new; the rhetoric works up to it confidently as the final telling detail. Everybody in Bristol knew that you could smell a Slaver five (or ten) miles to windward, and that the planks only lasted for five (or ten) voyages. However, while mulling over the first edition Coleridge felt that this point might not be obvious enough to everyone, so he wrote in the margin another verse, saying that the hulk was 'plankless' (l. 195). The modern reader needs this more than the contemporary ones did, being less accustomed to naked hulks, and the word 'merrily' is also a help – the gods of luck are not hypocrites, who blame their victims; 'they laugh and are glad and are terrible.' This verse must have been added early, before he went to Germany, because it is quite unlike the worried face-saving after the return. He thus had no opportunity to print the verse, and we have no reason to presume he would have rejected it if things had gone better.

If Coleridge wanted the poem to symbolize the maritime expansion, and it seems plain that the idea entered his mind fairly early in the process of composition, to give it a mystery about guilt would be an inherent part of the programme. The reports which he had read in such quantity often describe mal-treatment of natives, almost always without sense of guilt (but the English, coming later, sometimes boast that the natives where they beached gave them food and water because they both hated the cruel Spaniards). At this stage of his life, Coleridge was fond of saying that he judged a religion by its consequences, so he would often reflect as he read 'What *use* was their religion if it did not tell them that this was wrong?' When, he might ask, will they utter the anguished cry which is basic to the story of the Mariner, 'I did not know it was wrong when I did it'? In such a poem, too, their readiness to invent superstitions ought to be prominent, if only in justice to their courage; they pressed forward against terrors even greater than the real ones. They could not have done this without an appetite for marvels, also evident in the records, and here I think we reach the im-

portant sentiment 'Delight in Nature when terrible gives
strength to control her'. Most of the poem, indeed, coul[
derived from the one intention of celebrating the expans
though its parts had seemed to fall into place by successive bits
of luck, so that Coleridge may well have accepted the skeleton
ship before he saw how it 'fitted in'. And yet the crew of the
poem are quite unsmirched by this weighty background; they
never reach any natives, and seem never to have had any ob-
jective, just as they have no captain. Innocence could hardly be
carried further.

Many readers now, I have been sorry to find, feel that the
poem reeks of false sentiment and cranky self-righteousness
and a deceitful pretence of infantilism; it really does need
rescuing if possible. One obstacle is that practically all modern
critics, following the lead of the later Coleridge himself, pretend
that the Mariner commits a crime; even quite sensible ones
write down that shooting the Albatross was 'worse than a
murder ... the violation of a great sanctity' and things like
that. (It follows that the crew all deserved to be killed because
they at one stage approved of the crime – Gloss to l. 105.) A
student at Sheffield wrote in an essay for me that she would
have hanged the Mariner from the yard-arm with her own
hands; and she was not a vegetarian, I found, any more than
Coleridge was; she did not want to kill the men who killed
animals for her own pleasure. It seemed to me that she had been
given an official training in hypocrisy at her school. The critics,
as I understand, connive at this pretence because they assume
Coleridge was writing a Christian allegory of redemption
through suffering, and feel sure that any nonsense is permissible
in so good a cause. The idea does not get expressed clearly, but
I suppose their lurking awareness that the Mariner is innocent
makes him a yet closer parallel to Jesus Christ. He himself
readily provides what is called 'positive evidence in the text'
for such ideas, as in saying 'Instead of the cross, the Albatross
About my neck was hung' – he tries to apply the theology he
has been taught to his baffling and heart-freezing experiences.

But the author himself, when he wrote the poem, could not possibly have agreed with the hero; he considered the Redemption the main point where the Christian God became morally intolerable, and was prepared to make real sacrifices rather than give any countenance to a doctrine so plainly evil.

Indeed, he did not believe in guilt at all; or maybe he had recently started to, but he had not issued any warning. In a letter to Thelwall of 13th May '96, while scolding away at his friend's theoretical views, and saying that no man who acted on such views could be trusted, he throws in: '*Guilt* is out of the question – I am a Necessarian, and of course deny the possibility of it.' Lamb wrote to him on 10th January '97, confident that this point of doctrine was unchanged:

> Are you yet a Berkeleyan? Make me one. I rejoice in being, speculatively, a Necessarian. Would to God, I were habitually a practical one.

This is tender and noble, and intentionally so; but is it also intentionally funny? To be able to recognize oneself as incapable of moral decision is an odd thing to pray for. Lamb would probably be aware of the paradox, but anyway he knew the solution of it; the doctrine told you not to be censorious about other people – rather hard, of course, if you were always denouncing tyrants.

I have put into an Appendix an attempt to consider what Coleridge really believed in later life, and am concerned here with his opinions when first writing the poem. In 1789, the year after completing it, a Unitarian congregation offered to make him their salaried Minister, but he said they should not commit themselves till they had heard his sermon on why he could not administer the Lord's Supper. This tactful description had failed to remove from the ceremony all suggestion of sacrifice; and though, as a Unitarian, Coleridge need not profess that Jesus was God, he refused to worship a God who could be satisfied by the crucifixion of any innocent person, God or man. Just then a letter came from the Wedgwood brothers, offering him a pension, and our one chance of a clear statement by Coleridge of his youthful heresy disappeared. We only know the story because Hazlitt was there, and reports what Coleridge said on receiving the letter; he is not much of a witness, but he would not invent anything so creditable to Coleridge. Anyhow Coleridge had written the year before to Estlin (a Unitarian Minister then aged about fifty, his chief religious adviser and confidant) that if he took the sacrament himself, believing as he did, he would be 'eating and drinking condemnation'. I find it curious that my brother critics feel they can brush all this evidence breezily aside. From Coleridge's point of view, he had already renounced for his convictions a wealthy career in the Anglican Church (you may think this a delusion, but he said it for the rest of his life), so of course he would not now become a Moloch Priest, as he called it, celebrating a human sacrifice, and get a mere pittance in return; the proposal was absurd. And yet, consider how furious Sara would have been, with the second child on the way, after he had tossed aside his only chance of a salary.

Luckily we have a window through which to peer at his thoughts on guilt at this time: the synopsis for *The Wanderings of Cain*. Only a few years before he died, he printed a surviving chapter from this prose poem, with a chatty introduction, explaining that it had been planned as a collaboration with Wordsworth, but the theme did not suit Wordsworth, so 'the *Ancient Mariner* was written instead'.* Surely, one feels, the very inventor of murder would be treated as guilty, and now we learn that the Mariner was merely an alternative for him;

---

* The Oxford text (1912) prints the fragment from *Cain* as a year later than *The Ancient Mariner*, by a mistaken deduction from its use of Bartram's *Travels*. The great edition of the *Notebooks*, under 'General Note on entries 218–222' (1957), decides that he probably wrote it shortly before the *Mariner*, as he said he did. This same footnote in the Oxford text, giving the synopsis, refers us to an article in the *Athenæum* for 1894; but all you gain from looking it up is a bracketed query '(?)' after the word *accompanied* – an assurance that the slip in writing there was not made during transmission.

therefore the Mariner was a criminal too. The surviving chapter (whether doctored or not) gives an entirely orthodox appearance, and Coleridge innocently boasts that 'the draft of the plan . . . obtained favour in the eyes' of several good judges, so that he afterwards turned much of the work into verse, but practically all of it has got lost. In writing this, Coleridge would feel it was a safe bet that the obviously anti-Christian synopsis had got lost too. How agonized his ghost would become when the synopsis was printed, sixty years after his death; but the ghost soon lay quiet again, muttering as in life 'How I despise those who praise me'. It is given in the Oxford edition, p. 285, footnote 1, and proves that the young Coleridge was already examining the problem of guilt in an enlightened manner, as part of his search for a good God. Cain himself, of course, does feel guilt, and no one denies that he should, but the question is what should be done about it. His mental torments drive him to the wilderness, and there he is tempted by devils to commit atonement through bodily suffering, which is presented as a gross evil. He yields to the temptation to blind himself, even though he is intelligent enough to protest that his real fault had been a failure to make the proper use of his senses (this sounds very like Blake, but I suppose it is like Wordsworth too). Before sacrificing his eyes he addresses the landscape, and his eyes are saved by a prevision of the Redeemer; the devil reverts to its own shape, and flees down the gulfs of the mountains. (Acceptance of the ethics of Jesus, but revolt against the Father who enjoyed sacrifice, was of course a standard Romantic position.) The next devil disguises himself as the ghost of Abel, and tells Cain to sacrifice his son Enoch; this will satisfy not Cain's present God but the God of the Dead, whom Abel since he became dead has discovered to be far stronger. (A reader who was in the movement would easily recognize the God of the Dead as the God of the established Christian churches; he is Moloch again.) Just in time the real ghost of Abel appears; as regards his own murder he is entirely unreproachful, but he prevents the murder of Enoch

[34]

'with terror' – and naturally so, because it would be a blasphemy against the true God. Well, come now, our current mentors are free to despise the Enlightenment, but they cannot be much use as historical critics if they pretend that it never occurred. What redeems the Mariner is the opposite of pious self-torture; it is the return of spontaneous delight in the beauty of the world – the same protest against Christianity is here as in the synopsis for *Cain*. We do not know why Coleridge abandoned *Cain*; his pretence of telling us what happened is partly a joke. He may have become afraid of opposing Christianity so directly, or he may have persuaded himself that it had better not be attacked on such grounds. Anyway, the alternative plan that Wordsworth picked out of Shelvock's *Voyage* was more convenient for the basic purpose. If you regard the guilt-feeling as itself a problem, a case of imaginary guilt gives it a kind of chemical purity.

The remarks of Wordsworth in old age were perhaps meant to be rather debunking, but they are effective in clearing the air. The ballad needed a surprise, to make the story go, and an albatross which turned out to be a pet of the South Pole was very suitable. On this view, the reason for shooting it is of no significance – it was a thing anybody might have done, but it happened to bring bad luck. This is also the tone in Shelvock. The First Mate shot down a small dark albatross, which had been following the ship disconsolately for several days, because he thought this action might improve the direction of the wind; the Captain, who records the incident in his log, remarks that that this would have been the only sensible thing the First Mate had ever done, if it had worked; but did it? No. The weather continued to be intolerable. This bird fell into the sea, but we know that the one bagged by the Mariner was secured on board. I do not know why everyone excludes the usual reason for shooting a bird, especially among explorers: viz. to eat it. The huge white albatross tastes rancid, but the smaller dark one mentioned in Shelvock, which could be hung round a man's neck, might well be shared round as a soup protective against

[35]

scurvy. We know they have not touched land 'for weeks' and have worms in the hard tack. The Mariner claims they were the first ship to enter the Pacific, and Coleridge was not the man to think flippantly about starvation after reading the account of the first passage of the Magellan Strait. But I grant there is no hint of famine, only of a delicious feckless gaiety, when the Albatross

>... every day, for food or play,
>   Came to the Mariners' hollo.   (94)

They all feel the bird is numinous, full of magic whether for good or evil, so that shooting it might quite possibly bring good luck; and this is the most likely reason for the Mariner. He himself cannot tell us, because he has come to think it a great sin and cannot bear to remember the motive; he can hardly bring himself to report the fact, even though telling the whole story has become his routine.

Critics however often tell us that he shot it out of a random itch to exercise power, trivial though dreadful, and many of them cite an entry in Coleridge's Notebooks on the voyage to Malta, when he was reconsidering the poem. Note 2090, written in May 1804, reports how a hawk tried to find somewhere to rest, while the convoy was becalmed, but on each boat where it set foot the sailors shot at it, having nothing else to do; they always missed, but

> probably it perished from fatigue, and the attempt to rest on the wave. Poor hawk! O strange Lust of Murder in Man! It is not cruelty; it is mere non-feeling from non-thinking.

This is well said; and yet, after all, the reason why these characters were sailing in convoy was that they were at war with the French; plainly it was time they had a bit of target practice, if they were to carry guns at all. What is more important, Coleridge is writing a series of notes about sailors, and some of the other notes would support just the opposite interpretation of the poem. In April 27th (Note 2052) the

[*36*]

jovial captain orders out the rowboat so that he can catch a turtle:

> with the Sailor's whole Bustle and Bellow, and Life and Death Impatience, rapid, loud, eager, passionate Command, vehement reiteration, abrupt Transition, every the lightest order conveyed in the form of Reproach and Abuse, with Oaths intermixed. ....

Still, the captain could be quiet when he saw reason, because he himself plucked the turtle still asleep from the water. One sees that Coleridge was accustomed to monopolize the talk. By May 1st, as the calm continues, he has become positively suspicious of the captain:

> And the Captain begins to look round for the Jonas in the Fleet. Mem. One advantage of sailing in a *Convoy*. On a single vessel the Jonas must have been sought out amongst ourselves. [Anecdote about the suspicions of the Captain]. Here vexation, which in a Sailor's mind is always linked on to Reproach and Anger, makes the superstitious seek out an object of his superstition that can feel his anger. Else the Star, that dogged the Crescent or my 'cursed by the last Look of the waning moon' were better.

'Else ... better' has to mean that, if the poem were to tell the central truth about sailors, it wouldn't waste time on superstitions but just concentrate on their proneness to torment their scapegoats. Coleridge feels personally at risk, believing that he might easily have become a scapegoat, and he had already shown in the poem (ll. 100–5) that the crew blame the Mariner unreasonably. This is a more direct indication of the meaning of the poem than the rival one which is usually cited. In this Note, by the way, we get the first mention of a star 'dogging' the moon, which is used in the final text of the poem; he had composed the line of poetry in the quotation marks, about the waning moon, as a possible addition to the poem a few days before.

[37]

Then again, the crew do not literally curse the Mariner for shooting the Albatross, though they hang it round his neck, to make a pariah of him, when the weather turns bad. They curse him for calling the Ghost Ship; at least, that is the obvious occasion for their cursing, though they cannot speak to tell us so. I haven't noticed any of our pious critics joining in the cursing here, though it is not like them to miss an opportunity. The Mariner had made himself able to call the ship by biting his arm and sucking the blood, so that the parched throat could utter a cry, and this requires a convulsive muscular action outside the normal powers of the will; he could not have done it selfishly, one may hazard, but only for the sake of all his fellows. (When Wordsworth complained that the Mariner never acts, Coleridge ought to have told him to try doing this trick himself; it might also be recommended to our modern scolds.) Indeed, the obvious heroism of the Mariner at this point of the story, and its bleakly terrible reward, are what make it feel sensible to look back and consider whether he might have some good motive for shooting the bird in the first place. (And yet, he may only have been driven to heroic action by his need to recover the good-will of his comrades.) Sure enough, at his call, the Ghost Ship stops tacking about and bears down upon them, and they expect it to bring water; but at once the insulting dice allot Life-in-Death to the Mariner and Death to all the others. Even from a distance, the movements of this ship, in a dead calm, had made clear that it must be supernatural; and the crew were not quite unreasonable after so crushing a disappointment to complain that the Mariner had again got them into trouble with the spirits. It is widely believed that spirits, like the police, cannot cross your door unless invited, but once let in they cannot be ordered out. Thus the crew are acting by ancient principle, but the modern reader feels he cannot say that their curse is deserved; the Mariner is struck down by guilt, as by a mortal disease, and we are forced to realize that he is in a delusion. His story is at most only a parody of the Redemption.

[*38*]

The poem is therefore about Neurotic Guilt; it is the first major study of that condition, recognized as such. This is one of the most frequent mental disorders of civilized intelligent mankind, and among literary people it is practically normal. Large societies need to include a variety of groups with different moral codes or scales of value, and it is part of the business of a writer to act as a go-between; so their differences are liable to become a conflict within himself. The trouble is quite different from the deep internal causes of madness, though it easily combines with them. Dylan Thomas was accustomed to say it was curious he was such a martyr to Neurotic Guilt, as he led such an innocent life; and this was his settled conviction; but another part of his mind evidently regarded his life as his peasant aunt would have done. The experience of the Mariner is of course very unlike the familiar one of the literary man, indeed refreshingly unlike; and yet they are both, in a way, always present in the poem. All the time the adventures are being recited, the listening Guest is becoming sadder and wiser. Some critics have presented the Mariner himself as intellectually adventurous, an outcast because he is a progressive thinker, and we may be sure that this idea occurred to Coleridge; but he knew that his readers would much prefer the actual Mariner, who never argues in favour of his actions. (All the same, his mind is capable of the wicked whisper that stifled his prayer; it will have said 'God is unjust'.) People always find it hard to sympathize with Neurotic Guilt (in a world bursting with sin and misery, as Dr. Johnson said to the man who was afraid he had stolen his firm's pack-thread); indeed, this is what justifies the plot of the story, otherwise a rag-bag of accidents. Most readers, the author knew, would despise his own earnest convictions about the rights of animals (shooting birds was a very O.K. occupation); and therefore, if he expressed his views extravagantly enough, he could make the readers side with the Mariner, imagining themselves to oppose the author, who was plainly a muff. (The young Coleridge was brave about being laughed at, and rather prone to such innocent calculations.) But even the sporting reader does not want the Mariner to argue his case, and later on, after the whole crew have died because he fetched the Ghost Ship, he would be ridiculous if he lectured the silence on his good intentions. Destiny has made him appear in the wrong; he has been framed by the supreme powers. This makes him a peculiarly grand case of Neurotic Guilt, and might even suggest that his predicament is somehow universal.

I may be told that in all this I am only trying to argue away the obvious, because Coleridge really was a muff, that is, really did think it wicked to shoot the Albatross. And no wonder: the bird lives where nothing else can live, with no rest for its foot, and yet it is not at all unsociable; if anybody happens to turn up, it is ready to play and be friends. This puts it very high in the hierarchy of life, so that it deserves to be treated as a man and a brother – that is what the sailors mean by hailing it as a Christian soul, and probably most readers feel that to betray it was a crime. But all this agreement comes from an aristocratic sentiment, that the bird was high in the hierarchy; whereas the theory of Coleridge about Nature was democratic, and refused to accept our instincts at such a point. He did, indeed, for the 'Argument' before the second edition, when told to make the story more intelligible, invent the claim that the Mariner had acted 'against the laws of hospitality'; but here he still thinks of the Albatross as a kind of man. Most of the animals we fatten for eating are intelligent enough to trust us by the time we kill them; the conflict of sentiment here dates back to the Neolithic, and is evidently different from our spontaneous respect for the Albatross. If all animals have equal rights, the crew already deserve to be killed, long before they have 'made themselves accomplices to the crime', because they sacrificed all those innocent biscuit-worms to feed one hulking great Albatross. There is a similar, and poetically more important, logical gap about the creatures of the Pacific calm. That they crawl *with legs* upon the slimy sea is felt as an outrage against Nature herself (and well it may, since these legs can only be found upon our temperate horse-ponds); and yet the Mariner attains such a

[40]

pure sympathy with Nature that he loves them for the beauty of their movement. They have turned into water-snakes; it was very lucky for the Mariner that all their legs had dropped off, because he could not have loved them if they had still been crawly – though the hypocrisy of the doctrine insists that he could or should have loved them however crawly they were. The colours of the water when particularly disgusting (l. 135) are recalled in the colours of the delightful water-snakes (l. 315), and this is enough to bring the slimy things together with the snakes, though the contradiction is not rubbed home so hard in the poem as in the leering 'glosses'. Spontaneously, again, we feel that these crawlies are rather badly-made bits of machinery, whereas the snakes are recognized at once as being exquisitely co-ordinated – that, in fact, is *why* they are related to the subtlest beast of all the field, who was used by Satan as a tempter. The reason why the Mariner loved them was that he could see they are fairly high in the hierarchy of life; our instinctive feelings here are not mere delusion, though probably often bad shots, but are estimates of a creature's position on an evolutionary ladder. I cannot find that Coleridge ever accepted this idea, either in his Pantheist or his Christian periods, though he sometimes writes as if he understood it vividly; he would of course know about The Great Chain of Being, but had rejected it on political grounds. I once knew a scientist working on blackbeetles who said, 'They're very nice, really', and on making inquiry I found he meant that they have a kind of swagger in their deportment and the way they wave their whiskers, though he agreed that no one blackbeetle ever appreciates, or could be intended to appreciate, the swagger of any other blackbeetle. It struck me that his frame of mind was far more saintly in its view of Nature than anything Coleridge ever envisaged. Still, the feelings of Coleridge were good material to work upon, and if he had stuck to praising Nature he would be sure to make some resolution of their contradictions in later life. At the time, if told that his story was nonsense, he would probably have said that the moods of the spirits of Nature are what really matter, and that the behaviour of the animals merely expresses these moods. He did on some later occasion blame his own refusal when young to recognize a hierarchy in life, saying that this widespread heresy had caused the callousness about the lives of men evident during the Paris Terror (this would be a serious objection to pantheism, if at all plausible); but even then he only envisaged a two-storey class system, with men as the ruling class and all animals alike as the proles.

He was thus in a thorough revulsion against the whole doctrine of Nature, as well as an extremely bad nervous condition, when he added the marginal glosses to the poem for *Sybilline Leaves* (1817). This was well known at the time; Peacock's Mr. Flosky in *Nightmare Abbey* (1818) 'called the sun an *ignis fatuus*', which really does sum up the frame of mind of Coleridge; indeed *Biographia Literaria*, written just before, refuses to mention the ideas about Nature which had been crucial when he was a great poet. The turning-point is hard to date but must be put after the return from Malta, perhaps at his resistance as a journalist to Lord Erskine's Bill for the Prevention of Cruelty of Animals (thrown out in 1809). Erskine was a lawyer and had defended liberals bravely during the Police Terror, so he deserved well of Coleridge, who denounced his Bill as 'an example of the dangerous principle of extending PERSONALITY to things' (*Coleridge, Critic of Society*, J. Colmer, 1959). Pope Pius IX made the same rejection for the city of Rome, on the same grounds, later in the century. Coleridge was now wholly out of touch with *The Ancient Mariner*, and plainly inferior to the man who had written Note 1295, in 1802:

All animals have a sense of joke – calfs with their horns – Dogs biting – Women abusing their infants.

I am sorry that these introductory remarks have grown so long, but the poem raises large questions. We may now start on the text. In 1817 the marginal glosses were added; they say (what the poem does not) that the spirits who animate the corpses are angels. This makes nonsense of nearly all the details about them, so nothing can be done to clarify the poem until the parasitic growth has been removed. We have to proceed in reverse order of time, starting at the outside with the last corruption, and try to keep the stages distinct. A reader may be inclined to say, in defence of the glosses, that they must be expected to come as a surprise; they were added to let the poet tell us things which the narrator, the Mariner, could not have known. We may, indeed, sometimes observe the Old Coleridge trying to insinuate that he had 'meant it all along', as in the note at l. 349, saying that the angels 'had been sent down by the invocation of the guardian saint'. This does fit in, because the Mariner himself told us, only sixty lines before, expressing astonishment at the magical relief when he blesses the water-snakes, 'Sure my kind saint had pity on me, And I blessed them unaware.' Yes, but in the first edition, when the author and his intended audience had been enlightened people, they read this with a kindly smile for the naive piety of the Mariner; because the last thing a Christian saint would have told you to do, as they knew very well, was to treat an animal with bare decency, let alone love it. The inability of the religion to handle our relations with animals was one of its obvious gaps; this idea was very familiar to adherents of the Nature cult. Since the time of Coleridge, there have been efforts to raise St. Francis of Assisi into an exception, which were proved by Aldous Huxley (in *Do What You Will*) to rest on a very shaky foundation; but I have not found that Coleridge ever mentions him. To add in a later gloss that the saint not only restored the Mariner's intimacy with Nature but also threw in a platoon of angels, to handle the practical side, is a very cool bit of humbug. (Why the Mariner blesses the snakes is of course as much a mystery as why he shot the Albatross.) One point, I think, Coleridge did intend to clear up when he started the glosses, but their subsequent falsification made it impossible. The Mariner blesses the snakes in the tropical Pacific, and then goes into trance; this

[43]

gives the Polar Spirit an opportunity (requiring magic, whether he used speed or lapse of time) to move the ship south-west round the coast of Africa. That is why the Mariner wakes up feeling cold, and sees the *Aurora Borealis*, which as Coleridge well knew is only seen near the poles. The ship has now a straight run home, though of course a long one so that the Mariner has to be given another trance; thus the poem includes two arrivals at the Equator from the south, and this had better be explained. But Coleridge now wanted to say (gloss at l. 431) that the Polar Spirit only helps the Mariner 'in obedience to' the angels; he himself, not being a Christian spirit, merely craves for revenge. (We get the same sordid tone in Coleridge's *Philosophical Lectures* of the same period, accusing the *Enneads* and the *Gita* of worshipping the Devil, whereas Coleridge himself was the one who could not sleep without drugs because his God was so horrible.) But he could not alter the poem sufficiently; the spirits who animate the corpses fly down from the Aurora in a great wind, and therefore, when the Polar Spirit moves the ship south-west, they are not yet at work. The real poem assumed that both kinds of spirits are loyally, though rather confusedly, carrying out the decision of Death and Life-in-Death, so that there is no need for subordination; but now God's angels have to be in command, so the Polar Spirit must not do anything helpful till they arrive. It is a minor but definite example of the muddle caused by the change.

But why, in any case, do these angels need to have a Polar Spirit to do the heavy work for them, as if they were human magicians – what previous angels had been so feeble? Nay more, what other angels, in all human story, have needed to get inside corpses before they can so much as pull a rope? A legend told by a Bishop Paulinus, about some invisible angels who sailed a man's boat home, is regularly given as Coleridge's 'source' here; but it does not explain the one feature that needs explaining – why did the gruesome necessity of twitching corpses about arise in the case of the Mariner alone?

My answer is of course that these beings are not angels but

Spirits of Nature, as in *The Destiny of Nations,* and it is not surprising that they enter the corpses, because such beings are working inside our bodies all the time. In the broad traditional classification they are Spirits of the Air, but these ones appear to belong to a modern subgroup Spirits of Electricity; Coleridge was prone to describe Dorothy Wordsworth as a very electrometer of sensibility, so he would think highly of them. As Spirits of the Air they reach the ship in a big wind (l. 327; this was altered in the second edition because Southey found such a wind incredible, but it needs to be restored), and they come from the Aurora because Erasmus Darwin (*Botanical Garden,* Part I, Note I, 1791) had said it was electrical. They can enter corpses because Galvani in 1791 had published a book on the electric current, which he discovered from the twitching of some frogs' legs, hung up to dry for his dinner; the English translation was published in 1793, and Coleridge went on talking about Animal Magnetism for years. After all, Erasmus Darwin had well accustomed the public to popular science versified in terms of the spirits of the *Rape of the Lock,* and this was found cosy and reassuring; it was not sensible of the public to be shocked and astonished by the same thing in Coleridge.

Trying to handle this reaction, Coleridge added a verse in the second edition (1800), assuring the public that his spirits were not ghosts (l. 385). I have to take this detail out of its time-order and discuss it with the other evidence about angels, for fear someone may think that Coleridge in 1800 was 'already beginning' to think of the spirits as angels. In the added verse, the Mariner is made to tell the Guest that the corpses were animated by 'a troop of spirits blest', and many readers feel that this is practically a technical term for angels. But Coleridge, who anyway had his head full of blessed middle spirits, had a different reason for saying *blest* here, decisive when you realize that his ballad technique turned on the repetition of key words, so that to patch a verse in was a skilled technical operation. The relief now being given to the

[45]

Mariner is a result of having *blessed* the water-snakes, and the term is already echoed in the first edition, thirty lines later. Waking from trance, no longer tormented by drought, the Mariner felt so light and easy that he thought he might be 'a blessed ghost'. Nobody supposes this means he thought he was an angel; the phrase means 'not the kind of ghost that comes from Hell', whether or not it is also a mild kind of swearing. To fit in his added verse, Coleridge altered the start of the next one, giving: '... a troop of spirits blest. For, when it dawned, ...' – the spirits flew high up and sang hymns to the rising sun. *For* makes the Mariner imply: 'I knew they weren't ghosts, because they sang hymns to the rising sun', and this is a sensible argument; but surely angels would only sing hymns to God.

Three very good verses then describe the variety of their music – sometimes 'I heard the skylark sing', sometimes an orchestra, and at the climax 'now it is an angel's song'. Surely, if the creatures simply *were* angels, it would not make a climax to say they sang like themselves? There are no more indications of this kind till the ship is back in its home port; some bad spirits are now mysteriously threatening the Mariner, and the good spirits need to be sharply distinguished from them. 'A man all light, a seraph-man, on every corse there stood', and they are twice said to form a 'seraph-band' (ll. 566, 568, 572); each time there is a hyphen, making *seraph* a kind of adjective. Turning back to the earlier poems of Coleridge one finds that he regularly uses *seraph* in extended senses, whereas *angel* is used fairly strictly. 'On seraph wings I'll float a dream by night' he tells a young lady in 1794 (the word is already an adjective), and the unfortunate bride of the Prince Regent, imagining him before she met him, had 'shaped a seraph form, and named it Love'. Come now, if Prinny could be a seraph, surely a nature-spirit could too. I think that settles the matter.

We do not know when Coleridge first planned these marginal glosses, but one of them was too late for the 1817 edition; 'no twilight within the courts of the sun' was handwritten onto a presentation copy of it. Still, the plan to provide them was almost necessarily formed before the decision to turn the animating spirits into angels. The long note at l. 136, claiming a number of learned authorities for the belief in middle spirits, merely introduces the Spirit of the South Pole, but he is an extremely familiar type in the poetical tradition, like Father Tiber or Father Thames, and could not possibly need explaining; whereas Coleridge had actually met with the need to explain the middle spirits of Paracelsus and their intimacy with human bodies. However, the glosses are supposed to be written by a remote old pedant, and one cannot be sure what he might wish to explain. The events described in the poem happened about 1500 (before Magellan entered the Pacific in 1520), and we may imagine the poem to be composed about thirty years later, when the Mariner has settled down into his tireless course; then, around 1600, the manuscript fell into the hands of a scholarly editor, who added these comments in the margin, just as Hakluyt had done in the margins of the ships' captains' reports. This pedant is moralistic, and we may sometimes suppose the enlightened Coleridge to laugh at him for it, but he is abreast of the new learning; he needs to be, because Coleridge invented him as a bridge, to assure his modern readers that the superstitions of the ignorant old sailor could have been accepted by a seventeenth-century scientist. The note says:

> A Spirit had followed them; one of the invisible inhabitants of this planet, neither departed souls nor angels; concerning whom the learned Jew, Josephus, and the Platonic Constantinopolitan, Michael Psellus, may be consulted. They are very numerous, and there is no climate or element without one or more.

Planet shows that this editor accepted Copernicus, which by no means everyone did at his date: and this would probably mean that he accepted the 'new medicine' of Paracelsus as well; thus he would believe in active spirits, quite unlike Father Thames.

But the marginal glosses in their final form somehow do not ask us to believe in him; perhaps they made it easier for a pietist to laugh the spirits off, as a delusion of the sailors, while yet accepting the main part of the story and thinking that God's angels did all the work. Yet it is easy not to realize that the old Coleridge has ratted on the young one, because this editor still speaks confidently of 'middle spirits, neither of heaven or hell'. The pretence of seventeenth-century style is fairly perfunctory at times, as in:

> Death and Life-in-Death have diced for the ship's crew,
> and she (the latter) winneth the ancient Mariner.

Anyhow 'she (the latter)' ought to mean the ship. Still, the editor can give useful help in confusing the original story, as by saying 'The curse is finally expiated' (l. 441), merely because the Mariner finds himself able to look away from the cursing eyes of the ghastly crew. He then dare not look back, as if a 'frightful fiend' were behind him, so the reader does need a little distraction here if he is to remain confident that the crew are all angels. The comment on shooting the Albatross runs: 'The ancient Mariner inhospitably killeth the pious bird of good omen', and the word *pious* seems intended to make his attitude impossible for the reader; some tolerable implication might be found, but I can only see the Old Coleridge leering at the grown-ups; to insinuate: 'holy lies before the kiddies, eh?' As the tone of these notes is so very uncertain, even when they are not actively misleading, it seemed best not to let them distract a straight-forward reading of the poem. (They are given on p. 243.)

You should learn to collaborate with spirits, not giving them too much reverence or horror – that was the chief gift of Paracelsus to medicine. A broken bone heals itself, and obviously a spirit comes and does that wonderful thing; but the spirit isn't exactly sensible – a reasoning man has to tie the splint right, or the bone sets crooked. The spirits are always rather feckless, in all the authors who have celebrated them;

[*48*]

1. THE SAILORS AND THE ALBATROSS

One realizes the extreme cold and remoteness, the improbability of finding anything alive. The sailors at first sight of the bird know that it has magical powers, whether for good or evil. They temporize; they view it quizzically, as it views them; they jolly it along. The man in shadow, deciding to kill it for luck, is not really in a different mood.

they work confusedly and indirectly, rather like children imi-
tating the work of grown-ups (as in Wordsworth's *Intimations*).
And, therefore, when Coleridge turns his spirits into angels,
that is, immensely powerful beings under direct orders from
God, these angels are patently insincere; they are torturing the
Mariner under pretence of saving him, and sometimes the
pretence is reduced to a bare assertion (as in the note on 'finally
expiated'). This is what Gustav Doré insinuates about them, in
his searching illustrations to the poem (1875) which were at
the time thought so very pious and tender.

However, the 1817 text has at least one good addition.
This is first found in a *Note* of October 1806 (2880), soon after
Coleridge got back from Malta; the lines are written near the
start of a new notebook, in ink, which meant unusual care,
with two notes about Pindar and classical metres; probably
they were all written out again from memory, another note-
book having got lost in travel. Coleridge had found that a
change was needed in the poem, and set about it with readiness
and good humour. This happened on the voyage out; at least,
the notes do not tell us so, being only written for himself, and
often a bit reticent too, but I think they can be interpreted with
confidence. Notes 2047–50 are all written on the morning of
April 24th, shortly after the ship reached Gibraltar. It was after
midnight when Coleridge wrote down an observation about
the moon (2047), and the decisive conversation occurred at
breakfast with the ship's officers.

2047 ... a Halo with bright stars just within, and a perfectly
bright serene full moon in the center/. The planets larger/
the moon not/ why? –
2048 Eldridge and his Warts cured by rubbing them with
the hand of his Sister's dead Infant/knew a man who cured
one on his Eye by rubbing it with the dead Hand of his
Brother's – Comments on Ancient Mariner/ – Our Capt
'Damn me! I have no superstition, I had as soon sail on
Friday as on Saturday; but this I must say, that Sunday is

D [*49*]

really a lucky day to sail on/indeed to begin any sort of business upon/'

2049 Poem/ dim not feeble is the waning (moon)/the last curse of the waning moon/. The bright moon that follow'd suspended it, that when the moon waned again the Curse began to work, and was finished on the last day of the moon.

2050 Tuesday, April 24th Noon/Had a long and instructive walk with Major Adye, round Europa Point.

This is living at a great pace. I take it that the unpoetical tars explained to Coleridge about the rising of the moon; the good captain, who never gets his due from Coleridge, tactfully intervened when his officers had laughed long enough at the poet's error. From then on we often find his exercising his new-found skill (end of 2052, 2087, 2094, 2132, finally 2766); he evidently learned about it at that period, even if you query this particular conversation.

The poem as printed so far, in all three editions, had described a sunset (needed because the sun has to shine between the ribs of the Ghost Ship), then rapid dice-play, then 'With never a whisper in the Sea/ Off darts the Spectre-ship; /Till clomb above the eastern bar/The horned Moon with one bright Star /Almost atween the tips'. And the next verse began: 'One after one, by the horned Moon' – the crew at once die, dumb with thirst but cursing him with their eyes. So the horned moon got up just as the sun went down. Seven years after publication, the sailors told Coleridge that only a full moon can arise at sunset; a horned moon (the horns were needed, to insinuate a bad-luck star between them) could indeed rise later, during the night, but only if it were a waning, not a crescent moon. Coleridge must have been ignorant of this before, because he began composing verse about it at once, evidently to correct the poem; he would find nothing poetical in a merely wrong description of Nature.

He could see that there would be positive advantages in the correction. At first he tries to use the *suitableness* of a waning

[50]

moon, but on second thoughts this did not need rubbing in, at such a concentrated point. What he needed was some titanic or medically impossible action from the crew, as a retort to the Mariner's biting of his arm. To have them refuse to die till the moon rose, so they could use its light to curse the traitor (though dumb) with their glittering eyes, even then each waiting his turn till he can 'turn his face' and demand individual attention as he directs the glitter to the Mariner – that is adequate, and the lines which he inserted into the next edition of the poem are devoted to making us feel the agonizing slowness of this wait for the moon. However, though it is a magnificent idea, I have to confess I never saw the point before working on this edition. There is not enough to alert us for it; we need at least an occasion when the infuriated crew struggle to speak, and realize that they cannot curse the Mariner in words, being dumb through drought (which also means he has no opportunity to answer their unreasonable accusation). Such a verse is given by the first quatrain of the Notebook entry, which reads:

> With never a whisper on the main
> Off shot the Spectre ship;
> And stifled words and groans of pain
> Mix'd on each murmuring lip.

(The Oxford text gives *trembling* as written first and not erased, though *murmuring* is written above the line. The grand edition of the Notebooks, which is more reliable, gives *trembling* as erased.) This verse does not really give us enough, but it does give the right direction to our attention. The whole effect of the addition upon the built-up climax with the insistently repeated rhymes is I think very fine; and for the poet to tell us something about the reaction of the crew at this point is only normal.

So the next question is why Coleridge did not print it in 1817. His over-riding impulse in preparing *Sybilline Leaves* was an anxiety not to be jeered at any more, and not to give any

[*51*]

handle to insinuation; he might feel that the process of repetition here was too childlike, or, even worse, could be taken as a parody of the old ballad style, like the facetious lines excluded earlier. The technical trick here is to repeat or echo lines 3 and 4 of a quatrain in lines 1 and 2 of the following quatrain, so that the story of the ballad elbows its way forward, lumberingly (both versions of the text, with and without the disputed verse, are given on pp. 128 and 129). The first edition had used the same device earlier in the poem, though rather roughly: 'The Mariners all return'd to work. . . . The Mariners all gan pull the ropes' (ll. 416, 418); and here he had an evident reason for the cut, apart from any dislike of the metrical trick. Or again, the older Coleridge might fear that piling up four successive rhymes to *ship* would be thought childlike – as it is, and very good too. Mr. Pirie has also remarked that repetitions in the poem are used to mark delay, whereas here Coleridge wants to emphasize the speed of the nightfall and of the departure of the Ghost Ship; yes, but the reduced speed makes the ship imaginable, and leads in to the long dark wait which followed the sunset. Mr. Pirie maintains that the verse beginning *The sun's rim dips* was written as a substitute for the verse about the murmuring of the crew, so that Coleridge never intended to print them consecutively; if so, you understand, I cannot claim to be restoring the text to what it was before he mistakenly changed his mind. There is no decisive evidence here. But I think we have some indication of the dates of his changes of mind. We know that he was polishing the aphorism about 'no twilight' just as he sent the 1817 edition to the press, and it strikes me as merely a gimmick, a bit of 'imagery' (not even true, for that matter) which he dragged in to hide the gap where he had cut out the human drama.

The idea that it is somehow artistic not to let the sailors groan when they hear their fate strikes me as Eng. Lit. at its worst; I don't deny that something like that may have influenced Coleridge when he cut the lines in 1815, but if so we have an added reason for restoring what he planned when in a

[52]

healthier frame of mind. It was not long after the nervous breakdown, and soon after preparing *Biographia* and *Sybilline Leaves*, that he gave the particularly sectarian philosophy lectures; so this is the period when he was likely to turn the spirits into angels. In 1806, he could still half agree with the crew that their dying curse was likely to induce a faction of spirits to take up their cause; but in 1815 he was pretending that these spirits merely carry out the unknown plans of God, which in anyone else but God would often be called plainly unjust. Well then, no particular importance could attach to the indignation of the crew, or of anyone else. I think we should restore the drama as it was before the fatal change.

If this were all, the case would be on a par with our restoration of several other cuts made by the later Coleridge. But here he had thought of another improvement, quite independent, which needs to be in both lines (the one retained and the one restored). Ghost ships were usually reported as moving without wind, by magic, and presumably without the noises of wind; Coleridge at first felt he was merely being traditional in plugging the silence. Besides, it is always eerie to have the sea at peace (in a Victorian novel, when the sea is 'as calm as a millpond', the villain is likely to be drowned in the ensuing storm). But somehow the voyage to Malta made Coleridge realize he had carried the trick too far; the imagination jibs from any event at sea which is completely silent. Much better say that, as the water was so very calm, you could hear the hiss as the Ghost Ship cut through it, unpropelled, already far off, almost out of sight in the gathering dusk. Somehow the imagination accepts this at once. Coleridge seems to have invented it from the noise made by porpoises during the calm near the Straits of Gibraltar, when so many aspects of the poem came alive to him (Note 2052):

a noise of rushing, like that of a Vessel dashing on by Steam or other power within itself, through the Calm, and making the Billows and the Breeze which it did not find. Ancient Mariner.

(One need not think that the poet invented steamships; probably the ship's officers often lamented that they were so slow to come.)

This Note tells us that he already thought of using the idea in the poem, so it is surprising that he does not do it in the entry of 1806, but evidently he needed time to fit together the various good ideas which occurred to him on the voyage. However it came about, the note of 1806 reads 'with never a whisper', as do all previous editions, and only the 1817 edition has the triumphant improvement:

> With far-heard whisper, o'er the sea,
> Off shot the spectre-bark.

When therefore (on one page but not on the other) we print as the next lines:

> With far-heard whisper, on the main,
> Off shot the spectre-ship;

we are printing what Coleridge is not known to have written, but what he at least would have written if he had decided to keep the verse which he had long before designed for this place. Mr. Pirie feels that to do this goes beyond the rights of an editor, and I agree that it has the interest of a marginal case. The reader needs to be able to judge how the whole sequence feels, while not badgered by footnotes, and it seemed best to print both versions.

Following the policy of unwinding the cocoon in reverse order, I come next to the very queer business of the Latin epigraph, first printed in 1817 but copied into Coleridge's Notebook by the ladies at Keswick around the turn of 1801–2, among a series of other learned quotations. He would aim at printing it in the third edition of *Lyrical Ballads*, which came out at the end of 1802, but the poem there has no change from 1800 – evidently Wordsworth refused to accept any, and this would make Coleridge determined to print the epigraph when he could. The time did not come till 1817, when he had forgotten what the point of it was. The literary dishonesties of Coleridge are a baffling subject, because he seems not to have aimed at any normal gain by them, and yet they would make a gloomy kind of fun. Mr. W. J. Bate in his recent *Life of Coleridge* (1968) remarks that, when he translates entire paragraphs of Schelling and prints them as his own, he is always quoting 'pantheist' views which he longed to express but dared not allow himself to phrase; he could pretend before the world that he had said them, but before God he could only copy them out. Compared to that, the little cheat on Burnet is quite jolly. In the original passage, he was only talking about angels; one sentence does mention the 'middle spirits' praised by the Neoplatonists whom Coleridge admired, but the polite Latin is intended to jeer at their credulity (a modern reader tends to feel that the difference is almost invisible, but it had been considered important for a long time). It occurred to Coleridge that, as an epigraph is allowed to make cuts, only very little fudging was needed to make Burnet say the opposite. He inserted just five words of Latin, meaning 'Where do they live, and what do they do?' – of course, the creatures Burnet had in mind live in Heaven and do what God tells them, so this was enough to set them free. It would be interesting to know why he picked on Burnet, a Restoration Anglican whose Latin prose he admired. Burnet was keen on reconciling the geology of the Old Testament with modern science; for instance, the world was smooth when it was new, so only a little extra water could flood all the land areas – our high mountains and deep seas are a result of the resulting cataclysms. Coleridge thought that his descriptions of cataclysms deserved turning into Miltonic blank verse, but still, he was a prosy kind of man to be saddled with Undine and all her romantic kin. However, he was connected with the Cambridge Platonists, and best known for revolting against the eternity of Hell (*The Decline of Hell*, D. P. Walker, 1964). Coleridge would like him for that, but might have raised an eyebrow at one of the consequences of it. Finding the Biblical texts hard to evade, Burnet argued that God told us lies in the

Bible, though merely for a time, till we progress beyond the need for them; so Coleridge might feel that Burnet's own text deserved to be interpreted in a liberal way. Probably this little joke was a first stage in the invention of the 'marginal glosses'; Coleridge had already come to feel that he needed a seventeenth-century go-between, to assure his readers 'it would not be actually irreligious to believe what your pious ancestors did'. But, by the time he had finished ratting on the whole conception, there was no longer any point in taking these precautions. An honest quotation would actually have suited the final poem better.

Then again, if Coleridge had just wanted a respectable authority for believing in spirits, he could have quoted one near to his heart from his own century. (I owe the reference to Patricia Adair's *Waking Dream* of 1967, which is often good, and anticipates me in various points from the *Notebooks*. High time some of us used them.) This is the *Inquiry into the Nature of the Human Soul* by Andrew Baxter (1733), a Scots opponent of materialism who had inspired Priestley and was praised by Coleridge in his notes to Southey's *Joan of Arc* (1796). The strongest argument, as Baxter saw it, was one that his century had agreed to consider ludicrous. But it was the materialists who had been ludicrous, from Lucretius onwards, in their shifty attempts to explain dreams. Often a dream is not only quite unexpected, remote from a man's interests at the time, but seems to have been elaborately prepared, as when we find ourselves reading eagerly ahead in a non-existent book, or negotiating with a non-existent person whom we seem to have known intimately for years. If you said that the dreamer had prepared all this in some other region of his mind, you would give his mind an unwelcome complexity, indeed (here is a deep remark) 'the notion of consciousness would be rendered inconsistent' (1745 edition, II. 19). Far better to admit, like all the rest of mankind, including the classics and the Bible, that dreams are given us by spirits, some of them bad spirits who intend us harm, though their powers are mercifully limited.

[*56*]

Dreams are enchanting, but this word always means to Baxter something very disagreeable (II. 216), and he writes about it with energy:

> I may refer to the experience of most men, if they were ever sensible of a greater pleasure, than sometimes when they have wakened out of a dream, and found it was not real. (15)

Still, they are useful; 'real matters of fact have been discovered in dreams' (225). The book went on being reprinted and was praised by Warburton, but this part of it, the part with most observation and originality, could not escape from being considered ludicrous, and on the other hand was not old and quaint enough for Coleridge to make a pet of it. Still, I think it explains the confidence of his use of dreams in the *Mariner*.

I come now, still moving backwards, to the second edition of the poem (1800), where the changes are hardest to understand. He cannot already have lost his faith in Nature or otherwise fallen radically out of sympathy with the poem, so why did he make such extensive and harmful cuts? People used to say that he had become 'sunk in metaphysics', but he had not yet read the books which he brought home with him from Germany, where he had been meeting a variety of people and struggling to learn the language. And the reviews of the book, or even of this particular poem, were not rough; indeed, the *Edinburgh Review* was not founded till after the second edition; unfortunately perhaps, because the brassy dishonesty of its attacks would probably have stiffened Coleridge. The reviews might be called grudging and uninspired, but a second edition of the book was needed conveniently early. It is more to the point, I think, that Coleridge was already distressed by his failure to finish *Christabel*, and attached far more importance to it than he ever did to the *Mariner* (perhaps he would have been unable to finish the *Mariner* otherwise), so that spoiling the completed poem did not matter to him very greatly. But the main reason has to be that he was genuinely reverential towards

Wordsworth, and Wordsworth had become upset over the public reaction to the *Mariner*.

Both poets, after publishing the *Lyrical Ballads* (1798), set off with fine carelessness on the trip to Germany, leaving the public reaction to look after itself. Wordsworth came home first, with his sister, and the fine carelessness evaporated at once. He behaved oddly, and one would like to know why; it looks as if some documents have been suppressed, but the crucial things for Coleridge could be done by word of mouth. The result, more than a year later, was that the *Mariner* was reprinted (for the second edition, 1800) at the end of the *Lyrical Ballads*, instead of the beginning, with a dishonest note by Wordsworth. It begins:

> I cannot refuse myself the gratification of informing such readers as may have been pleased with this Poem, or with any part of it, that they owe their pleasure in some sort to me, as the Author himself was very desirous that it should be suppressed. This wish had arisen from a consciousness of the defects of the Poem, and from a knowledge that many persons had been much displeased by it. The Poem of my Friend has indeed great defects

– and in the course of listing the defects Wordsworth remarks 'the imagery is somewhat too laboriously accumulated', thus pretending that he has no idea what story is being told, what the point of the details could be, but regards them as random decorations, as in a carpet. He actually talks like a modern critic. If, as he claimed in later life, he had himself contributed the fatality of the Albatross and the corpses who sail the ship, his behaviour is worse, but not much. Before Coleridge got back from Germany, Wordsworth was already writing to the Bristol publisher Cottle saying that he would throw out the *Mariner* from the second edition; he had judged that:

> the *Mariner* had upon the whole been rather an injury to the volume; I mean that the old words and the strangeness of it have deterred readers from going on.

[*58*]

Before the end of the month he writes again, thanking the publisher for a payment, and says:

> nothing but pecuniary necessity will, I think, ever prevail on me to commit myself to the press again.

(*Early Letters of Wordsworth*, 95, 96, 98: July 1799). Probably he had still seen no reviews; when he sees Southey's one he writes to Cottle again, saying that Southey is supposed to be his friend, and

> knew that I had published these poems for money and money alone. If he could not conscientiously have spoken differently of the volume, he ought to have declined the task of reviewing it.   (99)

Coleridge after his return from Germany soon went north, hearing that Wordsworth was ill; there he met and fell in love with Sara Hutchinson, and also with the Lake District. Crucial decisions were necessarily made at this time, but no hint of them can be got from the only record, the Journal of Dorothy; except that Wordsworth was having a lot of his nervous stomach trouble. Then Coleridge went to London to earn money, and sent Wordsworth an encouraging letter about a Mr. G. who had praised the *Lyrical Ballads*. Wordsworth answers:

> The said Mr. G. I have often heard described as a puppy, one of the fawning, flattering kind; in short a polite liar, often perhaps without knowing himself to be so.   (105)

In a postscript, he adds:

> Take no pains to contradict the story that the L.B. are entirely yours. Such a rumour is the best thing that could befall them. Poor Cottle! Of this enough.

This is very rude behaviour from Wordsworth, and I hope the reader will not believe what he says. He is sponsoring a new religion; at this time, though afterwards tamed, he is 'else sinning greatly, a dedicated spirit', so he has a high motive for being so agitated over the reception of the *Lyrical Ballads*. As Cottle was a simple-minded Christian and easily shocked, it was important not to let him realize why Wordsworth was so anxious; money-talk for Cottle, then. But if Coleridge has harmed the new religion by the response to his part of the book, then there must be no weakness for friendship; Coleridge must go. Some kind of truth, known to Coleridge, must surely nestle behind the printed assertion that 'many persons had been much displeased' by the *Mariner*. Perhaps someone had laughed coarsely.

One should remember that Wordsworth had behaved generously to Coleridge in the first edition, by giving the *Mariner* first place. Coleridge had seemed to give solid intellectual support to the Nature-doctrine, from science and history, but now people said he had presented Nature as containing bad spirits, comically bad, practically vulgar. Obviously he could not be let write the Preface for the second edition. Wordsworth himself had been struggling in the cold German winter to put a good face upon the spirits of the tropics (in the poem *Ruth*), while not denying that they might encourage rather unbridled behaviour; this made it all the more exasperating if Coleridge had blurted out something tactless. However, on second thoughts, after Coleridge had offered to withdraw the *Mariner*, Wordsworth realized that there would be less risk of scandal if he reprinted it at the end of the book, with an easy note of chivalrous apology, and no admission that it had been thoroughly purged. So it came about that the poem which was fudged in 1815 to make it Christian had already been fudged in 1800 to make it Pantheist.

Coleridge was pathetically loyal and willing, and also was now becoming dependent on Wordsworth for what remained to him of domestic happiness; in any case, he would make the majority of the changes out of genuine conviction. It is very good luck that Wordsworth jolted him into removing the

comic Old English, which no doubt had been fun on the
original walking tour but was very out of key with the final
poem. Coleridge would readily feel excessive shame at this –
'awful facetiousness – my besetting vice – Pussy's Whiskers
again'. He shows his sincerity by removing cases of facetious-
ness which no one would have detected, for example:

> A Wind and Tempest strong!
> For days and weeks it play'd us freaks –
> Like chaff we drove along!

The double internal rhyme amounts to a parody of the old
ballad style, or of the modern imitators of it, though there are
no old words; Coleridge put instead 'And Southward still for
days and weeks'. But he kept the tone plucky and untroubled,
as is proper so early in the story; not till 1817 did he replace
chaff and *days and weeks* by a doom-laden word-painting of a
storm. (However, we have left that in too, since the modern
reader comes to the poem already expecting some such mood.)
It is now agreed that Wordsworth ought to have allowed *weft*
to stay in, since it was not archaic but merely nautical; that
would have required an explanatory footnote, but Words-
worth did not forbid them to himself – the third edition has a
footnote 'The Ten Commandments' under the word *Deca-
logue*. In the present edition we sometimes need to restore
verses from the first one, which the author would have altered
if they had been retained; and I do not think it would be unfair
to carry out his intention in such a case, except that I often do
not know how to do it. Fortunately, the poem is so full
of surprises that to have the Mariner break into dialect at
intimate moments, and that is what it feels like, should not be
painful.

Removing the 'old words' was thus fairly easy, but the other
assignment, of mitigating the 'strangeness', turned out hard.
Coleridge, when he realized that some readers had believed the
ghosts of the crew to have animated their own corpses (it
would be a form of vampirism), thought that he need only add

one verse to exclude the possibility; we can see him do it. I need to pause here and consider the background. A useful account of the treatment of the poem in the first reviews, and how the second edition reacted to them, is given by B. R. Elderry (*Studies in Philology*, 29); it shows that their complaints were patiently attended to, however trivial or wrongheaded, but there is no sign of this large misinterpretation. Indeed, the reviews do not bother to interpret the poem at all, but merely complain of obscurity; and Wordsworth became agitated before he had read them. The first readers can hardly be blamed for thinking about vampires, if the two poets had merely set out to make up a ballad suitable for the *Monthly Magazine*: in which the absurd *Alonzo* and *Ellenore* had been the two greatest successes. These ballads treat ghosts occupying their own corpses as practically the only known form of the supernatural. Or perhaps as the only form it was manly to believe in; a man who believed in fairies or pagan gods was unpleasantly silly, but he would be pig-headed if he disbelieved in ghosts altogether, even though they were commonly treated as a coarse joke. The feeling is evident in the standard work on the supernatural, which was sure to have been read by Coleridge early in life. It was by Calmet, a leading French theological scholar (1745, English translation 1759), and the English title is *Appearances of Angels, Devils and Ghosts* – which assumes that the French word 'esprits' meant ghosts only, and indeed the book hardly considers any other spirits.

As usual in sufferers from Neurotic Guilt, Coleridge was ready with the cry of the delinquent child 'No I Never', feeling that the point where he was innocent had better be made the most of, since he was probably guilty of something else, rather *like* that. I think he had been accepting the gamey side of Romantic ballad tradition quite freely, though it is rather ill-connected to his story and its moral; indeed, he refused to be frightened out of it. The ghastly calm on the tropical Pacific, which was so very exotic, continues in all editions to reek of the village churchyard:

About, about, in reel and rout,
　　The Death-fires danced at night;
　The water, like a witch's oils,
　　Burnt green and blue and white.　　(135)

The *O.E.D.* gives no previous authority for *death-fires*, a kind
of will-of-the-wisp seen over graves, already used by Coleridge
in the *Ode to the Departed Year*, l. 59; presumably he had
learned it from superstitious peasants. He never removed it.
Not till 1817 did he remove the verse describing Death, and
the cuts for that edition are usually if not always intended
merely to save his dignity:

　His bones were black with many a crack,
　　All black and bare, I ween;
　Jet-black and bare, save where with rust
　Of mouldy damps and charnel crust
　They're patch'd with purple and green.　　(200)

The second edition (1800) put 'They were' for 'They're'
presumably only to make it less informal, and this shows that
he positively intended to keep it in. So he should, because the
following verse, describing Life-in-Death, with italicized *Her*,
cries out for its companion. Mr. Roper comments in his
edition, as would many other critics: 'It is here and in [the
verse about the wind through his bones] that the poem comes
closest to the crudely horrific effects used by M. G. Lewis and
Bürger' (these were the patterns, the authors of *Alonzo* and
Ellenore). But the colours are so brisk; I can only see it as a
cover-design for the old *Saturday Evening Post*. Surely the
formula here is '*fun* with corpse-horror', even though he really
did want you, in the next verse, to feel disgusted by the
prostitute. I first wanted to conflate the alternative versions
here, as is so often done with Shakespeare, thus keeping in the
line *And she was far liker Death than he*. But after all she plainly
wasn't (Coleridge is telling a pious lie) so I thankfully agreed
with Mr. Pirie that conflation on a small scale, inside a verse, is

[*63*]

nearly always bad. In this case, the grim brooding which lay behind the 1817 edition has successfully heightened the original conception. Coming now to the verse about the wind among the bones of death (l. 215), retained in 1800 but cut in 1815, surely this cut makes a confusion, if you still allow Life-in-Death to whistle for a wind. Does it mean the goddess fails to raise the wind? But she sails off, as she had intended. (Coleridge at the start of the voyage to Malta observed the mate whistling for a wind, and noted doggishly 'a sweet image to precede a shipwreck': Note 2013). The ghost ship must not sail by the usual kind of wind, just as the Mariner, when his own ship is in the hands of spirits, feels on his cheek a wind that blows for himself alone. When the lady decides to leave her present company, and gives three sharp whistles, the spiritual wind uses the bones of Death as a musical instrument to reply 'Ay, ay, Ma'am'. The treatment of the wind in the poem is perhaps rather unsatisfying, but it is less bad when allowed to work itself out consistently. All this traditional and accepted part of the entertainment, then, which may be summed up as the church-yard flavour, Coleridge did not attempt to cut in 1800, and we need not suppose that Wordsworth made him try.

However, he was willing to admit that there might be room for misunderstanding, might even be a slip-up which he could no longer explain, in a verse which had not been complained about in any of the reviews. It is the most eerie moment of the whole poem. The spirits have just been seen in person, erect above the corpses they have abandoned, waving a farewell. The next verse says:

> Then vanish'd all the lovely lights;
>   The bodies rose anew;
> With silent pace, each to his place,
>   Came back the ghastly crew.
> The wind, that shade nor motion made,
>   On me alone it blew.   (l. 575)

Coleridge crossed this out, on a copy of the first edition; thus

[*64*]

2. WHY WE OMIT THE MARGINAL GLOSSES

Insufferably twee, the angels preen themselves among the corpses. But in this picture they have found another ploy; they make the ship appear tiny, like a mantelpiece ornament, so that all the sufferings of the crew become trivial. Doré contrives to make very clear that they are tormenting the Mariner under pretence of helping him. Coleridge inserted them nearly twenty years after writing the poem.

leaving no possible reason for the destruction of the ship which immediately follows. To replace it, he wrote in the margin:

> Then vanish'd all the lovely lights,
>   The spirits of the air;
> No souls of mortal men were they,
>   But spirits bright and fair.

This, by the way, is a decisive proof that he did not intend them to be angels; for a reader of Paracelsus, 'spirits of the air' was a technical term. But he never printed this verse; for one reason, he would prefer the reader to work out the answer for himself. Wordsworth on the other hand would at once say it was useless to delay the explanation of the spirits till they had gone; it should be given when they first appear. A more carefully planned verse (l. 385, already discussed) was fitted in there. We do not print as part of the poem the verse just quoted, because it was never intended to be conflated with the other verse, which we restore. What is particularly worth attention, I think, is that he must have taken this first step 'innocently', that is, supposing that all his spirits had been bright and fair.

It next occurred to him that he had made the same mistake earlier in the poem, just after the bodies are first animated; the spirits go away, and yet the bodies move. He would easily remember this because of the way he had composed; the whole poem is an echoing-chamber, taking to a wild extreme the ballad technique of repetition. So he hacked away another four verses here; and yet he would have known, if he had remembered the story, that there was no need for it. At dawn the spirits fly up for a choral service to greet the sun, but they came back to work as soon as it is over, and the corpses begin jerking about again. In the later passage, when he echoed this incident, the spirits have just made their farewell, so a different bit of story is needed if the verse is to be retained.

A reader may feel that these verses (ll. 411–426) are hardly worth putting back, but they tell us a good deal about the

E   [65]

character or frame of mind of the Mariner. I first thought that Coleridge deliberately removed all the 'psychology' from the second edition, perhaps in subservience to Wordsworth's belief that the Mariner has no character; but each of these cases turned out to be an accidental result of the anxiety about the nature of the spirits. Here the Mariner has described their singing with frank beauty, and it suddenly occurs to him that in this way he may lose his audience – the Guest may think he had a nice time on his travels. 'You never *heard* of anything so sad', he tells the Guest, insisting that this will make him rise next morning 'sadder and wiser': all the same, resuming his narrative, he had to admit that things went on peacefully. The effect of jamming together the two cut ends is to make a hideous cacophony: 'Singeth a quiet tune./Till noon we quietly sailed on', whereas the first draft, even when facetious, has a wonderfully sustained harmony of sound.

Another cut in the psychology was entailed by the explanatory verse telling you the spirits were not ghosts. The Mariner's nephew stood by him, knee to knee, while they pulled at one rope (so this corpse at least did not glare at him all the time):

> But he said nought to me.
> And I quak'd to think of my own voice,
> How frightful it would be!

> 'I fear thee, ancient Mariner!'
> Be calm, thou Wedding-Guest. . . .

Coleridge took out the two lines about the Mariner's voice when he added the calming verse that follows, and the only plausible reason is that he felt the sequence to be illogical; if the Mariner said he was afraid of ghosts, then the Guest could not have feared that the Mariner himself was a ghost. Or rather, Coleridge may have feared that his malignantly stupid reviewers would pretend so. The nephew, like the rest, had died of the thirst which made them all dumb; whatever magic had made uncle survive, he would feel shy of asking whether nephew could now speak – some painful change of expression at this thought will be what makes the Guest express horror. The two lines ought obviously to be restored.

The added verse is well planned as a self-justification, implying 'I never once *thought* of them as ghosts', and this also makes it fit the system of echoes. 'Twas not those souls that fled in pain/Which to their corses came again' echoes 'Their souls did from their bodies fly/They fled to bliss or woe'; and indeed, as the Mariner heard them pass like the whizz of his cross-bow, the poet was clearly not intending to make them return. It was heroic and selfless of the Mariner, one should recognize, while enduring the weight of their unreasonable curses, one after one as they died, to take an interest in each case and try to hear whether he went up or down.

At first these cuts appeared enough. But then Coleridge discovered, or was forced to admit, that the evil had been spreading like a cancer towards the end of the poem; five whole verses, of astonishing beauty in their context, had next to be destroyed. And now he could no longer claim to have been misunderstood (about ghosts); it became plain that he really had been envisaging bad spirits, not very bad, but on the wrong side in the story. He renounced them, but even so he was never again the trusted lieutenant of Wordsworth.

It may seem very unlikely that Coleridge could have forgotten the story of his own poem in so short a time. But I need not labour to make my theory plausible here; there can be no other explanation, I submit, of the very odd selection of cuts that he actually made, and the first alternative that he proposed. We should also remember that while composing he was engaged in a majestic process of echoing the crucial words and re-stating the themes in another key – he did also invent enough story to justify the way the poem needed to go on, but this work would be delegated to a sub-committee of his mind. In the same way, Shakespeare could always think at once of what had happened in the past lives of his characters, whenever there was occasion to mention it; but, on the next occasion, he was liable to think of something different. Then again, as Professor Jump suggested, Coleridge while composing may have felt a literary reminiscence; an echo of some epic battle by Ariosto was lightly sketched into the background (though, for the purpose of the story, it could not be treated lightly, and was in fact quite coherent). It never occurred to him that such a story would annoy Wordsworth (as indeed, why should it?), and when bully-ragged by Wordsworth he exuded immediately the cloud of unknowing of the cuttle-fish. If he had raised enough nerve to explain the story of the poem, after having remembered it, nobody could even have pretended to feel shocked, though Wordsworth might still feel cheated out of the expected hymn of praise for all Nature. The reason why he could not raise the nerve, I suspect, is that he had started off with the fatal 'No I Never' reaction. Both poets were still under thirty.

As the ship comes home we encounter two new groups of spirits, both of them earth-spirits, because they are tied to the locality; very alike, expect that one group is helping the Mariner and the other carrying out the curse laid upon him by the rest of the crew. The supporters of the crew succeed in occupying the corpses, apparently through a negligence of the spirits of the air (the ship is hurried north by some high power, after reaching the equator, so that they do not have to sail it). This first operation is achieved while the ship is still a few miles out, so that the Mariner does not yet know he is near home. Coleridge never felt that one was safe on coming home, and would probably feel a message in this part of the story: 'If you want to meet spirits, you had best go to remote deserts; but, once you have got the trick, you will find they clutter up the old home particularly badly.' All along, the sea has been a witches' cauldron, its lights hinting incessantly at beautiful or horrible life within – I have never seen a rotten herring glowing green in the dark, but apparently all Coleridge's friends had, and readily connected the sight with the *Aurora Borealis*; they

[68]

were well prepared for the central doctrine of the poem. The vision of the water-snakes has been described so magnificently that one feels confident the ocean has done its utmost; and so it has, but the port, when he arrives home, positively boils over.

The poet handles this approach to the climax, which as we should expect is left mysterious and tremendous, by writing six verses which form a detailed parallel to the six verses immediately preceding them. I cannot find that anybody spotted this before Mr. Pirie, almost two centuries after it was arranged, but Coleridge planned to make it obvious by repeating typically clumsy ballad forms, so that his earlier parodies of the ballad form, like Shakespeare's training in clownery, get caught up into his supreme achievement with the medium. The technique makes the opponents feel bewitchingly indistinguishable, though the ones on the Mariner's side presumably need to recall and reinforce the spirits of the air – we do not know how. The two lines:

> Till, rising from the same,
> Full many shapes, that shadows were

are repeated identically, and the first group of shapes are 'dark red' but the second 'crimson'. A picture could make these distinguishable, but one does not feel sure that they are different in character; it is more like a grand sporting event. The chief meaning of *shadows*, I think, has to be 'ghosts', but the Mariner is thoroughly bemused – never before has he been so like a dog in a dancing school. (I recall without comment the now widespread view that the angels are all cardinals.) The dark-red group are the ones opposed to the Mariner, and he finds them already occupying the corpses when he wakes from trance;

> All stood together on the deck,
>   For a charnel dungeon fitter,
> All fixed on me their stony eyes
>   That in the Moon did glitter.   (l. 490)

They had died with a curse in their eyes, and it 'had never

[69]

passed away'. In ordinary life, of course, it would do; the facial muscles relax, and a corpse often seems to have got younger, but dying of drought may be supposed to leave the muscles more fixed. However, the Mariner at first thought the animated corpses could not see him; it seems that the air-spirits could only use the bodies clumsily, for a few essential movements, jerking like lizards perhaps; so that they would not be spry enough to direct a scowl at him. But now they do, and their eyes are glittering again; it is an indignation meeting, and he dare not look away from them. But then something else, maybe a premonition of the homecoming, forces him to look ahead (this is all he need mean by 'the spell is snapped'; one might think that the good spirits do it for him, but they are out of power). A fair amount of time seems to pass before the ship enters harbour, and then the reinforcements for his opponents begin to emerge from the water; than a change in the lighting attracts his attention, and he looks back at the ghastly crew:

> I turned my head in fear and dread,
>   And by the holy rood,
> The bodies had advanced, and now
>   Before the mast they stood.

In a sailor's mouth, 'before the mast' meant the forecastle where the crew lived, apart from the officers, but Coleridge does not use these class terms; he means simply that the mast is no longer between them – the menace has come nearer. All the same, he is feeling *like* an officer confronted by a mutiny, so the term fits in well enough. At the moment however the revolting proletarians are calmly burning their uplifted right arms; the flames repeat the colour of their reinforcements. He prays and looks back at the shore, from which he may hope for help, and now the spirits bearing the other colours are rising from the water. Another shift in the light makes him turn his head again; the corpses have collapsed, and the spirits of the air now stand above them, shining in their turn and waving

[70]

their hands. One thinks of them as white, but they too should perhaps echo the colour of their assistants – diamonds upon crimson. The Pilot arrives in his rowboat a moment later, and would have taken a bit of time, so the 'signal to the land' which brought him out must have been the red one, from the enemy spirits. We are given no inkling of how either group drove out the other one from possession of the corpses, but the idea that they are in conflict gets heavily driven home; indeed, it is still plain enough in our standard version, after the mangling of the sequence; though I do not think anybody noticed it in print before Mr. Pirie.

It was a thrilling stroke to make the enemy spirits display Hands of Glory, effective even when not understood. But Coleridge would not think of it as obscure; the superstition had somehow come into notice – though not in Calmet, it is described in print several times during the thirty years before 1798. Thieves would cut off the hand of an executed criminal (whose body had been left exposed as a warning); this would be used to hold a candle, after both hand and candle had been prepared in a smelly Symbolist manner. Then, while a burglary was going on, the whole household would stay asleep (though the hand could not *send* anyone to sleep). It is a very placid bit of magic, intended to avoid bloodshed. J. L. Lowes, in *The Road to Xanadu*, hunting for a connection, recalled that corpses thought to be possessed by vampires had to be burned, with a stake through the heart; but the men who did that would decide they had made a mistake unless the corpses screamed and foamed at the mouth during the sanitary operation. The connection is much simpler; the air-spirits have gone to sleep, and these earth-spirits want to keep them asleep till plenty of reinforcements have arrived from the port; they are burglars, in a way, because they are trying to kidnap the Mariner. But then other local spirits turn up who support the Mariner (he is a native here too); maybe these ones just wake the air-spirits, who have superior powers, and indeed never seem to realize that anything was going wrong. They have completed their

[*71*]

assignment, now that the Mariner is home, and the Pilot is rowing out; so they make a gracious farewell and return to the stratosphere. Astonished at finding the corpses left vacant again, the enemy spirits try to use them for a last-minute coup, sailing the ship out of harbour; and therefore it has to be destroyed at once.

This is a good story, and yet one can hardly blame the readers of almost two centuries for failing to recognize it as one. In fact, the lines hardly do more than pretend to tell a story, because not enough is imagined about the actual methods and difficulties of the opposing parties; to recall a splendid phrase of I. A. Richards, the cloudy edge of play-time has not been crossed. Perhaps Coleridge was right to leave the spirits obscure, but he does the same thing about the plan of the crew to unite in putting their dying curse upon the Mariner; they have no need to discuss it, and could not, but act like a flock of birds. The story was never in sharp focus, one would think. Maybe there was even some truth in the suggestion of J. L. Lowes about the Hand-of-Glory; Coleridge was the more willing to destroy the whole splendid sequence because he felt he had been caught out using low-class peasant material (it was needed, to show that the enemy spirits are earth-bound, tied to the home port). Still, I think that he evidently did imagine this story, and that the poem is much improved when it is recognized.

We have next to consider who effects the rescue; a ballad would always be definite about that. Coleridge I think gave a very clear indication here, though of an odd kind. 'Part VI', which includes the spectral combat in the harbour, begins halfway through a conversation; between two senior spirits of the South Pole, whom the Mariner has the good fortune to overhear while in trance. This may seem absurdly convenient, but it had been a regular doctrine that one was capable of crossing wires when in that state. Ordinary dreams were merely sent by particular spirits and received passively, as when the crew are informed (l. 135) that the Polar Spirit is seeking revenge; but in the superior state of trance one had some power of seeking out the right place to eavesdrop. (The doctrine is mentioned by Calmet at I. 13 and II. 50, both times about Laplanders, which would win the attention of Coleridge). Anyhow, these spirits are merely floating above the ship, and their comments would obviously be worth hearing. They are loyal officials, concerned to implement the decision of Life and Life-in-Death; of course, events do not occur automatically merely because they are fated. They talk bad poetry, as the gods do in *Cymbeline*, and as the Fairy Queen in the panto was still doing when I was a boy; that is, you are meant to listen to it as a riddle, part of the plot, and not as 'imagery'. However, this is only so when Part VI has begun, which happens without any explanation; at the end of Part V they are talking good poetry, to express their detestation for men who shoot Albatrosses, and their relief at learning that the Mariner will have a long penance (it seems plain here that he is still undergoing penance whenever he repeats his story). With the new Part we enter the oracular style:

'Fly, brother, fly! More high, more high,
    Or we shall be belated.
For slow and slow that ship will go,
    When the Mariner's trance is abated.'

'Under what conditions', you are meant to think, 'would one reflect that speed was needed (even the use of the stratosphere) because a time would come when a ship would move slowly?' *If* a fight for possession of the ship is likely to occur while it is drifting after having reached harbour – there is only one answer to the riddle, I submit, once you admit it was meant to have an answer. Sure enough, the sea-lords arrive in the nick of time, with a tremendous roar which rushes up from far away, deep under water, and the ship goes down like lead. It has become intensely insanitary, very like the skeleton ship which had been a slave ship before it rotted away; it has a fiendish look, says the Pilot, making plain even to an uninstructed

[73]

reader that the ghastly crew would have done something very bad unless prevented in this decisive manner.

There is yet time for another important incident, which has been rather concealed by the grace of the description:

> Upon the whirl, where sank the ship,
> The boat swung round and round,
> And all was still, save where the hill
> Was telling of the sound.

Though knocked unconscious, the Mariner woke and recognized the urgency of this situation as soon as he was somehow dragged onto the spinning boat; he 'took the oars', and the Pilot's Boy, though mad with terror at the moment, paid him an involuntary tribute: 'The Devil knows how to row.' Unless he had rowed like a demon, they would have been sucked down by the whirlpool (I owe this point also to Mr. Pirie); as usual, the good spirits have behaved in a feckless manner likely to defeat their own purpose. It is still an adventure story; this time his heroic action succeeds, and saves the lives of all concerned, but they still give him no rational credit for it. And nor do most of his readers (especially perhaps if they have never been on a boat going round and round); the poetical detail of the immense calm which lay behind the echoing thunder of the shipwreck somehow tempts one to feel that nothing has happened.

The final moral has yet to be considered, and it has been much disliked. In the first place, I think it obvious that a poem is permitted to have a moral. The doctrinaire belief of modern Eng. Lit. that explicit statement of a moral is forbidden, or makes any poem bad, strikes me as merely one of the crotchets of Oscar Wilde. Maybe it is held because professional critics regard the moral as their own perquisite, so they will no more allow the author to speak up than a member of the Departments of History or Psychology. But the question need not be debated here. In this poem it is not the author who pronounces the moral, but the Mariner, and he cannot be expected to leave the Guest without a summing-up, because all along the offer of a revelation has been his only excuse for keeping the man from his pleasure. I grant that the incidents of the poem have made the moral look very dubious (because the experience of the Mariner has been rather like that of the Duchess of Malfi) but that is why, if you removed the moral, the poem would become hopelessly confused. It would then seem quite possible that the Mariner has turned into a vampire, whose pupils or victims set up as vampires when they graduate; after all, he has been greatly wronged, and is still suffering, and 'Those to whom evil is done Do evil in return'. If this had been the theory presented by the first readers to Wordsworth when he returned from Germany, it would have justified his queer behaviour; but they could not quite have said it, because the moral was there to prevent them. The last forty lines were never altered from the first edition, and accord with a vein of sentiment which Coleridge never rejected. Maybe the lines somehow connive at childishness, but both he and Words-worth were maintaining that children are mysteriously wise. You see what a confusion my opponents have got into; they both dislike having children called wise *and* dislike having them told 'Don't pull poor pussy's tail'. I am sure the children need to be told that, whether or not they have had the mysterious triumph of loving the slimy things of the great calm. Coleridge in later life, when asked about this topic, boasted of having snubbed Mrs. Barbauld, a lady who wrote moral books for children; and as they quarrelled quite early the conversa-tion must have happened around 1802. It has been long discussed, but I think without allowing for the degree of polite insincerity which is usual between enemy authors. Coleridge expressed regret that his poem had not been as aesthetically pure as the *Arabian Nights*, or so he boasted long after; but of course it *had* been, and so he had put the lady into a cleft stick. He considered that she harmed children by teaching them false morals, no use to them when they grew up (the possibility that his own methods might have harmed poor Hartley seems

[*75*]

never to have occurred to him). Surely the original poem is very sturdy on this point. The Mariner gets punished for killing a bird which merely happened to be a pet of the Polar Spirit, a thing he could not have foreseen; any more than the Arab, recalled by Coleridge, who happened to put out a spirit's eye while tossing a date-stone down a well. And indeed *The Ancient Mariner* continually tells us that life is a toss-up which a man must take as it comes; the second line *He stoppeth one of three* recalls a Biblical text which need mean no more (nowadays, when the young critic catches an old author quoting the Bible, he feels confident that the reference is 'significant', i.e. it means Hell-fire for the characters; but this one means 'it isn't his fault'). Surely the moral at the end is quite clear; it says that God made and loves us all, but not that all the accidents of the story are his calculated punishments for us (whereas some of the 'marginal glosses' really do attempt that greasy injustice).

In short, the kind of moral that Mrs. Barbauld wanted is immoral because, if all accidents are God's justice, nobody who has fallen down ought ever to be helped up. Consider on the other hand the third son in the fairy story, as he gives his last crust to the withered crone, while seeking his fortune; she is the Queen of the Fairies in disguise, and thus his fortune is secured. So far as we hear, it was just luck that he hit on the right crone, but the intention is to leave a child feeling that kind actions are quite likely to turn out worth while, or any-way are not so stupid as you might think. (And the grown-up has a better *aesthetic* appreciation of the story if he grasps this Intention, not only in its long-forgotten author but also in its innumerable reciters.) Here too the real moral of the poem is larger and more difficult than what the Mariner tells us; but we need not be surprised or irritated that he cannot say more. He has received an illumination, but he has understood it so little that he can only convey it by a technique of total recall, and we have seen him struggle to obtain a hearer. So I feel that, one way and another, the end of the poem is adequate even if rather flat, and certainly neither Mr. Pirie nor I would claim any right for an editor to remove it.

All the same, a wide variety of good critics have disliked the end of the poem, and maybe there is something else wrong with it. The young Coleridge was on principle reckless of absurdity, and here I think throws himself so eagerly into the part of a pious old man of 1500 that he becomes likely to be misunderstood. Several students had confronted me with evidence of this, but I resisted it till I came across an article by J. M. R. Purser (R.E.S. 1957). He finds the poem to be a spiritual allegory in which the neophyte (the Guest) is gradually beaten down until he attains 'a thorough acceptance of spiritual values', and after that, of course, he can't breed. Renouncing sex ('symbolized' by not arriving at the wedding party) is what matters, and telling an adventure story is only a technique to encourage it. The illustrator Doré, I now realize, was fully abreast of this interpretation; he makes the Guest look pathetically young and exasperated but increasingly in the toils of the Mariner. Of course, if the author at the time when he wrote the poem had accepted this analysis, he would think very wicked what Mr. Purser thinks pious and good: he might regard the Guest as becoming corrupted into one of the Priests of Night from *The Wanderings of Cain*. But he would feel he had done his best to avoid such misinterpretation, by writing the moral. At the time, he was still tolerably happy with his wife, and he never believed that 'spiritual values' entail celibacy. The Notebooks written in Malta and Sicily express a fierce hatred of the effects of Roman Catholicism. Still, I had to agree that the last pages contain something that corresponds to the eerie account of Mr. Purser.

It is only realistic to make the Mariner a bit of a spiritual bully. His behaviour is pointless unless he is eager to make a decisive impression upon the Guest, before they part for ever; he, rather than the author, needs a bang at the end. During the last forty lines, he inflates himself into a Mage very rapidly; he appears to claim the gift of tongues, and also ubiquity by levitation; these magical powers, we are to gather, enable him to pick out from all the world the young man most suited at the moment to hear his message, and it seems that no young man can refuse. If such is his mode of life, it is hard to see where he can have experienced what he calls the greatest happiness (far greater than a marriage-feast), that of walking placidly to the village church with one's fellow oldsters. The accusing spirits, we must remember, could not be drowned when the ship was sunk; that merely prevented them from killing the Mariner. They would next impose slanderous dreams on the magistrates at the court of inquiry, and no doubt had other techniques. So the Mariner would be driven into exile, probably on suspicion of having eaten the rest of the crew. No wonder he has to 'pass, like night, from land to land', as the slanders catch up with him. His life has always gone wrong, and surely one need not be surprised that his assurance 'all is well' rings hollow. The author does, I should recognize, speak the last two verses in his own person, and assures us that the Guest did rise next morning a wiser man. (We are not told that he slept.) There is no other comment on the views expressed by the Mariner.

Nor could there be, because Coleridge was using the simple Mariner to play a trick upon his Christian readers, 'boring from within' their system, using it to teach moral truths which were not its own. The moral says: 'Don't pull poor pussy's tail, because God loves all His creatures'; and the orthodox might cogently reply: 'But *where* does God give us any such instructions, in all Scripture, or tradition even?' – though the orthodox did not say this plainly, as it might not be good tactics. 'Tiresomely obvious' is the chief objection to the moral felt by a modern reader, and he feels this only because the trick it plays has been decisively successful. Coleridge of course did not invent the trick, but it had come gradually into use in England during the two previous generations, so that when he used it the fighting edge had not yet been dulled. If a reader is disgusted at the tone of pious unction suddenly adopted by the Mariner, he may without serious falsification regard Coleridge as writing a parody of it, with this purpose. Probably what Coleridge felt was more personal; the parsonic unction was a shameful temptation, to which he eventually succumbed, but here he could use it with a clear conscience.

One might thus expect to find a real moral for the poem, held by the author in reserve behind the too simple one of the Mariner. I said long ago in my book *Pastoral* that this moral was: 'Delight in Nature when terrible gives man strength to control it', and I still think this the normal form of the great theme, which is much neglected by literary critics. Indeed, it happened to Coleridge afterwards on Scafell; but the Mariner is hardly controlling Nature when the Albatross drops off his neck. Coleridge was almost pathologically lacking in the urge to take control, and perhaps this gives some excuse for the irrelevant complaints of Wordsworth against the Mariner. The Mariner does act heroically, but he never gets any return for it except fierce blame and wrong, and he never makes any complaint there; he is more staggeringly a good sport even than Sir Lancelot. A sufferer from Neurotic Guilt does of course become remarkably indifferent to the normal process of reward, craving only for relief; but I am not even sure what relief the Mariner found in telling his story, nor whether he felt it to serve some purpose, let alone what the Guest had not yet learned, to make him wiser, until he got out of bed next morning. The theme about Nature, I suppose, should be rephrased in the case of this poem as: 'Nature is often terrible; but one should take delight in her when one's own nature allows of it; and the reward if granted is the best thing that life has to offer.' No wonder it is hard to *find* a moral, because Wordsworth (even more than Coleridge) while making these moral claims for Nature refuses to present any case where Nature gives different advice from parent, teacher, or parson. *Nutting* does that; all the grown-ups told the child to be useful, but Nature told the child it was wicked to spoil the pretty hazel-trees – and so what happened? *Nutting* had to be excluded from *The Prelude*. The *Mariner*, to do it justice, is largely an adventure story; and an adventure story does not require any extra moral, because it celebrates continually the virtues of its hero. The spirits are even allowed to enjoy fighting each other, so long as we never learn how they do it. All the same, the moral needs to be spoken by the Mariner, partly to show that he does not know what his virtues are, partly because Christianity did not really teach it, and above all because the message will be profoundly reassuring to the reader, who is pretty sure to have the same neurosis as the Mariner. Such is the basic theory of the historical poem as conducted by Coleridge, and it does, you can hardly deny, enlarge the mind. I should confess that, after all this effort of understanding, the end of the poem still puts my teeth on edge; but that does not make it bad; such is what the poem ought to make you feel, when you consider the history which it is intended to sum up.

If the successive changes did the poem so much harm, a reader may object, it seems a bit curious that no one mentioned the changes at the time. At the time, however, even good critics considered what they called 'minute criticism' to be ungentlemanly, and it made them surprisingly careless readers. But Charles Lamb can be observed reacting correctly, though in the dark. When the second *Lyrical Ballads* (1800) came out, with the contemptuous apology for the *Mariner* by Wordsworth, Lamb sent him a protest:

> I was never so affected by any human tale. After first reading it I was totally possessed by it for many days.

He did not like 'the miraculous part', he goes on, but the feelings of the victim 'dragged me along like Tom Piper's magic whistle'. A month after Coleridge's death, and a few before his own, still amusing and unpretentious, Lamb was having a literary chat with a visitor (*Lamb recorded by his Contemporaries*, Edmund Blunden), and said that he –

> regarded *The Ancient Mariner* and *Christabel* as Coleridge's best productions in verse; the former, in his opinion, was

[*80*]

miserably clumsy in its arrangement, and the latter was injured by the 'mastiff bitch' at the beginning.

Not very deep, perhaps; but the story was what had bowled him over in the first edition, and, when he eventually read the poem again in some later edition, he found that had somehow faded away.

IV

Poems written by Coleridge earlier than *The Ancient Mariner* need to be examined for any light they may throw on that debated masterpiece, but the ones he wrote afterwards do not give much help, as his mind altered so rapidly. On the other hand, maybe this account of the *Mariner* helps to show why he could not finish *Christabel*. He tells us (*Biographia*, Chap. XIV) that those two poems and *The Dark Ladie* (for which *Love* was written as an introduction) were designed on the same plan, of making the reader understand or recreate a remote superstition by an appeal to his 'inward nature', that is, to something he already knows intimately. The later two poems would more nearly have realized his ideal, he says, if he had been able to finish them. After his triumph with the Renaissance, it would be natural for him to take on the Middle Ages, always a period of great interest to Romantics; and perhaps the basic trouble was a creditable one – he could not see any point in his medi-eval witch, after he had got her on the page: that is, could not see any satisfactory parallel to a modern mental disorder, from which he could deduce a satisfactory moral. No doubt he would again rely on the poetry to suggest a story as he went along. We know he wanted such a parallel, because he finally jammed onto the existing *Christabel*, as 'Conclusion to Part II', an observation about his own feelings for his child Hartley which he had posted to Southey several years earlier (cf. *Note* 1392). To give it any relevance, there had to be an absurd change in the thoughts of the rough Baron, so that he became a worrying introspective type (see Notes).

F

There are many complicating factors. The poem was to tell some deep truth about love, and while struggling to complete it Coleridge fell into a hopelessly frustrating love-affair with Sara Hutchinson, which made him promulgate sickly ideals of love; maybe we ought to thank the good sense of his unconsciousness for not allowing him to finish the poem so perversely as he came to intend. He had been inspired by St. Teresa, he told Allsop (*Recollections*, 1st edition, p. 42), who stood, to him, for Ladyhood of Nature. In his last years, he decided to make the Third Book consist merely of Christabel alone and waiting. Then again, we learn from Dorothy Wordsworth's *Journal* that her brother too around this time began to find great difficulty in finishing even short poems, and would 'hammer away at them till he was quite ill'. Both of them complained of a mysterious failure of inspiration, and in the case of Wordsworth you cannot blame opium or metaphysics, or even a nagging wife. Both, I submit, were losing faith in the special and challenging beliefs about Nature on which their earlier poetry had depended; though Wordsworth had never been so definite about the spirits, so that he could adjust himself more privately. His later poetry would otherwise have become very eccentric and isolated, and yet the grim decision gave him only one more great period, that of the first draft of the *Prelude*. All the same, I cannot see that this worry about the doctrine of Nature has any bearing on the failure to finish *Christabel*, which seems to have a completely different background from *The Ancient Mariner* (J. L. Lowes found that none of the same books are drawn upon). It is our misfortune if Coleridge, as he said, just happened to get repeatedly distracted from writing a whole first draft, while the impulse was fresh in his mind; but after all it is hard to believe that *The Dark Ladie* would ever have been any good.

There is no pretence, we should observe, that Christabel commits even a token sin, since to rescue another lady is not even a breach of decorum, and yet the effect of it is that she has begun turning into a snake before the fragment ends. It seems

[*82*]

odd that Wordsworth approved of *Christabel*, if he objected to a mere hint of vampirism in the *Mariner*; and yet, though he seemed to praise the Second Part to the author, who had carried it to him triumphantly across the mountains, two days later he inflicted the heavy blow of excluding both parts from the second edition of the *Ballads*. He was concerned with audience reaction, and may well have judged rightly; by the time the poem did get printed, Hazlitt was busily saying it was obscene. Like the *Mariner*, it treats the supernatural as obviously dubious, needing to be watched all the time; probably Coleridge would have claimed here to have expressed the ancient and permanent human sentiment on the matter. No wonder that Geraldine though some kind of witch is remorseful and admires goodness, and Christabel though as yet starry-eyed is already so infected as to copy her animal mannerisms. Somehow the poem feels complete after showing this; there is no need for the ladies to do anything further. Walter Scott, however, after hearing the poem read, could think of plenty more things for the ladies to do; so it is perhaps the only recent case of a whole poetical *genre* being founded by aural influence.

On the other hand, *Kubla Khan*, though abrupt, is a complete work which carries out the formula. It does of course look incomplete, so much so that Coleridge felt he could not show it to the public unless he fudged it in some way, and this he was brave enough to resist. Long afterwards he was coaxed by the kindly Byron to show his hoard of unpublished verse, and began lying to cover his shame when *Kubla Khan* turned up, and in this way came to realize that a bit of prose patter, making out that the poem was a curiosity which had happened to him in a dream, was all that was needed for print. Here, for once, he felt it would be shameful to spoil the poem merely to satisfy the public; compared to that, just telling some lies about it in prose felt quite innocent. This view of his rather puzzling behaviour has become widely accepted by scholarly opinion in recent years, though I think I belong to a minority in not ascribing any bad motive to Coleridge.

The poem describes what a Romantic poet should be and do, regarding him as in ideal perfection; but obviously Coleridge with his grinding sense of failure could not say that to Byron, who was actually doing those large things in the world that Coleridge could only comment on in his journalism. It was *because* the poem meant something so actual to Coleridge that he had to tell the public it was nonsense. However, though the poem is concerned with the Romantic poet, he had first set out, in accordance with his formula at the time, to describe the Mongol conquerors. After writing a rather accidental masterpiece about the Maritime Expansion, it was natural to have a shot at the previous conquest of the world, by Mongols on ponies, about as long ago again; and his formula required that he must compare the Mongols to something his readers understood intimately. The reason why the modern literary expert cannot look at the matter in this simple way, I am afraid, is that he cannot imagine a poet being directly interested in Kubla Khan. The theme is 'exotic', he will say, meaning 'I won't be bothered.' Thus a recent scholar argued that the poem must have been written before the trip to Germany, because Dorothy remarks in her *Journal* that at one German village she had to go and fill Kubla at the pump on the green. The little joke tells us that they pronounced Khan as 'can', which provides a rhyme, and I hope no one supposes that the poem was written after the trip. But you see the extraordinary assumption here; that Kubla must have been quite unknown until Coleridge read him up for some highly sophisticated 'aesthetic effect'. Anybody who was accustomed to hear Coleridge talking, as the evening wore on, would have heard about Kubla years before he wrote the poem. His Notebooks continue to record any odd bit of information about the Mongols that he comes across, such as that the present Khan had ordered a complete translation of the French *Encyclopaedia* (Note 424, May 1799). Not all writers were as world-minded as Coleridge, but Mr. Pirie has found that other Romantics at the time were interested in the Mongol Conquest too, and surely this was only

[*84*]

sensible of them, with Napoleon at their gates. The Khans were just going to destroy Europe, around 1240, when the death of Mangu called them back from the gates of Vienna to Karakorum, for a family share-out; and the next time they came west, a generation later, they had learned that the Moslem civilization was better worth looting, so they destroyed that instead. Hence our present superiority to the Moslems, which we find so natural; the idea that the Mongols were too remote to make any difference to us is ill-informed. Legend had it, though the name of the town must be wrong, that Hulagu the Hound of God made a pause before destroying Damascus, and the holy men of three religions came before him and pleaded for it, because they all held it sacred. 'You are mistaken', said Hulagu, 'the true God may be worshipped in any place'; and he laid waste the city for seven days. The point of the story is not that Hulagu is a monster of wickedness; he is immensely high-minded, but he has no idea what he is doing. Such was the traditional sentiment about the Mongols; Marlowe grasped it firmly for his *Tamburlane*, but modern readers are often puzzled by the result. (Surely he ought to be familiar to them from Science Fiction.) Europe, as I understand, did its best to praise the Mongols because they had saved us from the Moslems (so perhaps they were a wild kind of Christian); and they really had opened a secure land route to China, through which we learned important techniques – though who knew we were learning them would be hard to tell.

Hence there was a genuine point, though a remote and imaginative one, in saying that the Mongols were like the ideal Romantic artist, who creates a new era by expressing the cravings which his society dare not otherwise admit. Remote or not, the comparison became a cliché; from the time of Coleridge onward, a musician drawing upon the folk-tunes of a hitherto untapped part of Europe would be said to 'conquer Paris'. The practice of changing the fashions for ladies' dress every generation, so that every well-to-do girl grows up thinking 'Mum looked a frump when she was my age', became established at the time of the French Revolution and has fortunately never since then increased its pace; so that Coleridge lived in a society which had only recently become conscious of sudden changes of fashion. However, he would have been justly annoyed if told that this was what he meant by the poem. He would be likely to realize the grimness of this picture of what an *avant-garde* artist should do, so that he had a better reason than his personal failures for becoming shy about what the poem meant. But anyway, once you realize what material his mind was working on (as is now familiar, see *The Road to Xanadu*) the poem expresses its meaning very fully.

Mr. Pirie adopts a paragraph-break found in one manuscript, which helps to bring out the point. A long second paragraph, about the wild scenery, ends with Kubla hearing prophecies of war. A short third paragraph, about the calm garden of the palace, implies I think that such courts become a nursing-ground for artists after the conquest. Then in the last paragraph the resolution of the conflict makes the artist himself a conqueror. What advice it may give to the reader I am not so sure.

Fire, Famine etc. may have been written before the *Mariner*, though more probably it came later – Pitt went on treating the French revolutionaries in what Coleridge thought a provocative manner for a long time. A newspaper printed the poem anonymously in early 1798, and it appeared again with a few changes in Southey's *Annual Anthology* for 1800. The changes merely gear up the style to hit harder, and we need not puzzle much over the oracular 'eight years', as there was no attempt to adapt the date when reprinting. All this was plucky of Coleridge, as the Government was in a dangerous mood, and the authorship was not hard to discover.

Reprinting it for *Sybilline Leaves*, when the war was over, he introduced it with a long prose apology for having consigned his opponent to Hell; appearing to maintain that no theologian had really believed in Hell, even during the Wars of Religion, but had only used it, as here, for a sort of comic swearing – apart from a few actually *bad* men. The way he plumes himself

[86]

on this bit of reconciliation shows how irreconcilable to the religion he really was; but also, I suppose, the theological chat helped to distract attention from whether he had been a traitor at the time.

Fears in Solitude has the interest of an interim report. It was written in April, only three months after the publication of *Fire, Famine* etc., and appeared as a pamphlet the same year. Many other English liberals were experiencing this change of mind; they felt that the French invasion of Switzerland gave enough reason to decide that the revolutionaries had betrayed their ideals, and therefore need no longer be supported; the decision was welcome, as they were next expected to invade England. Coleridge was not inconsistent here; he continued to say that the arrogant insults of Pitt had forced war upon the revolutionaries, and maybe brought Napoleon to power – he said it even while demanding under the ministry of Fox that the war should be resumed, as a necessity of defence. All the same, the clerical unction and the desire to please are very prominent.

Love appears in the second edition of *Lyrical Ballads* (1800), and in a newspaper just before the turn of the century. Byron once remarked that it was Coleridge's best poem, liking it perhaps because it is especially wary about the supernatural. Feeling uneasy himself about trouble from that quarter, Byron could appreciate a character who, when he saw an Angel beautiful and bright, knew at once that it was a Fiend. Wordsworth must have accepted this poem while demanding the cuts in the *Mariner*; but then, it was only to the spirits of Nature that he forbad a darker side.

The Mad Monk has killed the woman he loves (apparently before he became a monk), and now all the beauty of Nature serves only to remind him of his crime. He begins a verse 'There was a time when . . .' – a time when the beauty of Nature was a source of inspiration, as it is no longer; the same phrase and context come in Coleridge's *Dejection* and Wordsworth's *Ode on Intimations*. This then (written in 1800) is the first of the series, and it firmly ascribes the loss of inspiration to feelings of guilt; in the poet, of course, they may be neurotic ones only.

Dejection (April 1802) is more natural and direct in its original form as a letter, which is given here, and many of the changes were plainly made only to avoid scandal or distress to individuals. The pruned and formalized version sometimes ascribes motives which are evidently wrong if you believe what the first draft tells you.

I. A. Richards, in *Coleridge on Imagination* (p. 152), pointed out that two opposed beliefs about Nature are considered in the poem, 'realistic' and 'projective' – the one saying that we merely imagine Nature, the other that we gain insight into her at moments of vision. He then boldly denied that the poem abandons one view and adopts the other, though that appears to be what it is doing; because the attempt repeatedly betrays itself – indeed, human language is not equipped to deny that we are somehow supported by Nature. We imagine we have two theories, but 'in the forms in which they are true, they combine to be a description of the fact of mind which is their ground and origin' (p. 157). Approaching the matter historically, H. W. Piper (op. cit. p. 168) said that *The Prelude* and *Prometheus Unbound* were written 'in celebration of the active universe' although both authors held a definite belief that 'the cause of mind is utterly unlike mind', so that he agrees with Richards that this could be done; but he denies that Coleridge could do it, by the time that Coleridge might have wanted to do it. As soon as Coleridge stopped believing in personal spirits of Nature, he stopped writing Nature-poetry. I think this has to be accepted, though it is also clear that I. A. Richards was propounding an important truth.

A fatal turning-point, or the rejection of a last chance, may I think be observed behind the *Hymn Before Sunrise, in the Vale of Chamounix* (published by the *Morning Post,* 11th September 1802). Early in August, Coleridge had made what he called an Excursion round the lake mountains, showing great vigour and staying-power, and each evening he would write up his

[88]

day in a letter to Sara Hutchinson. He claimed afterwards, while recommending the poem to Sotheby (Letter 459), that he had 'involuntarily poured forth a hymn in the manner of the Psalms' on Scafell, and in the letters to Sara there is only one passage where he says he spoke aloud. In his descent from the mountain he met a series of short cliffs, and the final one seemed impossible (Letter 451, August 6th):

My limbs were all of a tremble. I lay upon my Back to rest myself, and was beginning according to my custom to laugh at myself for a madman, when the sight of the crags above me on each side, and the impetuous Clouds just over them, posting so luridly and so rapidly to northward, overawed me. I lay in a state of almost prophetic Trance and Delight and blessed God aloud for the powers of Reason and the Will, which remaining no danger can overpower us! Oh God, I exclaimed aloud, how calm, how blessed I am now. I know not how to proceed, how to return, but I am calm and fearless and confident. If this reality were a Dream, if I were asleep, what agonies had I suffered! What screams!

After collecting himself in this way, he found a crack or chimney in the cliff; he satisfied himself that he would not get wedged in, and then 'slipped down as between walls, without any danger or difficulty'. He was triumphant about this, and indeed the recovery of his nerve had probably saved his life, but to him it would mean a great deal more; it proved that the doctrine about Nature was true. The poem as published, however, is addressed to Mont Blanc (the theme, Coleridge explained, 'seemed disproportionate to our humble mountains'), and praises that Grand-Tour mountain because, unlike a field of cows for example, it tactfully effaces itself so that one can see God instead:

I gazed upon thee,
Till thou, still present to my bodily eye,
Didst vanish from my thought; entranced in prayer
I worshipped the Invisible alone.

But the whole point of the incident, as he had described it to Sara, was that the scenery itself, or a mysterious feeling of intimacy with it, was what had recovered his nerve, as the water-snakes had healed the Mariner. If he had found himself alone with God on Scafell he would just have screamed, as he did in bed. The final poem is thus a betrayal of the experience which had set the process of writing it in motion.

He appears to realize this in Letter 457, another face-saver to Sotheby, which hints that his poems in the *Morning Post* are not intended for reprinting, being done for money presumably. One can calculate from Letter 464 (a report to Tom Wedgwood, earnestly confessional; see also Letter 447) that Coleridge's wife had agreed to stop scolding him, and try to make peace, during the period between his writing *Dejection* and having this triumph on Scafell. She had at last realized that her scolding only gave him stomach convulsions and did nothing at all to make him behave better, and her tears would do much to release him from the mood of *Dejection*; but he may have tried to show gratitude by betraying his genius, to make a saleable poem, as the only way he could please her. Even with this noble excuse, the case throws some doubt on the argument of *Dejection*, explaining why he cannot write poetry. He has again had an intimate experience with Nature; it has again brought him Joy and enabled him to write poetry; but none of this does him any good because the poetry cheats. Some might argue that it had to cheat, because he no longer believed in nature-spirits; and indeed, he had now reached the point of arguing against them, on grounds which he would previously have despised (see the excellent footnote to Letter 459); but the experience he described to Sara Hutchinson did not presume any such belief, and could have been treated in the style he so much revered in Wordsworth. He merely no longer wished to report what he had really felt. The face-saving letter 459, says Mr. Piper, is the occasion when he first applies the distinction between Imagination and Fancy to literary judgement – previously Imagination had meant for Coleridge an intuitive power to grasp the inwardness of Nature (as it had done for Paracelsus).

It would be fussy to blame him merely for writing a formal poem in an accepted mode, but surely it is exasperating to hear him prattle innocently to Sir George Beaumont about the much better poem that he has ruined. Sending a text of the *Hymn*, he added a note in the margin at the lines:

> O struggling with the darkness all the night,
> And visited all night by troops of stars . . .

'I had written a much finer line when Scafell was in my thoughts:

> O blacker than the darkness all the night,
> And visited . . .'

On a starry night, as he had seen, the mountain would define its shape by the stars which it hid, and if you watched long enough you would find stars successively disappearing into it, or re-emerging after their visit. In the idealistic style, on the other hand, any bit of Nature chosen for attention has to be regarded as 'struggling' on the side of goodness, though the poet may tacitly imply that there are bad forces in the confusion of Nature outside it, against which it struggles. Here he had merely allowed for perpetual snow on Mont Blanc, but he knew that his change of plan had spoiled the poem. He also admits that 'some Swiss poems' had helped the transformation (Letter 459), and of course did not deny that he had never seen Mont Blanc, only knowing about it from his reading; so the needling attack on the 'plagiarism' of the poem, made by De Quincey as soon as he was dead, was an irrelevant bit of punishment.

Next year the nightmares had become really bad. *The Pains of Sleep* (Sept. 1803), a great poem, written during his solitary return from a tour with the Wordsworths in Scotland, walking day after day with frightful vigour, is generally regarded as about the ill-effects of opium; truly enough, but it describes 'withdrawal symptoms', the effects of *not* taking opium.

[91]

Coleridge claimed in later years not to have known when he wrote it that the drug was *causing* the nightmares; he had thought opium was just a means of avoiding them, harmless except that he had better not become dependent upon it. When Coleridge sounds radiantly innocent he is pretty sure to be lying, or thinking that he is, even if what he says is true; here he does not want to let you know the real cause of the nightmares. The drug was on open sale, and many respectable Englishmen took it regularly throughout their successful careers. It is extremely habit-forming, and the effect is that one can go on taking a fixed amount every Saturday, for example, without trouble. One might argue that Coleridge, by stopping and starting in his ingenious way, extracted as much torture as was possible from the angel of mercy; and this would at least be more sensible than saying he had no 'will power', whereas most of his disasters were caused by his pigheadedness. But anyhow, Wordsworth describes himself as having very similar nightmares, in which he spoke hopelessly against false accusations, as a result of his divided loyalty between England and the French Revolution. (*Prelude*, X. 400; the text implies an unjust French trial, under the Terror, but what really disturbed Wordsworth would be the thought of a just accusation at an English one.) Coleridge was involved in that too, but also much more involved in theological conflicts than Wordsworth. His parson brother George would not have been backward in threatening him with Hell, we may be sure, and he spends a lot of time arguing Hell away. I do not deny that he had other sources of guilt-feeling, above all the powerful scolding of the wife who had been foisted on him by Southey, and also that he was driven to overdoses by mere bodily pain, especially from 'neuralgia' whether neurotic or not; but the decisive craving for an overdose would come at night from fear of Hell.

A month after he had written *The Pains of Sleep*, when they had all got back from the tour (Oct. 1803), he had Hazlitt staying with him to paint his portrait (at the end of this visit,

[*92*]

Coleridge gave the philandering Hazlitt a stout pair of shoes, to escape over the mountains from the infuriated villagers). On the evening of the 26th Wordsworth took the side of Hazlitt in jeering at Coleridge's God, and Coleridge answered excitedly but was not apparently upset. Next day he prepared for the evening, and he reports himself (Note 1619) as giving a triumphant metaphysical disproof of the malignity of the Deity, but then, he says:

> went to bed after tea – and in about two hours absolutely summoned the whole Household to me by my screams, from all the chambers – and I continued screaming even after Mrs. Coleridge was sitting and speaking to me. O me! O me!

In December of the same year we find him writing to Matthew Coates, a Bristol Quaker:

> You were the first man from whom I heard that article of my faith enunciated that is nearest to my heart, I mean the absolute Impersonality of the Deity.

It is hard to see how your God can remain impersonal while you are discussing whether he is malignant, but that is a minor problem; what does seem to emerge is that Coleridge's God could not be trusted to remain impersonal after Coleridge had got to sleep. During 1803 he himself suggests this explanation of his nightmares in letters to his brother George and to Coates (523, 529), giving a convincing denial; but then, what he wants to promise them is that he had nothing on his conscience – there is no *real* guilt driving him to these nightmares. I suppose nobody denies now that it was an almost pure case of Neurotic Guilt, not even the people who say it was his own fault for taking opium. Ten years later, after a period when he had to be watched all the time (he says) to keep him from suicide, he no longer troubles about the distinction; e.g. Letter 910, of December 1813: 'The Terrors of the Almighty have been around and against me', or Letter 933 of May 1814:

'I have had more than a glimpse of what is meant by the Death, and utter Darkness, and the Worm that dieth not' – and the rest of the sentence does seem convincing evidence that he now believed in Hell, though he began arguing it away again when he felt better. He is just about ripe now to destroy *The Ancient Mariner*, as he did in the following year.

Psyche is a witty epigram (1808), but it becomes very grim when put beside a letter of Dorothy Wordsworth in 1810, describing the end of Coleridge's love for Sara Hutchinson (E. K. Chambers, *Coleridge*, p. 222). She had been coaxing him into dictating *The Friend*, and writing it all down for him, but Dorothy believed she would have become seriously ill if she had gone on any longer; she was much fretted by his incessant demand for attention and reassurance. One could not invent a more decisive moral object-lesson in favour of adultery. Coleridge always understood such things beforehand, though it never did him any good; here he understands that love without bodily pleasure to support it, in his own case at least, was sure to turn into something disagreeable. His high-flown language about ideal love is always eerily irrelevant to his own needs, which were masculine enough in their way and very stubborn; even more than most men, he required the support of placid domestic comfort, and had only lost it through the scheming of young Southey. To be fair to Southey, who went on helping, however fretfully, with the wife and children, the young Coleridge had been so much mangled by his upbringing that his sexual preferences were rather hard to discover; consider a detail of the important Notebook entry 2398:

> ... I have always been preyed upon by some dread ... then ... then ... then a state of struggling with madness from an incapability of hoping I should be able to marry Mary Evans.

The same grim outlook on love is the point of his *Song* (published 1828), a parody of the splendid and already well-known song by Byron 'So we'll go no more a-roving' – 'For the sword outwears its sheath, And the Soul wears out the Breast.' Byron thinks of human love as our most immortal part, and no doubt did keep it bright by regular scouring; but Coleridge was right to answer that the sword was far more likely to decay than the sheath. (When I was young, you still had to clean the knives at once after a meal, or they rusted.) Of course the two poets mean by 'love' quite different things, and to explain the poem of Coleridge one must first explain the poem of Byron. Coleridge has in view a chaste devotion, such as had ended dismally for Sara Hutchinson about fifteen years before. Byron was writing to Hobhouse about Carnival Week in Venice, saying that he had had very little 'actual debauchery' but is so tired after going to one club ball after another, night after night (he could not dance), that he will write letters this evening instead. The exquisite song follows with hardly any change of tone. A man addresses a male friend, the song presumes, and last evening they went out together in the town each seeking a female partner. What Coleridge writes about under cover of the same literary form is quite different. It was very bad luck for Coleridge, and improbable as well, to have Southey convert him to chastity in 1794, at the age of 21, a plan which would have astonished his orthodox tutors at Cambridge; to do that and then force him to marry a scold was brutally destructive. The Notebooks written in Malta, especially, leave no doubt that chastity was bad for Coleridge.

In *Human Life* (1817) we find Coleridge writing a poem about a conclusion from his philosophy, as one might expect him to have done more often. It will be remembered that *Biographia Literaria*, Chap. XII, by way of giving us a taste of the philosophy, proves that the existence of things without us is inherently involved in our immediate self-consciousness. He was prepared to carry the process further; the existence of other people, and hence the existence of the moral law, could be shown to have the same transcendental security. He thought he had done it again for immortality, or nearly at any rate; but then, many a man does not recognize that his immediate self-consciousness tells him he cannot die, whereas the other three beliefs may be called universal. Still, anybody who does not recognize it must be profoundly at odds with himself, and find life empty, and such is what the poem attempts to describe. The first sonnet manages to keep to this theme; it only becomes good, I think, when it describes (apparently only to deny) the mystery of Nature's unconscious creativeness, but that cannot be thought irrelevant. The second sonnet is not so lifeless, and evidently this is because it tells us things about the experience of Coleridge. He ought not to have been at odds with himself, because he did recognize that his self-consciousness gave him this message. But he was, and what the poem really tells you, I find, is that life becomes empty if a religious scruple cuts you off from domestic affection. 'Coleridge knew well' as Stephen Potter wrote with unexpected firmness (*Coleridge and STC*, p. 59), 'that to live up to principles which were not grounded in his experience was the only sin.' And indeed, he often says in the notebooks that the scruple was disabling him from doing valuable work, and attempts no rational defence for it, so one must agree with his own terrible phrase that 'his heart mantled in its own delight' (Note 2990); he fell in love with his chains.

In the splendid *Epitaph*, posted off to two or three friends in the year before his death, he contrives a last riddle about himself, equivocal rather than profound. 'Mercy for praise, to be forgiven for fame' is a paradox that might be interpreted in several ways, and Coleridge while posting off one of the later copies becomes uneasy about it, fearing perhaps that it gave too much away. He had bumped his nose so often that he had come to expect everything to go wrong, so he would have begged mercy for any success he had achieved, and the only kind which was at all familiar was applause. All his life he had wanted praise, from a circle of co-believers, from the whole dinner party, from the cold public itself; he could not bear to speak out about religion because he was an affectionate man to whom general acceptance by the society he lived in was a primary need (cf. Note 1418). No wonder he asked mercy for

[*96*]

that, forgiveness for all that endless fobbing off and talking down, which really had brought praise and fame. Probably he remembered the terrible intimacy of a sonnet of Donne, doubting whether he could endure to see God face to face:

> That thou remember them, some claim as debt;
> I think it mercy if thou wilt forget.

And yet he has to write, in a covering note introducing the poem to one of a few friends before whom he is playing out the drama of his death: 'N.B. "for" in the sense "instead of" ' – thus labouring to throw away the whole point of the line. In his heart, I suppose, he always blamed himself for writing good poetry because it was showing off – the better the poetry the worse, so he must hide that too at the end, just as he had tried to muddle up the text all along. He has always the fascination of the most extreme case of something.

APPENDIX

Many critics have felt sure that *The Ancient Mariner* is an allegory of the Atonement, or at least that it was turned into one when the author became a Christian and realized its meaning. But this doctrine was his chief point of resistance to Christianity, a resistance that he never fully abandoned, so that he was very unlikely to have celebrated the doctrine in the *Mariner*.

Nearly all the Romantic poets complained at having been taught that God was 'satisfied' by the crucifixion of Jesus, as is well shown in Vol. III of *Religious Trends in English Poetry* by H. N. Fairchild (1949), an impartial witness because he can see no force in their objections. It was so firmly rooted in the mind of Coleridge that he even confessed to it in *Biographia Literaria*, though that work is largely concerned to pretend that none of the thoughts of his youth had ever been dangerous ones. He had had doubts, he says:

concerning the Incarnation and the Redemption by the cross; which I could neither reconcile in reason with the impassiveness of the Divine Being, nor in my moral feelings with the sacred distinction between things and persons, the vicarious payment of a debt and the vicarious expiation of guilt. A more thorough revolution in my philosophic principles, and a deeper insight into my own heart, were yet wanting. Nevertheless, . . . my final conversion to the whole truth in Christ. . . .

He thus insinuates that he has swallowed the belief in God striking a bargain ('redemption' is a metaphor drawn from the slave-market) but does not tell what he now considers the 'whole truth' to be. Not long before, he he was writing to his old Unitarian adviser Estlin, explaining comfortingly that his opinions had really changed very little (Letter 719, 3rd December 1808):

> The differences between us are rather philosophical than theological.
> ... the Calvinist tenet of a vicarious Satisfaction I reject not without some horror – and though I believe that Redemption by Christ implies more than what the Unitarians understand by the phrase, yet I use it rather as an XYZ, an unknown quantity, than as words to which I pretend to attach clear notions.

He had written much the same earlier, in an attempt to make peace with his brother George (Letter 443, July 1802). However, he might understandably change his mind after the breakdown when he had to be kept from suicide. But in May 1821, according to Thomas Allsop, an enlightened young business man who had made friends with him through his public lectures, he was saying that Lord Byron, if he had done some further research,

> would have been able to upset all the evidences of Christianity, upheld as it is at present, by simple confutation. It is possible to assent to the doctrine of redemption as at present promulgated, that the moral death of an unoffending being should be a consequence of the transgression of humanity *and its atonement?*

Allsop adds in a footnote:

> Let it always be borne in mind that this and other expressions in these pages were the opinions he expressed *to me*, and are not to be taken as expressions of doubt generally, but of disbelief in the corruptions of the vulgar Christianity in vogue.

The book was published in 1836, soon after the death of Coleridge, and caused great indignation; there was much talk in the reviews of cowardly slander. Wordsworth, in a letter dated 9th January 1836, remarks that he has glanced into the book, on finding it lying about, and found that the bad effects were from 'trying to scrape together *the whole truth* about his departed friend', often using details which Allsop himself had not fully understood. But on 17th January the diarist Crabbe Robinson gives a summary of answers about religion given to him by Wordsworth recently, very mild and uncertain, except for one bit:

> The thought that an infinitely pure being can receive satisfaction from the sufferings of Jesus Christ and accept them as a satisfaction for the

sins of the guilty is declared by Coleridge to be an outrage upon common sense. It is a hard saying, nor can I interpret it to my satisfaction.

One can feel the word 'satisfaction' sticking in his gullet. (Do not be distracted by Mr. Fairchild, who ascribes this paragraph to 1826, nor by the editor T. Sadler, who ascribes it to Dr. Thomas Arnold.) Evidently, Wordsworth has been reminded of this habit of Coleridge by his tiny peep into the book. He had been on a small Continental tour with Coleridge in 1828, and would surely know if his opinions on the point had altered. One may deduce that, although Wordsworth felt it proper to speak of the book with sad patience, as a grave wrong done through ignorance, in his own mind he felt that it simply gives a true record. The third edition (1864) came out when Allsop was elderly and respected, and has an impressive introduction; he is still angry with the clergy who 'make use' of Coleridge ('I distinctly state that Coleridge ever retained the convictions of his earnest early youth'), and reprints some of the scurrility attacking the first edition. For that edition, he says, he had wanted to make a full statement of the esoteric views of Coleridge, but the publishers would not allow it, which proves that they have a secret method of imposing censorship. All the same, one need not believe that this esoteric doctrine was in tidy order. Coleridge always talked to please his hearer, and evidently found it delightful to lecture a generous-minded enlightened young man, like the friends of his youth, after his long struggle to please the grisly Christians. I think one could even point out the places where he yielded insincerely, as in agreeing that a really good government would not inflict any punishments at all, whereas most of the time his agreement was eager, and supporting arguments would bubble up. But to discount his talk to Allsop, even in a stronger degree than I have ventured, does not make it any less real as one of the permanent factions in the battlefield of his mind. One gets a similar impression, for example, when he is writing a long note in a copy of the *Sermons* of Jeremy Taylor, who became almost as bad as the Restoration Archbishop Tillotson, who offered a broad comforting view of the basic Christian doctrines, whereas Coleridge considered his offers a delusion, tantamount to Socinianism (*Coleridge on the Seventeenth Century*, R. Brinkley, p. 284). Do not be deluded, he urges the reader:

> Above all, do not dwell too much on the apparent Absurdity and Horror of the doctrine he opposes; but examine what he puts in its place.

The Absurdity and Horror which Coleridge finds so apparent is what he had undertaken to defend for the rest of his life, and he gives it this

[*99*]

description as a matter of course. One is tempted to hope that Lamb was right when he said, with his unshakeable loyalty, 'It's only Coleridge's fun.' But nobody could think this about his remarks, a year before he died, on the achievement of Negro Emancipation (*Table Talk*, 17th June '33). He hopes it may not do the great harm he expects. Only a purely Christian motive can possibly produce good results, and here the Nonconformists have been allowed to meddle, so it isn't Christian at all. Mr. Pecksniff might have talked so, if he had been High Church; it is really horrifying. But he continued to be jovial at parties, so far as his health allowed, in his last years, and I suppose we should agree with his friends that there was a kind of atonement in that.

To the Author of 'The Robbers'

Schiller! that hour I would have wish'd to die.
If thro' the shuddering midnight I had sent
From the dark dungeon of the Tower time-rent
That fearful voice, a famish'd Father's cry —
Lest in some after moment aught more mean   5
Might stamp me mortal! A triumphant shout
Black Horror scream'd, and all her *goblin* rout
Diminish'd shrunk from the more withering scene!
Ah! Bard tremendous in sublimity!
Could I behold thee in thy loftier mood   10
Wandering at eve with finely-frenzied eye
Beneath some vast old tempest-swinging wood!
Awhile with mute awe gazing I would brood:
Then weep aloud in a wild ecstasy!

Monologue to a Young Jack Ass in Jesus Piece. Its mother near it chained to a log

Poor little Foal of an oppresséd race!
I love the languid patience of thy face:
And oft with gentle hand I give thee bread,
And clap thy ragged coat and scratch thy head.
But what thy dulled spirit hath dismay'd,   5

That never thou dost sport along the glade?
And (most unlike the nature of things young)
That still to earth thy moping head is hung?
Doth thy prophetic soul anticipate,
Meek Child of Misery! thy future fate? 10
The starving meal, and all the thousand aches
'That patient Merit of the Unworthy takes'?
Or is thy sad heart thrill'd with filial pain
To see thy wretched mother's shorten'd chain?
And truly, very piteous is *her* lot – 15
Chain'd to a log upon a narrow spot,
Where the close-eaten grass is scarcely seen,
While sweet around her waves the tempting green!

Poor Ass! thy master should have learnt to show
Pity – best taught by fellowship of Woe! 20
For much I fear me that *He* lives like thee,
Half famish'd in a land of Luxury!
How *askingly* its steps toward me tend?
It seems to say, 'And have I then *one* friend?'
Innocent foal! thou despised and forlorn! 25
I hail thee *Brother* – spite of the fool's scorn!
And fain I'd take thee with me, to the Dell
Where high-soul'd Pantisocracy shall dwell!
Where Mirth shall tickle Plenty's ribless side,
And smiles from Beauty's Lip on sunbeams glide, 30
Where Toil shall wed young Health that charming Lass!
And use his sleek cows for a looking-glass –
Where Rats shall mess with Terriers hand-in-glove
And Mice with Pussy's Whiskers sport in Love!
How thou wouldst toss thy heels in gamesome play, 35
And frisk about, as lamb or kitten gay!
Yea! and more musically sweet to me
Thy dissonant harsh bray of joy would be,
Than Handel's softest airs that soothe to rest
The tumult of a scoundrel Monarch's Breast. 40

[*102*]

The Eolian Harp

My pensive Sara! thy soft cheek reclined
Thus on mine arm, most soothing sweet it is
To sit beside our Cot, our Cot o'ergrown
With white-flower'd Jasmin, and the broad-leav'd Myrtle,
And watch the clouds, that late were rich with light,   5
Slow saddening round, and mark the star of eve
Shine opposite! How exquisite the scents
Snatch'd from yon bean-field! and the world *so* hush'd!
Hark! the still murmur of the distant Sea
Tells us of silence.
              And th' Eolian Lute,   10
How by the desultory breeze caress'd,
Like some coy maid half yielding to her lover,
It pours such sweet upbraidings, as must needs
Tempt to repeat the wrong! And now, its strings
Boldlier swept, the long sequacious notes   15
Over delicious surges sink and rise,
Such a soft floating witchery of sound
Methinks, it should have been impossible
Not to love all things in a World like this,
Where e'en the Breezes of the simple Air   20
Possess the power and Spirit of Melody!

And thus, my Love! as on the midway slope
Of yonder hill I stretch my limbs at noon,
Whilst through my half-clos'd eye-lids I behold
The sunbeams dance, like diamonds, on the main,   25
And tranquil muse upon tranquillity;
Full many a thought uncall'd and undetain'd,
And many idle flitting phantasies,
Traverse my indolent and passive brain,
As wild and various as the random gales   30
That swell and flutter on this subject Lute!
   Or what if all of animated nature

[*103*]

Be but organic Harps diversely fram'd,
That tremble into thought, as o'er them sweeps
Plastic and vast, one intellectual breeze,   35
At once the Soul of each, and God of all?
    But thy more serious eye a mild reproof
Darts, O belovéd Woman! nor such thoughts
Dim and unhallow'd dost thou not reject
And biddest me walk humbly with my God.   40
Meek Daughter in the family of Christ!
Well hast thou said and holily disprais'd
These shapings of the unregenerate mind;
Bubbles that glitter as they rise and break
On vain Philosophy's aye-babbling spring.   45
For never guiltless may I speak of him,
The Incomprehensible! save when with awe
I praise him, and with Faith that inly *feels*;
Who with his saving mercies healéd me,
A sinful and most miserable man,   50
Wilder'd and dark, and gave me to possess
Peace, and this Cot, and thee, dear honoured Maid!

From *Reflections on Entering into Active Life*

Low was our pretty Cot: our tallest Rose
Peep'd at the chamber-window. We could hear
At silent noon, and eve, and early morn,
The Sea's faint murmur. In the open air
Our Myrtles blossom'd; and across the porch   5
Thick Jasmins twined: the little landscape round
Was green and woody, and refresh'd the eye.
It was a spot which you might aptly call
The Valley of Seclusion! Once I saw

(Hallowing his Sabbath-day by quietness)   10
A wealthy son of Commerce saunter by,
Bristowa's citizen – he paus'd, and look'd
With a pleased sadness and gaz'd all around,
Then eye'd our cottage and gaz'd round again,
And said, it was a *blessed little place.*   15
And we *were* bless'd. Oft with patient ear
Long-listening to the viewless sky-lark's note
(Viewless, or haply for a moment seen
Gleaming on sunny wings) in whisper'd tones
I've said to my Belovéd, 'Such sweet Girl!   20
The inobtrusive song of Happiness,
Unearthly minstrelsy! then only heard
When the Soul seeks to hear; when all is hush'd,
And the Heart listens!'
                              But the time, when first
From that low Dell, steep up the stony Mount   25
I climb'd with perilous toil and reach'd the top,
Oh! what a goodly scene! *Here* the bleak mount,
The bare bleak mountain speckled thin with sheep;
Grey clouds, that shadowing spot the sunny fields;
And river, now with bushy rocks o'er-brow'd,   30
Now winding bright and full, with naked banks;
And seats, and lawns, the Abbey and the wood,
And cots, and hamlets, and faint city-spire;
The Channel *there*, the Islands and white sails,
Dim coasts, and cloud-like hills, and shoreless Ocean – 35
It seem'd like Omnipresence! God, methought,
Had built him there a Temple: the whole World
Was *imag'd* in its vast circumference:
No *wish* profan'd my overwhelméd heart.
Blest hour! It was a luxury, – to be!   40

From *Religious Musings*

　　　　　　　　　Lovely was the death
Of Him whose life was Love! Holy with power
He on the thought-benighted Sceptic beamed
Manifest Godhead, melting into day
What floating mists of dark idolatry　　　　　　　　5
Broke and misshaped the omnipresent Sire:
And first by Fear uncharmed the drowséd Soul.
Till of its nobler nature it 'gan feel
Dim recollections; and thence soared to Hope.
Strong to believe whate'er of mystic good　　　　　10
The Eternal dooms for His immortal sons.
From Hope and firmer Faith to perfect Love
Attracted and absorbed: and centered there
God only to behold, and know, and feel,
Till by exclusive consciousness of God　　　　　　15
All self-annihilated it shall make
God its Identity: God all in all!
We and our Father one!
　　　　　　　　　　And blest are they,
Who in this fleshly World, the elect of Heaven,
Their strong eye darting through the deeds of men,　　20
Adore with steadfast unpresuming gaze
Him Nature's essence, mind, and energy!

　　　　*　　　*　　　*　　　*

There is one Mind, one omnipresent Mind,
Omnific. His most holy name is Love.
Truth of subliming import! with the which　　　　　25
Who feeds and saturates his constant soul,
He from his small particular orbit flies
With blest outstarting! From himself he flies,
Stands in the sun, and with no partial gaze
Views all creation; and he loves it all,　　　　　　30
And blesses it, and calls it very good!

This is indeed to dwell with the Most High!
Cherubs and rapture-trembling Seraphim
Can press no nearer to the Almighty's throne.
But that we roam unconscious, or with hearts   35
Unfeeling of our universal Sire,
And that in His vast family no Cain
Injures uninjured (in her best-aimed blow
Victorious Murder a blind Suicide)
Haply for this some younger Angel now   40
Looks down on Human Nature: and, behold!
A sea of blood bestrewed with wrecks, where mad
Embattling Interests on each other rush
With unhelmed rage!
                'Tis the sublime of man,
Our noontide Majesty, to know ourselves   45
Parts and proportions of one wondrous whole!
This fraternises man, this constitutes
Our charities and bearings. But 'tis God
Diffused through all, that doth make all one whole;
This the worst superstition, him except   50
Aught to desire, Supreme Reality!
The plenitude and permanence of bliss!
O Fiends of Superstition! not that oft
The erring Priest hath stained with brother's blood
Your grisly idols, not for this may wrath   55
Thunder against you from the Holy One!
But o'er some plain that steameth to the sun,
Peopled with Death; or where more hideous Trade
Loud-laughing packs his bales of human anguish;
I will raise up a mourning, O ye Fiends!   60
And curse your spells, that film the eye of Faith,
Hiding the present God; whose presence lost,
The moral world's cohesion, we become
An Anarchy of Spirits! Toy-bewitched,
Made blind by lusts, disherited of soul,   65
No common centre Man, no common sire

Knoweth! A sordid solitary thing,
Mid countless brethren with a lonely heart
Through courts and cities the smooth savage roams
Feeling himself, his own low self the whole;   70

                *   *   *   *

Thee to defend, meek Galilaean! Thee
And thy mild laws of Love unutterable,
Mistrust and Enmity have burst the bands
Of social peace: and listening Treachery lurks
With pious fraud to snare a brother's life;   75
And childless widows o'er the groaning land
Wail numberless; and orphans weep for bread!
Thee to defend, dear Saviour of Mankind!
Thee, Lamb of God! Thee, blameless Prince of Peace!
From all sides rush the thirsty brood of War! –   80

                *   *   *   *

Nor least in savagery of holy zeal,
Apt for the yoke, the race degenerate,
Whom Britain erst had blushed to call her sons!
Thee to defend the Moloch Priest prefers
The prayer of hate, and bellows to the herd,   85
That Deity, Accomplice Deity
In the fierce jealousy of wakened wrath
Will go forth with our armies and our fleets
To scatter the red ruin on their foes!

                *   *   *   *

            O ye numberless,   90
Whom foul Oppression's ruffian gluttony
Drives from Life's plenteous feast! O thou poor Wretch
Who nursed in darkness and made wild by want,
Roamest for prey, yea thy unnatural hand
Dost lift to deeds of blood! O pale-eyed form,   95
The victim of seduction, doomed to know
Polluted nights and days of blasphemy;
Who in loathed orgies with lewd wassailers

Must gaily laugh, while thy remembered Home
Gnaws like a viper at thy secret heart!   100
O agéd Women, ye who weekly catch
The morsel tossed by law-forced charity,
And die so slowly, that none call it murder!
O loathly suppliants! ye, that unreceived
Totter heart-broken from the closing gates   105
Of the full Lazar-house; or, gazing, stand,
Sick with despair! O ye to Glory's field
Forced or ensnared, who, as ye gasp in death,
Bleed with new wounds beneath the vulture's beak!
O thou poor widow, who in dreams dost view   110
Thy husband's mangled corse, and from short doze
Start'st with a shriek; or in thy half-thatched cot
Waked by the wintry night-storm, wet and cold
Cow'rst o'er thy screaming baby! Rest awhile
Children of Wretchedness! More groans must rise,   115
More blood must stream, or ere your wrongs be full.
Yet is the day of Retribution nigh:

          *   *   *   *

               Believe thou, O my soul,
Life is a vision shadowy of Truth;
And vice, and anguish, and the wormy grave,   120
Shapes of a dream! The veiling clouds retire,
And lo! the Throne of the redeeming God
Forth flashing unimaginable day
Wraps in one blaze earth, heaven and deepest hell.

Contemplant Spirits! ye that hover o'er   125
With untired gaze the immeasurable fount
Ebullient with creative Deity!
And ye of plastic power, that interfused
Roll through the grosser and material mass
In organizing surge! Holies of God!   130
(And what if Monads of the infinite mind?)
I haply journeying my immortal course

Shall sometime join your mystic choir! Till then
I discipline my young and novice thought
In ministeries of heart-stirring song,
And aye on Meditation's heaven-ward wing
Soaring aloft I breathe the empyreal air
Of Love, omnific, omnipresent Love . . .

From *The Destiny of Nations*

For what is Freedom, but the unfettered use
Of all the powers which God for use had given?
But chiefly this, him First, him Last to view
Through meaner powers and secondary things
Effulgent, as through clouds that veil his blaze.   5
For all that meets the bodily sense I deem
Symbolical, one mighty alphabet
For infant minds; and we in this low world
Placed with our backs to bright Reality,
That we may learn with young unwounded ken   10
The substance from its shadow. Infinite Love,
Whose latence is the plenitude of All,
Thou with retracted beams, and self-eclipse
Veiling, revealest thine eternal Sun.

But some there are who deem themselves most free   15
When they within this gross and visible sphere
Chain down the wingéd thought, scoffing ascent,
Proud in their meanness: and themselves they cheat
With noisy emptiness of learnéd phrase,
Their subtle fluids, impacts, essences,   20
Self-working tools, uncaused effects, and all
Those blind Omniscients, those Almighty Slaves,

Untenanting creation of its God.
    But Properties are God: the naked mass
(If mass there be, fantastic guess or ghost)   25
Acts only by its inactivity.
Here we pause humbly. Others boldlier think
That as one body seems the aggregate
Of atoms numberless, each organized;
So by a strange and dim similitude   30
Infinite myriads of self-conscious minds
Are one all-conscious Spirit, which informs
With absolute ubiquity of thought
(His one eternal self-affirming act!)
All his involvéd Monads, that yet seem   35
With various province and apt agency
Each to pursue its own self-centering end.
Some nurse the infant diamond in the mine;
Some roll the genial juices through the oak;
Some drive the mutinous clouds to clash in air,   40
And rushing on the storm with whirlwind speed,
Yoke the red lightnings to their volleying car.
Thus these pursue their never-varying course,
No eddy in their stream. Others, more wild,
With complex interests weaving human fates,   45
Duteous or proud, alike obedient all,
Evolve the process of eternal good.

    And what if some rebellious, o'er dark realms
Arrogate power? yet these train up to God,
And on the rude eye, unconfirmed for day,   50
Flash meteor-lights better than total gloom.
As ere from Lieule-Oaive's vapoury head
The Laplander beholds the far-off Sun
Dart his slant beam on unobeying snows,
While yet the stern and solitary Night   55
Brooks no alternate sway, the Boreal Morn
With mimic lustre substitutes its gleam,

Guiding his course or by Niemi lake
Or Balda Zhiok, or the mossy stone
Of Solfar-kapper, while the snowy blast   60
Drifts arrowy by, or eddies round his sledge,
Making the poor babe at its mother's back
Scream in its scanty cradle: he the while
Wins gentle solace as with upward eye
He marks the streamy banners of the North,   65
Thinking himself those happy spirits shall join
Who there in floating robes of rosy light
Dance sportively. For Fancy is the power
That first unsensualises the dark mind,
Giving it new delights; and bids it swell   70
With wild activity; and peopling air,
By obscure fears of Beings invisible,
Emancipates it from the grosser thrall
Of the present impulse, teaching Self-control,
Till Superstition with unconscious hand   75
Seat Reason on her throne. Wherefore not vain,
Nor yet without permitted power impressed,
I deem those legends terrible, with which
The polar ancient thrills his uncouth throng:
Whether of pitying Spirits that make their moan   80
O'er slaughter'd infants, or that Giant Bird
Vuokho, of whose rushing wings the noise
Is Tempest, when the unutterable Shape
Speeds from the mother of Death and utters once
That shriek, which never murderer heard, and lived.   85

    *   *   *   *

If there be Beings of higher class than Man,
I deem no nobler province they possess,
Than by disposal of apt circumstance
To rear up kingdoms: and the deeds they prompt,
Distinguishing from mortal agency,   90
They choose their human ministers from such states

As still the Epic song half fears to name,
Repelled from all the minstrelsies that strike
The palace-roof and soothe the monarch's pride.
And such, perhaps, the Spirit, who (if words   95
Witnessed by answering deeds may claim our faith)
Held commune with that warrior-maid of France
Who scourged the Invader.

This Lime-Tree Bower My Prison

Well – they are gone: and here must I remain,
Lam'd by the scathe of fire, lonely & faint,
This lime-tree bower my prison. They, meantime,
My friends, whom I may never meet again,
On springy heath, along the hill-top edge,   5
Wander delighted, and look down, perchance,
On that same rifted Dell, where many an Ash
Twists it's wild limbs beside the ferny rock,
Whose plumy ferns for ever nod and drip
Spray'd by the waterfall. But chiefly Thou,   10
My gentle-hearted CHARLES! thou, who hast pin'd
And hunger'd after Nature many a year
In the great City pent, winning thy way,
With sad yet bowed soul, thro' evil & pain
And strange calamity. – Ah slowly sink   15
Behind the western ridge; thou glorious Sun!
Shine in the slant beams of the sinking orb,
Ye purple Heath-flowers! Richlier burn, ye Clouds!
Live in the yellow Light, ye distant Groves!
And kindle, thou blue Ocean! So my friend   20
Struck with joy's deepest calm, and gazing round
On the wide view, may gaze till all doth seem
Less gross than bodily, a living Thing

That acts upon the mind, and with such hues
As cloathe the Almighty Spirit, when he makes   25
Spirits perceive His presence!
                         A Delight
Comes sudden on my heart, and I am glad
As I myself were there! Nor in this bower
Want I sweet sounds or pleasing shapes. I watch'd
The sunshine of each broad transparent Leaf   30
Broke by the shadows of the Leaf or Stem,
Which hung above it: and that Wall-nut Tree
Was richly ting'd: and a deep radiance lay
Full on the ancient ivy which usurps
Those fronting elms, and now with blackest mass   35
Makes their dark foliage gleam a lighter hue
Thro' the last twilight. -- And tho' the rapid bat
Wheels silent by and not a swallow twitters,
Yet still the solitary humble-bee
Sings in the bean flower. Henceforth I shall know   40
That nature ne'er deserts the wise & pure,
No scene so narrow, but may well employ
Each faculty of sense, and keep the heart
Awake to Love & Beauty: and sometimes
'Tis well to be bereav'd of promis'd good   45
That we may lift the soul, & contemplate
With lively joy the joys, we cannot share.
My Sister & my Friends! when the last Rook
Beat it's straight path along the dusky air
Homewards, I bless'd it; deeming, it's black wing   50
Cross'd, like a speck, the blaze of setting day,
While ye stood gazing; or when all was still,
Flew creaking o'er your heads, & had a charm
For you, my Sister & my Friends! to whom
No sound is dissonant, which tells of Life!   55

The Foster-mother's Tale. A Narration in Dramatic Blank Verse

MARIA. But that entrance, Mother!
FOSTER-MOTHER. Can no one hear? It is a perilous tale!
MARIA. No one.
FOSTER-MOTHER. My husband's father told it me,
Poor old Leoni! – Angels rest his soul!   5
He was a woodman, and could fell and saw
With lusty arm. You know that huge round beam
Which props the hanging wall of the old Chapel?
Beneath that tree, while yet it was a tree,
He found a baby wrapt in mosses, lined   10
With thistle-beards, and such small locks of wool
As hang on brambles. Well, he brought him home,
And rear'd him at the then Lord Velez' cost.
And so the babe grew up a pretty boy,
A pretty boy, but most unteachable –   15
And never learnt a prayer, nor told a bead,
But knew the names of birds, and mock'd their notes,
And whistled, as he were a bird himself:
And all the autumn 'twas his only play
To get the seeds of wild flowers, and to plant them   20
With earth and water, on the stumps of trees.
A Friar, who gather'd simples in the wood,
A grey-haired man – he lov'd this little boy,
The boy lov'd him – and, when the Friar taught him,
He soon could write with the pen: and from that time,   25
Lived chiefly at the Convent or the Castle.
So he became a very learnéd youth.
But Oh! poor wretch! – he read, and read, and read,
Till his brain turn'd – and ere his twentieth year,
He had unlawful thoughts of many things: 30
And though he prayed, he never lov'd to pray
With holy men, nor in a holy place –

[117]

But yet his speech, it was so soft and sweet,
The late Lord Velez ne'er was wearied with him.
And once, as by the north side of the Chapel   35
They stood together, chain'd in deep discourse,
The earth heav'd under them with such a groan,
That the wall totter'd, and had well-nigh fallen
Right on their heads. My Lord was sorely frighten'd;
A fever seiz'd him, and he made confession   40
Of all the heretical and lawless talk
Which brought this judgment: so the youth was seiz'd
And cast into that cell. My husband's father
Sobb'd like a child – it almost broke his heart:
And once as he was working in the cellar,   45
He heard a voice distinctly; 'twas the youth's,
Who sung a doleful song about green fields,
How sweet it were on lake or wild savannah,
To hunt for food, and be a naked man,
And wander up and down at liberty.   50
Leoni doted on the youth, and now
His love grew desperate; and defying death,
He made that cunning entrance I describ'd:
And the young man escap'd.
MARIA. 'Tis a sweet tale: 55
And what became of him?
FOSTER-MOTHER. He went on shipboard
With those bold voyagers, who made discovery
Of golden lands. Leoni's younger brother
Went likewise, and when he return'd to Spain,   60
He told Leoni, that the poor mad youth,
Soon after they arriv'd in that new world,
In spite of his dissuasion, seiz'd a boat,
And all alone, set sail by silent moonlight
Up a great river, great as any sea,   65
And ne'er was heard of more: but 'tis suppos'd,
He liv'd and died among the savage men.

The Dungeon

And this place our forefathers made for man!
This is the process of our love and wisdom,
To each poor brother who offends against us –
Most innocent, perhaps – and what if guilty?
Is this the only cure? Merciful God!   5
Each pore and natural outlet shrivell'd up
By Ignorance and parching Poverty,
His energies roll back upon his heart,
And stagnate and corrupt; till chang'd to poison,
They break out on him, like a loathsome plague-   10
    spot;
Then we call in our pamper'd mountebanks –
And this is their best cure! uncomforted
And friendless solitude, groaning and tears,
And savage faces, at the clanking hour,
Seen through the steams and vapour of his   15
    dungeon,
By the lamp's dismal twilight! So he lies
Circled with evil, till his very soul
Unmoulds its essence, hopelessly deform'd
By sights of ever more deformity!

With other ministrations thou, O Nature!   20
Healest thy wandering and distemper'd child:
Thou pourest on him thy soft influences,
Thy sunny hues, fair forms, and breathing sweets,
Thy melodies of woods, and winds, and waters,
Till he relent, and can no more endure   25
To be a jarring and a dissonant thing,
Amid this general dance and minstrelsy;
But, bursting into tears, wins back his way,
His angry spirit heal'd and harmoniz'd
By the benignant touch of Love and Beauty.   30

[117]

On a Ruined House in a Romantic Country

(From *Sonnets Attempted in the Manner of Contemporary Writers*)

And this reft house is that the which he built,
Lamented Jack! And here his malt he pil'd,
Cautious in vain! These rats that squeak so wild,
Squeak, not unconscious of their father's guilt.
'Did ye not see her gleaming thro' the glade?   5
Belike, 'twas she, the maiden all forlorn.
What though she milk no cow with crumpled horn,
Yet *aye* she haunts the dale where *erst* she stray'd;
And *aye* beside her stalks her amorous knight!
Still on his thighs their wonted brogues are worn,   10
And thro' those brogues, still tatter'd and betorn,
His hindward charms gleam an unearthly white;
As when thro' broken clouds at night's high noon
Peeps in fair fragments forth the full-orb'd harvest-
    moon!

The Rime of the Ancient Mariner

In Seven Parts

ARGUMENT

How a Ship having passed the Line was driven by storms to
the cold Country towards the South Pole; and how from
thence she made her course to the tropical Latitude of the Great
Pacific Ocean; and of the strange things that befell; and in
what manner the Ancient Mariner came back to his own
Country.

EPIGRAPH
(1817)

(From Thomas Burnet's *Archaeologiae Philosophicae* of 1692, in Derek
Roper's translation.)

I can readily believe that in the sum of existing things there
are more invisible beings than visible, [and that there are more
angels in heaven than there are fishes in the sea.*] 1. But who
will explain this great family to us – their ranks, their
relationships, their differences, and their respective duties?
[What do they do, and where do they live?†] 2. Man's
intelligence has always sought knowledge of these matters,
but has never attained it. Meanwhile, I do not deny that it
pleases me sometimes to contemplate in my mind, as in a
picture, the idea of a greater and better world; lest the mind,
grown used to dealing with the small matters of everyday life,
should dwindle and be wholly submerged in petty thoughts.
Nevertheless we should be vigilant of truth and keep a sense of
proportion, so that we may discriminate between things certain
and things uncertain, daylight and darkness.

* Omitted by Coleridge.
† Added by Coleridge.

PART I

It is an ancient Mariner,
    And he stoppeth one of three.
'By thy long grey beard and glittering eye,
    Now wherefore stopp'st thou me?

The Bridegroom's doors are opened wide   5
    And I am next of kin;
The guests are met, the feast is set: –
    May'st hear the merry din.'

But still he holds the Wedding-Guest –
    'There was a ship,' quoth he –   10
'Nay, if thou'st got a laughsome tale,
    Mariner! come with me.'

He holds him with his skinny hand,
    Quoth he, 'there was a Ship' –
'Now get thee hence, thou grey-beard loon!   15
    Or my Staff shall make thee skip.'

He holds him with his glittering eye –
    The Wedding-Guest stood still,
And listens like a three years' child:
    The Mariner hath his will.   20

The Wedding-Guest sat on a stone:
    He cannot choose but hear;
And thus spake on that ancient man,
    The bright-eyed Mariner.

'The ship was cheered, the harbour cleared,   25
    Merrily did we drop
Below the kirk, below the hill,
    Below the lighthouse top.

The Sun came up upon the left,
    Out of the sea came he!   30
And he shone bright, and on the right
    Went down into the sea.

Higher and higher every day,
    Till over the mast at noon' –
The Wedding-Guest here beat his breast,   35
    For he heard the loud bassoon.

The bride hath paced into the hall,
    Red as a rose is she;
Nodding their heads before her goes
    The merry minstrelsy.   40

The Wedding-Guest he beat his breast,
    Yet he cannot choose but hear;
And thus spake on that ancient man,
    The bright-eyed Mariner.

'Listen, Stranger! Storm and Wind,   45
    A Wind and Tempest strong!
For days and weeks it play'd us freaks –
    Like chaff we drove along.
                [121]

With sloping masts and dipping prow,
    As who pursued with yell and blow   50
    Still treads the shadow of his foe,
And forward bends his head,
    The ship drove fast, loud roared the blast,
And southward aye we fled.

And now there came both mist and snow,   55
    And it grew wondrous cold:
And ice, mast-high, came floating by
    As green as emerald.

And through the drifts the snowy clifts
    Did send a dismal sheen: 60
Nor shapes of men nor beasts we ken –
    The ice was all between.

The ice was here, the ice was there,
    The ice was all around:
It cracked and growled, and roared and howled,   65
    Like noises in a swound!

At length did cross an Albatross,
    Thorough the fog it came;
As if it had been a Christian soul,
    We hailed it in God's name.   70

The mariners gave it biscuit-worms,
    And round and round it flew.
The ice did split with a thunder-fit;
    The helmsman steered us through!

And a good south wind sprung up behind;   75
    The Albatross did follow,
And every day, for food or play,
    Came to the mariner's hollo!

In mist or cloud, on mast or shroud,
    It perched for vespers nine;   80
Whiles all the night, through fog-smoke white,
    Glimmered the white Moon-shine.'

'God save thee, ancient Mariner!
    From the fiends, that plague thee thus! –
Why look'st thou so?' – With my cross-bow   85
    I shot the Albatross.

PART II

The Sun came up upon the right,
    Out of the sea came he;
And broad as a weft upon the left
    Went down into the sea.   90

And the good south wind still blew behind,
    But no sweet bird did follow,
Nor any day for food or play
    Came to the mariners' hollo!

And I had done a hellish thing,   95
    And it would work 'em woe:
For all averred, I had killed the bird
    That made the breeze to blow.
Ah wretch! said they, the bird to slay,
    That made the breeze to blow!   100

Nor dim nor red, like God's own head,
    The glorious Sun uprist:
Then all averred, I had killed the bird
    That brought the fog and mist.
'Twas right, said they, such birds to slay,   105
    That bring the fog and mist.

The fair breeze blew, the white foam flew,
    The furrow followed free;
We were the first that ever burst
    Into that silent sea.   110

Down dropt the breeze, the sails dropt down,
    'Twas sad as sad could be;
And we did speak only to break
    The silence of the sea!

All in a hot and copper sky,   115
    The bloody Sun, at noon,
Right up above the mast did stand,
    No bigger than the Moon.

Day after day, day after day,
    We stuck, nor breath nor motion;   120
As idle as a painted ship
    Upon a painted ocean.

Water, water, every where,
    And all the boards did shrink;
Water, water, every where,   125
    Nor any drop to drink.

The very deep did rot: O Christ!
    That ever this should be!
Yea, slimy things did crawl with legs
    Upon the slimy sea.   130

About, about, in reel and rout
    The death-fires danced at night;
The water, like a witch's oils,
    Burnt green, and blue and white.

And some in dreams assuréd were   135
    Of the Spirit that plagued us so;
Nine fathom deep he had followed us
    From the land of mist and snow.

And every tongue, through utter drought,
    Was withered at the root;   140
We could not speak, no more than if
    We had been choked with soot.

Ah! well a-day! what evil looks
    Had I from old and young!
Instead of the cross, the Albatross   145
    About my neck was hung.

PART III

There passed a weary time. Each throat
    Was parched, and glazed each eye.
A weary time! a weary time!
    How glazed each weary eye,   150
When looking westward, I beheld
    A something in the sky.

At first it seemed a little speck,
    And then it seemed a mist;
It moved and moved, and took at last   155
    A certain shape, I wist.

A speck, a mist, a shape, I wist!
    And still it neared and neared:
As if it dodged a water-sprite,
    It plunged and tacked and veered.   160

With throats unslaked, with black lips baked,
    We could nor laugh nor wail;
Then while through drought all dumb they stood
I bit my arm and sucked the blood
    And cried, A sail! a sail!   165

With throats unslaked, with black lips baked,
  Agape they heard me call:
Gramercy! they for joy did grin,
And all at once their breath drew in,
  As they were drinking all.   170

See! see! (I cried) she tacks no more!
  Hither to work us weal;
Without a breeze, without a tide,
  She steadies with upright keel!

The western wave was all a-flame.   175
  The day was well nigh done!
Almost upon the western wave
  Rested the broad bright Sun;
When that strange shape drove suddenly
  Betwixt us and the Sun.   180

And straight the Sun was flecked with bars,
  (Heaven's Mother send us grace!)
As if through a dungeon-grate he peered
  With broad and burning face.

Alas! (thought I, and my heart beat loud)   185
  How fast she nears and nears!
Are those *her* sails that glance in the Sun,
  Like restless gossameres?

Are those *her* ribs through which the Sun
  Did peer, as through a grate?   190
And is that Woman all her crew?
Is that a Death? and are there two?
  Is Death that woman's mate?

This Ship it was a plankless thing,
    – A bare Anatomy!   195
A plankless spectre – and it mov'd
    Like a Being of the Sea!
The Woman and a fleshless Man
    Therein sate merrily.

His bones were black with many a crack,   200
    All black and bare, I ween;
Jet-black and bare, save where with rust
Of mouldy damps and charnel crust
    They're patched with purple and green.

Her lips were red, *her* looks were free,   205
    Her locks were yellow as gold:
Her skin was as white as leprosy,
The Night-mare Life-in-Death was she
Who thicks man's blood with cold.

The naked hulk alongside came,   210
    And the twain were casting dice;
'The game is done! I've won! I've won!'
    Quoth she, and whistles thrice.

A gust of wind sterte up behind
    And whistled through his bones;   215
Through the holes of his eyes and the hole of his
      mouth
    Half-whistles and half-groans.

The Sun's rim dips; the stars rush out
    At one stride comes the dark;
With far-heard whisper, o'er the sea,   220
    Off shot the spectre-bark.

With far-heard whisper on the main
    Off shot the spectre-ship;
And stifled words and groans of pain
    Mix'd on each murmuring lip.   225

We listened and looked sideways up!
    Fear at my heart, as at a cup,
    My life-blood seemed to sip!
The stars were dim, and thick the night,
The steersman's face by his lamp gleamed white;   230
    From the sails the dews did drip –
Till clomb above the eastern bar
The horned Moon, with one bright star
    Within the nether tip.

The Sun's rim dips; the stars rush out: 235
    At one stride comes the dark;
With far-heard whisper, o'er the sea,
    Off shot the spectre-bark.

We listened and looked sideways up!
Fear at my heart, as at a cup,   240
    My life-blood seemed to sip!
The stars were dim, and thick the night,
The steersman's face by his lamp gleamed white;
    From the sails the dews did drip –
Till clomb above the eastern bar   245
The horned Moon, with one bright star
    Within the nether tip.

See Notes, p. 229, and Critical Introduction, p. 51. The lines here are numbered consecutively, to avoid suggesting any preference for one of the versions.

One after one, by the star-dogged Moon,
  Too quick for groan or sigh,
Each turned his face with a ghastly pang,   250
  And cursed me with his eye.

Four times fifty living men,
  (And I heard nor sigh nor groan)
With heavy thump, a lifeless lump,
  They dropped down one by one.   255

The souls did from their bodies fly, –
  They fled to bliss or woe!
And every soul, it passed me by,
  Like the whizz of my cross-bow!

PART IV

'I fear thee, ancient Mariner!   260
  I fear thy skinny hand!
And thou art long, and lank, and brown,
  As is the ribbed sea-sand.

I fear thee and thy glittering eye,
  And thy skinny hand, so brown.' –   265
Fear not, fear not, thou Wedding-Guest!
  This body dropt not down.

Alone, alone, all, all alone,
  Alone on a wide wide sea!
And Christ would take no pity on   270
  My soul in agony.

The many men, so beautiful!
  And they all dead did lie:
And a million million slimy things
  Lived on; and so did I.   275

[130]

I looked upon the rotting sea,
    And drew my eyes away;
I looked upon the rotting deck,
    And there the dead men lay.

I looked to heaven, and tried to pray;   280
    But or ever a prayer had gusht,
A wicked whisper came, and made
    My heart as dry as dust.

I closed my lids, and kept them close,
    And the balls like pulses beat;   285
For the sky and the sea, and the sea and the sky
Lay like a load on my weary eye,
    And the dead were at my feet.

The cold sweat melted from their limbs,
    Nor rot nor reek did they: 290
The look with which they looked on me
    Had never passed away.

An orphan's curse would drag to hell
    A spirit from on high;
But oh! more horrible than that   295
    Is the curse in a dead man's eye!
Seven days, seven nights, I saw that curse,
    And yet I could not die.

The moving Moon went up the sky,
    And no where did abide: 300
Softly she was going up,
    And a star or two beside –

Her beams bemocked the sultry main,
  Like April hoar-frost spread;
But where the ship's huge shadow lay,
The charméd water burnt alway
  A still and awful red.

Beyond the shadow of the ship,
  I watched the water-snakes:
They moved in tracks of shining white,
And when they reared, the elfish light
  Fell off in hoary flakes.

Within the shadow of the ship
  I watched their rich attire:
Blue, glossy green, and velvet black,
They coiled and swam; and every track
  Was a flash of golden fire.

O happy living things! no tongue
  Their beauty might declare:
A spring of love gushed from my heart,
  And I blessed them unaware:
Sure my kind saint took pity on me,
  And I blessed them unaware.

The self-same moment I could pray;
  And from my neck so free
The Albatross fell off, and sank
  Like lead into the sea.

PART V

Oh sleep! it is a gentle thing,
  Beloved from pole to pole!
To Mary Queen the praise be given!
She sent the gentle sleep from Heaven,
  That slid into my soul.

305

310

315

320

325

330

[*132*]

The silly buckets on the deck,
    That had so long remained,
I dreamt that they were filled with dew;   335
    And when I awoke, it rained.

My lips were wet, my throat was cold,
    My garments all were dank;
Sure I had drunken in my dreams,
    And still my body drank.   340

I moved, and could not feel my limbs:
    I was so light – almost
I thought that I had died in sleep,
    And was a blessèd ghost.

And soon I heard a roaring wind: 345
    It did not come anear;
But with its sound it shook the sails,
    That were so thin and sere.

The upper air burst into life!
    And a hundred fire-flags sheen,   350
To and fro they were hurried about!
And to and fro, and in and out,
    The wan stars danced between.

And the coming wind did roar more loud,
    And the sails did sigh like sedge;   355
And the rain poured down from one black cloud;
    The Moon was at its edge.

The thick black cloud was cleft, and still
    The Moon was at its side:
Like waters shot from some high crag,   360
The lightning fell with never a jag,
    A river steep and wide.

The strong wind reach'd the ship: it roar'd
    And dropp'd down, like a stone!
Beneath the lightning and the Moon   365
    The dead men gave a groan.

They groaned, they stirred, they all uprose,
    Nor spake, nor moved their eyes;
It had been strange, even in a dream,
    To have seen those dead men rise.   370

The helmsman steered, the ship moved on;
    Yet never a breeze up-blew;
The mariners all 'gan work the ropes,
    Where they were wont to do;
They raised their limbs like lifeless tools –   375
    We were a ghastly crew.

The body of my brother's son
    Stood by me, knee to knee:
The body and I pulled at one rope,
    But he said nought to me.   380
And I quak'd to think of my own voice
    How frightful it would be!

'I fear thee, ancient Mariner!'
    Be calm, thou wedding-guest!
'Twas not those souls, that fled in pain,   385
Which to their corses came again,
    But a troop of Spirits blest.

For when it dawned – they dropped their arms,
    And clustered round the mast:
Sweet sounds rose slowly through their mouths,   390
    And from their bodies passed.

Around, around, flew each sweet sound,
    Then darted to the Sun;
Slowly the sounds came back again,
    Now mixed, now one by one.   395

Sometimes a-dropping from the sky
    I heard the sky-lark sing;
Sometimes all little birds that are,
How they seemed to fill the sea and air
    With their sweet jargoning!   400

And now 'twas like all instruments,
    Now like a lonely flute;
And now it is an angel's song,
    That makes the heavens be mute.

It ceased; yet still the sails made on   405
    A pleasant noise till noon,
A noise like of a hidden brook
    In the leafy month of June,
That to the sleeping woods all night
    Singeth a quiet tune.   410

Listen, O listen, thou Wedding-Guest!
    'Mariner! thou hast thy will:
For that, which comes out of thine eye, doth make
    My body and soul to be still.'

Never sadder tale was told   415
    To a man of woman born:
Sadder and wiser thou Wedding-Guest!
    Thou'lt rise tomorrow morn.

Never sadder tale was heard
    By man of woman born: 420
The mariners all return'd to work
    As silent as beforne.
                [135]

The mariners all 'gan pull the ropes,
    But look at me they n'old:
Thought I, I am as thin as air –   425
    They cannot me behold.

Till noon we quietly sailed on,
    Yet never a breeze did breathe:
Slowly and smoothly went the ship,
    Moved onward from beneath.   430

Under the keel nine fathom deep,
    From the land of mist and snow,
The spirit slid: and it was he
    That made the ship to go.
The sails at noon left off their tune,   435
    And the ship stood still also.

The Sun, right up above the mast,
    Had fixed her to the ocean:
But in a minute she 'gan stir,
    With a short uneasy motion –   440
Backwards and forwards half her length
    With a short uneasy motion.

Then like a pawing horse let go,
    She made a sudden bound:
It flung the blood into my head,   445
    And I fell down in a swound.

How long in that same fit I lay,
    I have not to declare;
But ere my living life returned,
I heard and in my soul discerned   450
    Two voices in the air.

'Is it he?' quoth one, 'Is this the man?
    By him who died on cross,
With his cruel bow he laid full low
    The harmless Albatross.   455

The spirit who bideth by himself
    In the land of mist and snow,
He loved the bird that loved the man
    Who shot him with his bow.'

The other was a softer voice,   460
    As soft as honey-dew:
Quoth he, 'The man hath penance done,
    And penance more will do'.

PART VI

First Voice

'But tell me, tell me! speak again,
    Thy soft response renewing –   465
What makes that ship drive on so fast?
    What is the ocean doing?'

Second Voice

'Still as a slave before his lord,
    The ocean hath no blast;
His great bright eye most silently   470
    Up to the Moon is cast –

If he may know which way to go;
    For she guides him smooth or grim.
See brother, see! how graciously
    She looketh down on him.'   475

'But why drives on that ship so fast,
    Without or wave or wind?'

Second Voice

'The air is cut away before,
    And closes from behind.

Fly, brother, fly! more high, more high!   480
    Or we shall be belated:
For slow and slow that ship will go,
    When the Mariner's trance is abated.'

I woke, and we were sailing on
    As in a gentle weather: 485
'Twas night, calm night, the moon was high;
    The dead men stood together.

All stood together on the deck,
    For a charnel-dungeon fitter:
All fixed on me their stony eyes,   490
    That in the Moon did glitter.

The pang, the curse, with which they died,
    Had never passed away:
I could not draw my eyes from theirs,
    Nor turn them up to pray.   495

And now this spell was snapt: once more
    I viewed the ocean green,
And looked far forth, yet little saw
    Of what had else been seen –

Like one, that on a lonesome road
    Doth walk in fear and dread,
And having once turned round walks on,
    And turns no more his head;
Because he knows, a frightful fiend
    Doth close behind him tread.

But soon there breathed a wind on me,
    Nor sound nor motion made:
Its path was not upon the sea,
    In ripple or in shade.

It raised my hair, it fanned my cheek
    Like a meadow-gale of spring –
It mingled strangely with my fears,
    Yet it felt like welcoming.

Swiftly, swiftly flew the ship,
    Yet she sailed softly too:
Sweetly, sweetly blew the breeze –
    On me alone it blew.

Oh! dream of joy! is this indeed
    The light-house top I see?
Is this the hill? is this the kirk?
    Is this mine own countree?

We drifted o'er the harbour-bar,
    And I with sobs did pray –
O let me be awake, my God!
    Or let me sleep alway.

500

505

510

515

520

525

The harbour-bay was clear as glass,
    So smoothly it was strewn!
And on the bay the moonlight lay,
    And the shadow of the Moon.

The moonlight bay was white all o'er,   530
    Till rising from the same,
Full many shapes, that shadows were,
    Like as of torches came.

A little distance from the prow
    Those dark-red shadows were;   535
But soon I saw that my own flesh
    Was red as in a glare.

I turn'd my head in fear and dread,
    And by the holy rood,
The bodies had advanc'd, and now   540
    Before the mast they stood.

They lifted up their stiff right arms,
    They held them strait and tight;
And each right-arm burnt like a torch,
    A torch that's borne upright.   545
Their stony eye-balls glitter'd on
    In the red and smoky light.

I pray'd and turn'd my head away
    Forth looking as before.
There was no breeze upon the bay,   550
    No wave against the shore.

See pp. 69 and 239 for a discussion of this parallelism.

The rock shone bright, the kirk no less,
　　That stands above the rock:
The moonlight steeped in silentness
　　The steady weathercock.　　　　　　　555

And the bay was white with silent light,
　　Till rising from the same,
Full many shapes, that shadows were,
　　In crimson colours came.

A little distance from the prow　　　　560
　　Those crimson shadows were:
I turned my eyes upon the deck –
　　Oh, Christ! what saw I there!

Each corse lay flat, lifeless and flat,
　　And, by the holy rood!　　　　　　565
A man all light, a seraph-man,
　　On every corse there stood.

This seraph-band, each waved his hand:
　　It was a heavenly sight!
They stood as signals to the land,　　570
　　Each one a lovely light;

This seraph-band, each waved his hand,
　　No voice did they impart –
No voice; but oh! the silence sank
　　Like music on my heart.　　　　　575

But soon I heard the dash of oars,
　　I heard the Pilot's cheer;
My head was turned perforce away
　　And I saw a boat appear.

Then vanish'd all the lovely lights;   580
    The bodies rose anew:
With silent pace, each to his place,
    Came back the ghastly crew.
The wind, that shade nor motion made,
    On me alone it blew.   585

The Pilot and the Pilot's boy,
    I heard them coming fast:
Dear Lord in Heaven! it was a joy
    The dead men could not blast.

I saw a third – I heard his voice: 590
    It is the Hermit good!
He singeth loud his godly hymns
    That he makes in the wood.
He'll shrieve my soul, he'll wash away
    The Albatross's blood.   595

PART VII

This Hermit good lives in that wood
    Which slopes down to the sea.
How loudly his sweet voice he rears!
He loves to talk with marineres
    That come from a far countree.   600

He kneels at morn, and noon, and eve –
    He hath a cushion plump:
It is the moss that wholly hides
    The rotted old oak-stump.

The skiff-boat neared: I heard them talk,   605
    'Why, this is strange, I trow!
Where are those lights so many and fair,
    That signal made but now?'

'Strange, by my faith!' the Hermit said –
    'And they answered not our cheer!   610
The planks look warped! and see those sails,
    How thin they are and sere!
I never saw aught like to them,
    Unless perchance it were

Brown skeletons of leaves that lag   615
    My forest-brook along;
When the ivy-tod is heavy with snow,
And the owlet whoops to the wolf below,
    That eats the she-wolf's young.'

'Dear Lord! it hath a fiendish look – '   620
    (The Pilot made reply)
'I am a-feared' – 'Push on, push on!'
    Said the Hermit cheerily.

The boat came closer to the ship,
    But I nor spake nor stirred;   625
The boat came close beneath the ship,
    And straight a sound was heard.

Under the water it rumbled on,
    Still louder and more dread:
It reached the ship, it split the bay;   630
    The ship went down like lead.

Stunned by that loud and dreadful sound,
    Which sky and ocean smote,
Like one that hath been seven days drowned
    My body lay afloat;   635
But swift as dreams, myself I found
    Within the Pilot's boat.

Upon the whirl, where sank the ship,
  The boat spun round and round;
And all was still, save that the hill   640
  Was telling of the sound.

I moved my lips – the Pilot shrieked
  And fell down in a fit;
The holy Hermit raised his eyes,
  And prayed where he did sit.   645

I took the oars: the Pilot's boy,
  Who now doth crazy go,
Laughed loud and long, and all the while
  His eyes went to and fro.
'Ha! ha!' quoth he, 'full plain I see,   650
  The Devil knows how to row.'

And now all in my own countree,
  I stood on the firm land!
The Hermit stepped forth from the boat,
  And scarcely he could stand.   655

'O shrieve me, shrieve me, holy man!'
  The Hermit crossed his brow.
'Say quick,' quoth he, 'I bid thee say –
  What manner of man art thou?'

Forthwith this frame of mine was wrenched   660
  With a woful agony,
Which forced me to begin my tale;
  And then it left me free.

Since then, at an uncertain hour,
  That agony returns: 665
And till my ghastly tale is told,
  This heart within me burns.

I pass, like night, from land to land;
    I have strange power of speech;
That moment that his face I see,   670
I know the man that must hear me:
    To him my tale I teach.

What loud uproar bursts from that door!
    The wedding-guests are there:
But in the garden-bower the bride   675
    And bride-maids singing are:
And hark the little vesper bell,
    Which biddeth me to prayer!

O Wedding-Guest! this soul hath been
    Alone on a wide wide sea: 680
So lonely 'twas, that God himself
    Scarce seeméd there to be.

O sweeter than the marriage-feast,
    'Tis sweeter far to me,
To walk together to the kirk   685
    With a goodly company! –

To walk together to the kirk,
    And all together pray,
While each to his great Father bends,
Old men, and babes, and loving friends   690
    And youths and maidens gay!

Farewell, farewell! but this I tell
    To thee, thou Wedding-Guest!
He prayeth well, who loveth well
    Both man and bird and beast.   695

He prayeth best, who loveth best
    All things both great and small;
For the dear God who loveth us,
    He made and loveth all.

K   [145]

The Mariner, whose eye is bright,   700
    Whose beard with age is hoar,
Is gone: and now the Wedding-Guest
    Turned from the bridegroom's door.

He went like one that hath been stunned,
    And is of sense forlorn: 705
A sadder and a wiser man,
    He rose the morrow morn.

Christabel

'Tis the middle of night by the castle clock,
And the owls have awakened the crowing cock;
Tu-u-whoo! Tu-u-whoo!
And hark, again! the crowing cock,
How drowsily it crew.   5

Sir Leoline, the Baron rich,
Hath a toothless mastiff bitch;
From her kennel beneath the rock
She makes answer to the clock,
Four for the quarters, and twelve for the hour;   10
Ever and aye, moonshine or shower,
Sixteen short howls, not over loud;
Some say, she sees my lady's shroud.

[*146*]

Is the night chilly and dark?
The night is chilly, but not dark.   15
The thin gray cloud is spread on high,
It covers but not hides the sky.
The moon is behind, and at the full;
And yet she looks both small and dull.
The night is chill, the cloud is gray: 20
'Tis a month before the month of May,
And the Spring comes slowly up this way.

The lovely lady, Christabel,
Whom her father loves so well,
What makes her in the woods so late,   25
A furlong from the castle gate?
She had dreams all yesternight
Of her own betrothéd knight;
And she in the midnight wood will pray
For the weal of her lover that's far away.   30

She stole along, she nothing spoke,
The breezes they were still also,
And naught was green upon the oak
But the moss and mistletoe:
She knelt beneath the huge oak tree,   35
And in silence prayeth she.

The lady leaps up suddenly,
The lovely lady, Christabel!
It moaned as near, as near can be,
But what it is she cannot tell. –   40
On the other side it seems to be,
Of the huge, broad-breasted, old oak tree.

The night is chill; the forest bare;
Is it the wind that moaneth bleak?
There is not wind enough to twirl   45

The one red leaf, the last of its clan,
That dances as often as dance it can,
Hanging so light, and hanging so high,
On the topmost twig that looks out at the sky.

Hush, beating heart of Christabel!   50
Jesu, Maria, shield her well!
She folded her arms beneath her cloak,
And stole to the other side of the oak.
        What sees she there?

        A damsel bright,   55
Clad in a silken robe of white,
Her neck, her feet, her arms were bare,
And the jewels were tumbled in her hair.
I guess, 'twas frightful there to see
A lady so richly clad as she –   60
Beautiful exceedingly!

Mary mother, save me now!
Said Christabel, And who art thou?

The lady strange made answer meet,
And her voice was faint and sweet: –   65
Have pity on my sore distress,
I scarce can speak for weariness:
Stretch forth thy hand, and have no fear!
Said Christabel, How camest thou here?
And the lady, whose voice was faint and sweet,   70
Did thus pursue her answer meet: –

My sire is of a noble line,
And my name is Geraldine:
Five ruffians seized me yestermorn,
Me, even me, a maid forlorn;   75
They chok'd my cries with wicked might,
And tied me on a palfrey white.
The palfrey was as fleet as wind,

And they rode furiously behind.
They spurred amain, their steeds were white: 80
And twice we crossed the shade of night.
As sure as Heaven shall rescue me,
I have no thought what men they be;
Nor do I know how long it is
(For I have lain in fits I wis)   85
Since one, the tallest of the five,
Took me from the palfrey's back,
A weary woman, scarce alive.
Some muttered words his comrade spoke:
He placed me underneath this oak;   90
They swore they would return with haste;
Whither they went I cannot tell –
I thought I heard, some minutes past,
Sounds as of a castle bell.
Stretch forth thy hand (thus ended she),   95
And help a wretched maid to flee.

Then Christabel stretched forth her hand,
And comforted fair Geraldine,
Saying that she should command
The service of Sir Leoline   100
And straight be convoy'd, free from thrall
Back to her noble father's hall.

So up she rose and forth they passed
With hurrying steps yet nothing fast.
Her lucky stars the lady blest,   105
And Christabel she sweetly said –
All our household are at rest,
Each one sleeping in his bed,
Sir Leoline is weak in health,
And may not awakened be,   110
So to my room we'll creep in stealth,
And you to-night must sleep with me.

They cross'd the moat, and Christabel
Took the key that fitted well;
A little door she opened straight,   115
All in the middle of the gate;
The gate that was ironed within and without,
Where an army in battle array had marched out.
The lady sank, belike through pain,
And Christabel with might and main   120
Lifted her up, a weary weight,
Over the threshold of the gate:
Then the lady rose again,
And moved, as she were not in pain.

So free from danger, free from fear,   125
They crossed the court: right glad they were.
And Christabel she sweetly cried
To the lady by her side,
O praise the Virgin all divine
Who hath rescued thee from thy distress!   130
Alas, alas! said Geraldine,
I cannot speak for weariness.
So free from danger, free from fear,
They crossed the court: right glad they were.

Outside her kennel, the mastiff old   135
Lay fast asleep, in moonshine cold.
The mastiff old did not awake,
Yet she an angry moan did make!
And what can ail the mastiff bitch?
Never till now she uttered yell   140
Beneath the eye of Christabel.
Perhaps it is the owlet's scritch:
For what can ail the mastiff bitch?

They passed the hall, that echoes still,
Pass as lightly as you will!   145

The brands were flat, the brands were dying,
Amid their own white ashes lying;
But when the lady passed, there came
A tongue of light, a fit of flame;
And Christabel saw the lady's eye,   150
And nothing else she saw thereby,
Save the boss of the shield of Sir Leoline tall,
Which hung in a murky old nitch in the wall.
O softly tread, said Christabel,
My father seldom sleepeth well.   155

Sweet Christabel her feet she bares,
And they are creeping up the stairs,
Now in glimmer, and now in gloom,
And now they pass the Baron's room,
As still as death, with stifled breath!   160
And now have reached her chamber door;
And now they with their feet press down
The rushes of her chamber floor.

The moon shines dim in the open air,
And not a moonbeam enters here.   165
But they without its light can see
The chamber carved so curiously,
Carved with figures strange and sweet,
All made out of the carver's brain,
For a lady's chamber meet: 170
The lamp with twofold silver chain
Is fastened to an angel's feet.

The silver lamp burns dead and dim;
But Christabel the lamp will trim.
She trimmed the lamp, and made it bright,   175
And left it swinging to and fro,
While Geraldine, in wretched plight,
Sank down upon the floor below.

[153]

O weary lady, Geraldine,
I pray you, drink this spicy wine!   180
It is a wine of virtuous powers;
My mother made it of wild flowers.
Nay, drink it up, I pray you do!
Believe me it will comfort you.
And will your mother pity me,   185
Who am a maiden most forlorn?
Christabel answered – Woe is me!
She died the hour that I was born.
I have heard the grey-haired friar tell
How on her death-bed she did say,   190
That she should hear the castle-bell
Strike twelve upon my wedding-day.
O mother dear! that thou wert here!
I would, said Geraldine, she were!

But soon with altered voice, said she –   195
'Off, woman, off! this hour is mine –
Off, woman, off! 'tis given to me.'

Then Christabel knelt by the lady's side,
And raised to heaven her eyes so blue –
Alas! said she, this ghastly ride –   200
Dear lady! it hath wildered you!
The lady wiped her moist cold brow,
And faintly said, I'm better now!

Again the wild-flower wine she drank:
Her fair large eyes 'gan glitter bright,   205
And from the floor wheron she sank,
The lofty lady stood upright:
She was most beautiful to see,
Like a lady of a fair countree.

And thus the lofty lady spake –   210
'All they, who live in the upper sky,
Do love you, holy Christabel!
And you love them, and for their sake
And for the good which me befel,
Even I in my degree will try,   215
Fair maiden, to requite you well,
But now unrobe yourself; for I
Must pray, ere yet in bed I lie.'

Quoth Christabel, So let it be!
And as the lady bade, did she.   220
Her gentle limbs did she undress,
And lay down in her loveliness.
But through her brain of weal and woe
So many thoughts moved to and fro,
That vain it were her lids to close;   225
So half-way from the bed she rose,
And on her elbow did recline
To look at the lady Geraldine.

Beneath the lamp the lady bowed,
And slowly rolled her eyes around;   230
Then drawing in her breath aloud,
Like one that shuddered, she unbound
The cincture from beneath her breast:
Her silken robe, and inner vest,
Dropt to her feet, and full in view,   235
Behold! her bosom, and half her side –
Are lean and old and foul of hue.
A sight to dream of, not to tell!
And she is to sleep with Christabel.
She took two paces and a stride,   240
And lay down by the Maiden's side! –
And in her arms the maid she took,
        Ah wel-a-day!
        [*153*]

And with sad voice and doleful look
These words did say:
'In the touch of my bosom there worketh a spell,   245
Which is lord of thy utterance, Christabel!
Thou knowest to-night, and wilt know to-morrow,
The mark of my shame, the seal of my sorrow;
       But vainly thou warrest,
       For this is alone in   250
       Thy power to declare,
       That in the dim forest
       Thou heard'st a low moaning,
And found'st a bright lady, surpassingly fair;
And didst bring her home with love and with charity,   255
To shield her and shelter her from the damp air.'

THE CONCLUSION OF BOOK THE FIRST

It was a lovely sight to see
The lady Christabel, when she
Was praying at the old oak tree.
       Amid the jagged shadows   260
       Of mossy leafless boughs,
       Kneeling in the moonlight,
       To make her gentle vows;
Her slender palms together prest,
Heaving sometimes on her breast;   265
Her face resigned to bliss or bale –
Her face, oh call it fair not pale,
And both blue eyes more bright than clear,
Each about to have a tear.

With open eyes (ah woe is me!)   270
Asleep, and dreaming fearfully,
Fearfully dreaming, yet, I wis,
Dreaming that alone, which is –
O sorrow and shame! Can this be she,

The lady, that knelt at the old oak tree?   275
And lo! the worker of these harms,
That holds the maiden in her arms,
Seems to slumber still and mild,
As a mother with her child.

A star hath set, a star hath risen,   280
O Geraldine! since arms of thine
Have been the lovely lady's prison.
O Geraldine! one hour was thine –
Thou'st had thy will! By tairn and rill,
The night-birds all that hour were still.   285
But now they are jubilant anew,
From cliff and tower, tu-whoo! tu-whoo!
Tu-whoo! tu-whoo! from wood and fell!
And see! the lady Christabel
Gathers herself from out her trance;   290
Her limbs relax, her countenance
Grows sad and soft; the smooth thin lids
Close o'er her eyes; and tears she sheds –
Large tears that leaves the lashes bright!
And oft the while she seems to smile   295
As infants at a sudden light!

Yea, she doth smile, and she doth weep,
Like a youthful hermitess,
Beauteous in a wilderness,
Who, praying always, prays in sleep.   300
And, if she move unquietly,
Perchance, 'tis but the blood so free
Comes back and tingles in her feet.
No doubt, she hath a vision sweet.
What if her guardian spirit 'twere,   305
What if she knew her mother near?
But this she knows, in joys and woes,
That saints will aid if men will call:
For the blue sky bends over all!

Each matin bell, the Baron saith,   310
Knells us back to a world of death.
These words Sir Leoline first said,
When he rose and found his lady dead:
These words Sir Leoline will say
Many a morn to his dying day!   315

And hence the custom and law began
That still at dawn the sacristan,
Who duly pulls the heavy bell,
Five and forty beads must tell
Between each stroke – a warning knell,   320
Which not a soul can choose but hear
From Bratha Head to Wyndermere.

Saith Bracy the bard, So let it knell!
And let the drowsy sacristan
Still count as slowly as he can!   325
There is no lack of such, I ween,
As well fill up the space between.
In Langdale Pike and Witch's lair,
And Dungeon-ghyll so foully rent,
With ropes of rock and bells of air   330
Three simple sextons' ghosts are pent,
Who all give back, one after t'other,
The death-note to their living brother;
And oft too, by the knell offended,
Just as their one! two! three! is ended,   335
The devil mocks the doleful tale
With a merry peal from Borrowdale.
The air is still! through many a cloud
That merry peal comes ringing loud;
And Geraldine shakes off her dread,   340
And rises lightly from her bed;

[156]

Puts on her simple vestments white,
And tricks her hair in lovely plight,
And nothing doubting of her spell
Awakens the lady Christabel.   345
'Sleep you, sweet lady Christabel?
I trust that you have rested well.'

And Christabel awoke and spied
The same who lay down by her side –
O rather say, the same whom she   350
Raised up beneath the old oak-tree!
Nay, fairer yet! and yet more fair!
For she belike, hath drunken deep
Of all the blessedness of sleep!
And while she spake, her looks, her air   355
Such gentle thankfulness declare,
That (so it seemed) her girded vests
Grew tight beneath her heaving breasts.
'Sure I have sinn'd' said Christabel,
'Now heaven be praised if all be well!'   360
And in low faltering tones, yet sweet,
Did she the lofty lady greet
With such perplexity of mind
As dreams too lively leave behind.

So quickly she rose, and quickly arrayed   365
Her maiden limbs, and having prayed
That He, who on the cross did groan,
Might wash away her sins unknown,
She forthwith led fair Geraldine
To meet her sire, Sir Leoline.   370

The lovely maid and the lady tall
Are pacing both into the hall,
And pacing on through page and groom,
Enter the Baron's presence-room.

[*157*]

The Baron rose, and while he prest   375
His gentle daughter to his breast,
With cheerful wonder in his eyes
The lady Geraldine espies,
And gave such welcome to the same,
As might beseem so bright a dame!   380

But when he heard the lady's tale,
And when she told her father's name,
Why waxed Sir Leoline so pale,
Murmuring o'er the name again,
Lord Roland de Vaux of Tryermaine?   385
Alas! they had been friends in youth;
But whispering tongues can poison truth;
And constancy lives in realms above;
And life is thorny; and youth is vain;
And to be wroth with one we love   390
Doth work like madness in the brain.
And thus it chanced, as I divine,
With Roland and Sir Leoline.
Each spake words of high disdain
And insult to his heart's best brother: 395
And parted – ne'er to meet again!
And never either found another
To free the hollow heart from paining –
They stood aloof, the scars remaining,
Like cliffs which had been rent asunder;   400
A dreary sea now flows between; –
But neither heat, nor frost, nor thunder,
Shall wholly do away, I ween,
The marks of that which once hath been.

Sir Leoline, a moment's space,   405
Stood gazing on the damsel's face:
And the youthful Lord of Tryermaine
Came back upon his heart again.
                    [158]

O then the Baron forgot his age,
His noble heart swelled high with rage;   410
He swore by the wounds in Jesu's side
He would proclaim it far and wide,
With trump and solemn heraldry,
That they, who thus had wronged the dame,
Were base as spotted infamy!   415
'And if they dare deny the same,
My herald shall appoint a week,
And let the recreant traitors seek
My tourney court – that there and then
I may dislodge their reptile souls   420
From the bodies and forms of men!'
He spake: his eye in lightning rolls!
For the lady was ruthlessly seized; and he kenned
In the beautiful lady the child of his friend!

And now the tears were on his face,   425
And fondly in his arms he took
Fair Geraldine, who met the embrace,
Prolonging it with joyous look.
Which when she viewed, a vision fell
Upon the soul of Christabel,   430
The vision foul of fear and pain!
She shrunk and shuddered, and saw again –
(Ah woe is me! Was it for thee,
Thou gentle maid! such sights to see?)
Again she saw that bosom old,   435
Again she felt that bosom cold,
And drew in her breath with a hissing sound:
Whereat the Knight turned wildly round,
And nothing saw, but his own sweet maid
With eyes upraised, as one that prayed.   440

The pang, the sight, had passed away,
And in its stead that vision blest,

Which comforted her after-rest
While in the lady's arms she lay,
Had put a rapture in her breast,   445
And on her lips and o'er her eyes
Spread smiles like light!
              With new surprise,
'What ails then my beloved child?'
The Baron said – His daughter mild
Made answer, 'All will yet be well!'   450
I ween, she had no power to tell
Aught else: so mighty was the spell.

Yet he, who saw this Geraldine,
Had deemed her sure a thing divine:
Such sorrow with such grace she blended,   455
As if she feared she had offended
Sweet Christabel, that gentle maid!
And with such lowly tones she prayed
She might be sent without delay
Home to her father's mansion.   460
              'Nay!
Nay, by my soul!' said Leoline.
'Ho! Bracy the bard, the charge be thine!
Go thou, with music sweet and loud,
And take two steeds with trappings proud,
And take the youth whom thou lov'st best   465
To bear thy harp, and learn thy song,
And clothe you both in solemn vest,
Lest wandering folk, that are abroad,
Detain you on the valley road.

'And when he has crossed the Irthing flood,   470
My merry bard! he hastes, he hastes
Up Knorren Moor, through Halegarth Wood,
And reaches soon that castle good
Which stands and threatens Scotland's wastes.

'Bard Bracy! bard Bracy! your horses are fleet,   475
Ye must ride up the hall, your music so sweet,
More loud than your horses' echoing feet!
And loud and loud to Lord Roland call,
Thy daughter is safe in Langdale hall!
Thy beauteous daughter is safe and free –   480
Sir Leoline greets thee thus through me!
He bids thee come without delay
With all thy numerous array
And fetch thy lovely daughter home:
And he will meet thee on the way   485
With all his numerous array
White with their panting palfreys' foam:
And, by mine honour! I will say,
That I repent me of the day
When I spake words of fierce disdain   490
To Roland de Vaux of Tryermaine! –
– For since that evil hour hath flown,
Many a summer's suns have shone;
Yet ne'er found I a friend again
Like Roland de Vaux of Tryermaine.   495

The lady fell, and clasped his knees,
Her face upraised, her eyes o'erflowing;
And Bracy replied, with faltering voice,
His gracious Hail on all bestowing! –
'Thy words, thou sire of Christabel,   500
Are sweeter than my harp can tell;
Yet might I gain a boon of thee,
This day my journey should not be,
So strange a dream hath come to me,
That I had vowed with music loud   505
To clear yon wood from thing unblest,
Warned by a vision in my rest!
For in my sleep I saw that dove,
That gentle bird, whom thou dost love,

And call'st by thy own daughter's name – 510
Sir Leoline! I saw the same
Fluttering, and uttering fearful moan,
Among the green herbs in the forest alone.
Which when I saw and when I heard,
I wonder'd what might ail the bird; 515
For nothing near it could I see,
Save the grass and the green herbs underneath the old tree.

'And in my dreams methought I went
To search out what might there be found;
And what the sweet bird's trouble meant, 520
That thus lay fluttering on the ground.
I went and peered, and could descry
No cause for her distressful cry;
But yet for her dear lady's sake
I stooped, methought, the dove to take, 525
When lo! I saw a bright green snake
Coiled around its wings and neck.
Green as the herbs on which it couched,
Close by the dove's its head it crouched;
And with the dove it heaves and stirs, 530
Swelling its neck as she swelled hers!
I woke; it was the midnight hour,
The clock was echoing in the tower;
But though my slumber was gone by,
This dream it would not pass away – 535
It seem'd to live upon my eye!
And thence I vowed this self-same day
With music strong and saintly song
To wander through the forest bare,
Lest aught unholy wander there.' 540

Thus Bracy said: the Baron, the while,
Half-listening heard him with a smile;
Then turned to Lady Geraldine,

[*162*]

His eyes made up of wonder and love;
And said in courtly accents fine,   545
'Sweet maid, Lord Roland's beauteous dove,
With arms more strong than harp or song,
Thy sire and I will crush the snake!'
He kissed her forehead as he spake,
And Geraldine in maiden wise   550
Casting down her large bright eyes,
With blushing cheek and curtsey fine
She turned her from Sir Leoline;
Softly gathering up her train,
That o'er her right arm fell again;   555
And folded her arms across her chest,
And couched her head upon her breast,
And looked askance at Christabel –
Jesu, Maria, shield her well!

A snake's small eye blinks dull and shy;   560
And the lady's eyes they shrunk in her head,
Each shrunk up to a serpent's eye,
And with somewhat of malice, and more of dread,
At Christabel she looked askance! –
One moment – and the sight was fled!   565
But Christabel in dizzy trance
Stumbling on the unsteady ground
Shuddered aloud with hissing sound;
And Geraldine again turned round,
And like a thing, that sought relief,   570
Full of wonder and full of grief,
She rolled her large bright eyes divine
Wildly o'er Sir Leoline.

The maid, alas! her thoughts are gone,
She nothing sees – no sight but one!   575
The maid, devoid of guile and sin,
I know not how, in fearful wise,
So deeply had she drunken in

[*163*]

That look, those shrunken serpent eyes,
That all her features were resigned   580
To this sole image in her mind:
And passively did imitate
That look of dull and treacherous hate!
And thus she stood, in dizzy trance,
Still picturing that look askance   585
With forced unconscious sympathy
Full before her father's view –
As far as such a look could be
In eyes so innocent and blue!

But when the trance was o'er, the maid   590
Paused awhile, and inly prayed:
Then falling at her Father's feet,
'By my mother's sould do I entreat
That thou this woman send away!'
She said: and more she could not say: 595
For what she knew she could not tell,
O'er-mastered by that mighty spell.

Why is thy cheek so wan and wild,
Sir Leoline? Thy only child
Lies at thy feet, thy joy, thy pride,   600
So fair, so innocent, so mild;
The same, for whom thy lady died!
O by the pangs of her dear mother
Think thou no evil of thy child!
For her, and thee, and for no other,   605
She prayed the moment ere she died:
Prayed that the babe for whom she died,
Might prove her dear lord's joy and pride!
    That prayer her deadly pangs beguiled,
        Sir Leoline!   610
    And wouldst thou wrong thy only child,
        Her child and thine?

Within the Baron's heart and brain
If thoughts, like these, had any share,
They only swelled his rage and pain,   615
And did not work confusion there.
His heart was cleft with pain and rage,
His cheeks they quivered, his eyes were wild,
Dishonoured thus in his old age;
Dishonoured by his only child,   620
And all his hospitality
To th' insulted daughter of his friend
By more than woman's jealousy
Brought thus to a disgraceful end –
He rolled his eye with stern regard   625
Upon the gentle minstrel bard,
And said in tones abrupt, austere –
'Why, Bracy! dost thou loiter here?
I bade thee hence!' The bard obeyed;
And turning from his own sweet maid,   630
The agéd knight, Sir Leoline,
Led forth the lady Geraldine!

Fire, Famine and Slaughter

The Scene a desolated Tract in La Vendée. Famine is dis-
covered lying on the ground; to her enter Fire and Slaughter.

    FAM. Sisters! sisters! who sent you here?
    SLAU. (to Fire). I will whisper it in her ear.
    FIRE. No! no! no!
          Spirits hear what spirits tell:
          'Twill make a holiday in Hell.   5
          No! no! no!
          Myself, I named him once below,
          And all the souls, that damnéd be,

Leaped up at once in anarchy,
Clapped their hands and danced for glee.   10
They no longer heeded me;
But laughed to hear Hell's burning rafters
Unwillingly re-echo laughters!
No! no! no!
Spirits hear what spirits tell: 15
'Twill make a holiday in Hell!

FAM. Whisper it, sister! so and so!
In a dark hint, soft and slow.

SLAU. Letters four do form his name –
And who sent you?

BOTH The same! the same!   20

SLAU. He came by stealth, and unlocked my den,
And I have drunk the blood since then
Of thrice three hundred thousand men.

BOTH Who bade you do't?

SLAU.   The same! the same!
Letters four do form his name.   25
He let me loose, and cried Halloo!
To him alone the praise is due.

FAM. Thanks, sister, thanks! the men have bled,
Their wives and their children faint for bread.
I stood in a swampy field of battle;   30
With bones and skulls I made a rattle,
To frighten the wolf and carrion-crow
And the homeless dog – but they would not go.
So off I flew: for how could I bear
To see them gorge their dainty fare?   35
I heard a groan and a peevish squall,
And through the chink of a cottage-wall –
Can you guess what I saw there?

BOTH Whisper it, sister! in our ear.

FAM. A baby beat its dying mother: 40
I had starved the one and was starving the other!

BOTH Who bade you do't?

[166]

FAM.   The same! the same!
          Letters four do form his name.
          He let me loose, and cried, Halloo!
          To him alone the praise is due.   45
FIRE Sisters! I from Ireland came!
          Hedge and corn-fields all on flame,
          I triumph'd o'er the setting sun!
          And all the while the work was done,
          On as I strode with my huge strides,   50
          I flung back my head and I held my sides,
          It was so rare a piece of fun
          To see the sweltered cattle run
          With uncouth gallop through the night,   55
          Scared by the red and noisy light!
          By the light of his own blazing cot
          Was many a naked Rebel shot:
          The house-stream met the flame and hissed,
          While crash! fell in the roof, I wist,
          On some of those old bed-rid nurses,   60
          That deal in discontent and curses.
BOTH Who bade you do't?
FIRE   The same! the same!
          Letters four do form his name.
          He let me loose, and cried Halloo!
          To him alone the praise is due.   65
ALL   He let us loose, and cried Halloo!
          How shall we yield him honour due?
FAM. Wisdom comes with lack of food.
          I'll gnaw, I'll gnaw the multitude,
          Till the cup of rage o'erbrim: 70
          They shall seize him and his brood –

SLAU. They shall tear him limb from limb!
FIRE O thankless beldames and untrue!
      And is this all that you can do
      For him, who did so much for you?   75
      Ninety months he, by my troth!
      Hath richly catered for you both;
      And in an hour would you repay
      An eight years' work? – Away! away!
      I alone am faithful! I   80
      Cling to him everlastingly.

Frost at Midnight

The Frost performs its secret ministry,
Unhelped by any wind. The owlet's cry
Came loud – and hark, again! loud as before.
The inmates of my cottage, all at rest,
Have left me to that solitude, which suits   5
Abstruser musings: save that at my side
My cradled infant slumbers peacefully.
'Tis calm indeed! so calm, that it disturbs
And vexes meditation with its strange
And extreme silentness. Sea, hill, and wood,   10
This populous village! Sea, and hill, and wood,
With all the numberless goings-on of life,
Inaudible as dreams! the thin blue flame
Lies on my low-burnt fire, and quivers not;
Only that film, which fluttered on the grate,   15
Still flutters there, the sole unquiet thing.
Methinks, its motion in this hush of nature
Gives it dim sympathies with me who live,
Making it a companionable form,

Whose puny flaps and freaks the idling Spirit   20
By its own moods interprets, every where
Echo or mirror seeking of itself,
And makes a toy of Thought.
                    But O! how oft,
How oft, at school, with most believing mind,
Presageful, have I gazed upon the bars,   25
To watch that fluttering *stranger*! and as oft
With unclosed lids, already had I dreamt
Of my sweet birth-place, and the old church-tower,
Whose bells, the poor man's only music, rang
From morn to evening, all the hot Fair-day,   30
So sweetly, that they stirred and haunted me
With a wild pleasure, falling on mine ear
Most like articulate sounds of things to come!
So gazed I, till the soothing things, I dreamt,
Lulled me to sleep, and sleep prolonged my dreams!   35
And so I brooded all the following morn,
Awed by the stern preceptor's face, mine eye
Fixed with mock study on my swimming book:
Save if the door half opened, and I snatched
A hasty glance, and still my heart leaped up,   40
For still I hoped to see the *stranger's* face,
Townsman, or aunt, or sister more beloved,
My play-mate when we both were clothed alike!

   Dear Babe, that sleepest cradled by my side,
Whose gentle breathings, heard in this deep calm,   45
Fill up the interspersèd vacancies
And momentary pauses of the thought!
My babe so beautiful! it thrills my heart
With tender gladness, thus to look at thee,
And think that thou shalt learn far other lore,   50
And in far other scenes! For I was reared
In the great city, pent 'mid cloisters dim,

And saw nought lovely but the sky and stars.
But *thou*, my babe! shalt wander like a breeze
By lakes and sandy shores, beneath the crags   55
Of ancient mountain, and beneath the clouds,
Which image in their bulk both lakes and shores
And mountain crags: so shalt thou see and hear
The lovely shapes and sounds intelligible
Of that eternal language, which thy God   60
Utters, who from eternity doth teach
Himself in all, and all things in himself.
Great universal Teacher! he shall mould
Thy spirit, and by giving make it ask.

Therefore all seasons shall be sweet to thee,   65
Whether the summer clothe the general earth
With greenness, or the redbreast sit and sing
Betwixt the tufts of snow on the bare branch
Of mossy apple-tree, while the nigh thatch
Smokes in the sun-thaw; whether the eave-drops fall   70
Heard only in the trances of the blast,
Or if the secret ministry of frost
Shall hang them up in silent icicles,
Quietly shining to the quiet Moon.

From *Fears in Solitude*

                    From east to west
A groan of accusation pierces Heaven!
The wretched plead against us; multitudes
Countless and vehement, the sons of God,
Our brethren! Like a cloud that travels on,   5
Steamed up from Cairo's swamps of pestilence,
Even so, my countrymen! have we gone forth
And borne to distant tribes slavery and pangs,

And, deadlier far, our vices, whose deep taint
With slow perdition murders the whole man,   10
His body and his soul! Meanwhile, at home,
All individual dignity and power
Engulfed in Courts, Committees, Institutions
Associations and Societies,
A vain, speech-mouthing, speech-reporting Guild,   15
One Benefit-Club for mutual flattery,
We have drunk up, demure as at a grace,
Pollutions from the brimming cup of wealth;
Contemptuous of all honourable rule,
Yet bartering freedom and the poor man's life   20
For gold, as at a market! The sweet words
Of Christian promise, words that even yet
Might stem destruction, were they wisely preached,
Are muttered o'er by men, whose tones proclaim
How flat and wearisome they feel their trade: 25
Rank scoffers some, but most too indolent
To deem them falsehoods or to know their truth.
Oh! blasphemous! the Book of Life is made
A superstitious instrument, on which
We gabble o'er the oaths we mean to break,   30
For all must swear – all and in every place,
College and wharf, council and justice-court;
All, all must swear, the briber and the bribed,
Merchant and lawyer, senator and priest,
The rich, the poor, the old man and the young;   35
All, all make up one scheme of perjury,
That faith doth reel; the very name of God
Sounds like a juggler's charm; and, bold with joy,
Forth from his dark and lonely hiding-place,
(Portentous sight!) the owlet Atheism,   40
Sailing on obscene wings athwart the noon,
Drops his blue-fringéd lids, and holds them close,
And hooting at the glorious sun in Heaven,

[171]

Cries out, 'Where is it?'
                              Thankless too for peace,
(Peace long preserved by fleets and perilous seas)   45
Secure from actual warfare, we have loved
To swell the war-whoop, passionate for war!
Alas! for ages ignorant of all
Its ghastlier workings, (famine or blue plague,
Battle, or siege, or flight through wintry snows,)   50
We, this whole people, have been clamorous
For war and bloodshed; animating sports,
The which we pay for as a thing to talk of,
Spectators and not combatants! No guess
Anticipative of a wrong unfelt,   55
No speculation on contingency,
However dim and vague, too vague and dim
To yield a justifying cause; and forth,
(Stuffed out with big preamble, holy names,
And adjurations of the God in Heaven,)   60
We send our mandates for the certain death
Of thousands and ten thousands! Boys and girls,
And women, that would groan to see a child
Pull off an insect's leg, all read of war,
The best amusement for our morning meal!   65
The poor wretch, who has learnt his only prayers
From curses, who knows scarcely words enough
To ask a blessing from his Heavenly Father,
Becomes a fluent phraseman, absolute
And technical in victories and defeats,   70
And all our dainty terms for fratricide;
Terms which we trundle smoothly o'er our tongues
Like mere abstractions, empty sounds to which
We join no feeling and attach no form!
As if the soldier died without a wound;   75
As if the fibres of this godlike frame
Were gored without a pang; as if the wretch,
Who fell in battle, doing bloody deeds,

Passed off to Heaven, translated and not killed;
As though he had no wife to pine for him,   80
No God to judge him! Therefore, evil days
Are coming on us, O my countrymen!
And what if all-avenging Providence,
Strong and retributive, should make us know
The meaning of our words, force us to feel   85
The desolation and the agony
Of our fierce doings?

     *   *   *   *

But, O dear Britain! O my Mother Isle!
Needs must thou prove a name most dear and holy
To me, a son, a brother, and a friend,   90
A husband, and a father! who revere
All bonds of natural love, and find them all
Within the limits of thy rocky shores.
O native Britain! O my Mother Isle!
How shouldst thou prove aught else but dear and holy   95
To me, who from thy lakes and mountain-hills,
Thy clouds, thy quiet dales, thy rocks and seas,
Have drunk in all my intellectual life,
All sweet sensations, all ennobling thoughts,
All adoration of the God in nature,   100
All lovely and all honourable things,
Whatever makes this mortal spirit feel
The joy and greatness of its future being?

     *   *   *   *

And now, belovéd Stowey! I behold
Thy church-tower, and, methinks, the four huge elms   105
Clustering, which mark the mansion of my friend;
And close behind them, hidden from my view,
Is my own lowly cottage, where my babe
And my babe's mother dwell in peace! With light
And quickened footsteps thitherward I tend,   110

Remembering thee, O green and silent dell!　　　110
And grateful, that by nature's quietness
And solitary musings, all my heart
Is softened, and made worthy to indulge
Love, and the thoughts that yearn for human kind.　　115

The Nightingale

No cloud, no relique of the sunken day
Distinguishes the West, no long thin slip
Of sullen light, no obscure trembling hues.
Come, we will rest on this old mossy bridge!
You see the glimmer of the stream beneath,　　　5
But hear no murmuring: it flows silently,
O'er its soft bed of verdure. All is still,
A balmy night! and though the stars be dim,
Yet let us think upon the vernal showers
That gladden the green earth, and we shall find　　10
A pleasure in the dimness of the stars.
And hark! the Nightingale begins its song,
'Most musical, most melancholy' bird!
A melancholy bird? Oh! idle thought!
In Nature there is nothing melancholy.　　　15
But some night-wandering man whose heart was pierced
With the remembrance of a grievous wrong,
Or slow distemper, or neglected love,
(And so, poor wretch! filled all things with himself,
And made all gentle sounds tell back the tale　　20
Of his own sorrow) he, and such as he,
First named these notes a melancholy strain.
And many a poet echoes the conceit;
Poet who hath been building up the rhyme

When he had better far have stretched his limbs   25
Beside a brook in mossy forest-dell,
By sun or moon-light, to the influxes
Of shapes and sounds and shifting elements
Surrendering his whole spirit, of his song
And of his fame forgetful! so his fame   30
Should share in Nature's immortality,
A venerable thing! and so his song
Should make all Nature lovelier, and itself
Be loved like Nature! But 'twill not be so;
And youths and maidens most poetical,   35
Who lose the deepening twilights of the spring
In ball-rooms and hot theatres, they still
Full of meek sympathy must heave their sighs
O'er Philomela's pity-pleading strains.

My Friend, and thou, our Sister! we have learnt   40
A different lore: we may not thus profane
Nature's sweet voices, always full of love
And joyance! 'Tis the merry Nightingale
That crowds, and hurries, and precipitates
With fast thick warble his delicious notes,   45
As he were fearful that an April night
Would be too short for him to utter forth
His love-chant, and disburthen his full soul
Of all its music!
                      And I know a grove
Of large extent, hard by a castle huge,   50
Which the great lord inhabits not; and so
This grove is wild with tangling underwood,
And the trim walks are broken up, and grass,
Thin grass and king-cups grow within the paths.
But never elsewhere in one place I knew   55
So many nightingales; and far and near,
In wood and thicket, over the wide grove,
They answer and provoke each other's song,

[175]

With skirmish and capricious passagings,
And murmurs musical and swift jug jug,   60
And one low piping sound more sweet than all –
Stirring the air with such a harmony,
That should you close your eyes, you might almost
Forget it was not day! On moonlight bushes,
Whose dewy leaflets are but half-disclosed,   65
You may perchance behold them on the twigs,
Their bright, bright eyes, their eyes both bright and full,
Glistening, while many a glow-worm in the shade
Lights up her love-torch.

                    A most gentle Maid,
Who dwelleth in her hospitable home   70
Hard by the castle, and at latest eve
(Even like a Lady vowed and dedicate
To something more than Nature in the grove)
Glides through the pathways; she knows all their notes,
That gentle Maid! and oft, a moment's space,   75
What time the moon was lost behind a cloud,
Hath heard a pause of silence; till the moon
Emerging, hath awakened earth and sky
With one sensation, and those wakeful birds
Have all burst forth in choral minstrelsy,   80
As if some sudden gale had swept at once
A hundred airy harps! And she hath watched
Many a nightingale perch giddily
On blossomy twig still swinging from the breeze,
And to that motion tune his wanton song   85
Like tipsy Joy that reels with tossing head.

Farewell, O Warbler! till to-morrow eve,
And you, my friends! farewell, a short farewell!
We have been loitering long and pleasantly,
And now for our dear homes. – That strain again!   90

Full fain it would delay me! My dear babe,
Who, capable of no articulate sound,
Mars all things with his imitative lisp,
How he would place his hand beside his ear,
His little hand, the small forefinger up,   95
And bid us listen! And I deem it wise
To make him Nature's play-mate. He knows well
The evening-star; and once, when he awoke
In most distressful mood (some inward pain
Had made up that strange thing, an infant's dream –)   100
I hurried with him to our orchard-plot,
And he beheld the moon, and, hushed at once,
Suspends his sobs, and laughs most silently,
While his fair eyes, that swam with undropped tears,
Did glitter in the yellow moon-beam! Well! –   105
It is a father's tale: But if that Heaven
Should give me life, his childhood shall grow up
Familiar with these songs, that with the night
He may associate joy. – Once more, farewell,
Sweet Nightingale! once more, my friends! farewell.   110

Kubla Khan

In Xanadu did Kubla Khan
A stately pleasure-dome decree:
Where Alph, the sacred river, ran
Through caverns measureless to man
    Down to a sunless sea.   5
So twice five miles of fertile ground
With walls and towers were girdled round:
And there were gardens bright with sinuous rills,
Where blossomed many an incense-bearing tree;

And here were forests ancient as the hills,   10
Enfolding sunny spots of greenery.

But oh! that deep romantic chasm which slanted
Down the green hill athwart a cedarn cover!
A savage place! as holy and enchanted
As e'er beneath a waning moon was haunted   15
By woman wailing for her demon-lover!
And from this chasm, with ceaseless turmoil seething,
As if this earth in fast thick pants were breathing,
A mighty fountain momently was forced:
Amid whose swift half-intermitted burst   20
Huge fragments vaulted like rebounding hail,
Or chaffy grain beneath the thresher's flail:
And 'mid these dancing rocks at once and ever
It flung up momently the sacred river.
Five miles meandering with a mazy motion   25
Through wood and dale the sacred river ran,
Then reached the caverns measureless to man,
And sank in tumult to a lifeless ocean:
And 'mid this tumult Kubla heard from far
Ancestral voices prophesying war!   30

    The shadow of the dome of pleasure
    Floated midway on the waves;
    Where was heard the mingled measure
    From the fountain and the caves.
It was a miracle of rare device,   35
A sunny pleasure-dome with caves of ice!

    A damsel with a dulcimer
    In a vision once I saw:
    It was an Abyssinian maid,
    And on her dulcimer she played,   40
    Singing of Mount Abora.
    Could I revive within me

Her symphony and song,
    To such a deep delight 'twould win me,
That with music loud and long,   45
I would build that dome in air,
That sunny dome! those caves of ice!
And all who heard should see them there,
And all should cry, Beware! Beware!
His flashing eyes, his floating hair!   50
Weave a circle round him thrice,
And close your eyes with holy dread,
For he on honey-dew hath fed,
And drunk the milk of Paradise.

Lines Composed in a Concert-Room

Nor cold, nor stern, my soul! yet I detest
    These scented Rooms, where, to a gaudy throng,
Heaves the proud Harlot her distended breast,
    In intricacies of laborious song.

These feel not Music's genuine power, nor deign   5
    To melt at Nature's passion-warbled plaint;
But when the long-breathed singer's uptrilled strain
    Bursts in a squall – they gape for wonderment.

Hark! the deep buzz of Vanity and Hate!
    Scornful, yet envious, with self-torturing sneer   10
My lady eyes some maid of humbler state,
    While the pert Captain, or the primmer Priest,
Prattles accordant scandal in her ear.

O give me, from this loathsome scene released,
    To hear our old Musician, blind and grey,   15
(Whom stretching from my nurse's arms I kissed,)
    His Scottish tunes and warlike marches play,
By moonshine, on the balmy summer-night,

The while I dance amid the tedded hay
With merry maids, whose ringlets toss in light.   20
Or lies the purple evening on the bay
Of the calm glossy lake, O let me hide
    Unheard, unseen, behind the alder-trees,
Around whose roots the fisher's boat is tied,
    On whose trim seat doth Edmund stretch at ease,   25
And while the lazy boat sways to and fro,
    Breathes in his flute sad airs, so wild and slow,
That his own cheek is wet with quiet tears.

But O, dear Anne! when midnight wind careers,
And the gust pelting on the out-house shed   30
    Makes the cock shrilly in the rainstorm crow,
    To hear thee sing some ballad full of woe,
Ballad of ship-wreck'd sailor floating dead,
    Whom his own true-love buried in the sands!
Thee, gentle woman, for thy voice remeasures   35
Whatever tones and melancholy pleasures
    The things of Nature utter; birds or trees,
Or moan of ocean-gale in weedy caves,
Or where the stiff grass mid the heath-plant waves,
    Murmur and music then of sudden breeze.   40

Dear Maid! whose form in solitude I seek,
    Such songs in such a mood to hear thee sing,
    It were a deep delight! – But thou shalt fling
Thy white arm round my neck, and kiss my cheek,
    And love the brightness of my gladder eye   45
    The while I tell thee what a holier joy

It were in proud and stately step to go,
    With trump and timbrel clang, and popular shout,
    To celebrate the shame and absolute rout
Unhealable of Freedom's latest foe,   50
    Whose tower'd might shall to its centre nod.

When human feelings, sudden, deep and vast,
As all good spirits of all ages past
   Were armied in the hearts of living men,
Shall purge the earth, and violently sweep   55
These vile and painted locusts to the deep.

Introduction to the Tale of the Dark Ladie

O leave the Lily on its stem;
   O leave the Rose upon the spray;
O leave the Elder-bloom, fair Maids!
   And listen to my lay.

A Cypress and a Myrtle bough,   5
   This morn around my harp you twin'd,
Because it fashion'd mournfully
   Its murmurs in the wind.

And now a Tale of Love and Woe,
   A woeful Tale of Love I sing: 10
Hark, gentle Maidens, hark! it sighs
   And trembles on the string.

But most, my own dear Genevieve!
   It sighs and trembles most for thee!
O come and hear the cruel wrongs   15
   Befel the dark Ladie!

Few sorrows hath she of her own,
   My hope, my joy, my Genevieve!
She loves me best whene'er I sing
   The songs that make her grieve.   20

[*181*]

All thoughts, all passions, all delights,
  Whatever stirs this mortal frame,
All are but ministers of Love,
  And feed his sacred flame.

O ever in my waking dreams,   25
  I dwell upon that happy hour,
When midway on the Mount I sate
  Beside the ruin'd Tow'r.

The moonshine, stealing o'er the scene,
  Had blended with the lights of eve,
And she was there, my hope! my joy!   30
  My own dear Genevieve!

She lean'd against the armed Man
  The statue of the armed Knight –
She stood and listen'd to my harp,   35
  Amid the ling'ring light.

I play'd a sad and doleful air,
  I sang an old and moving story,
An old rude song, that fitted well
  The ruin wild and hoary.   40

She listen'd with a flitting blush,
  With downcast eyes and modest grace:
For well she knew, I could not choose
  But gaze upon her face.

I told her of the Knight that wore   45
  Upon his shield a burning brand,
And how for ten long years he woo'd
  The Ladie of the Land:

I told her, how he pin'd, and ah!
  The deep, the low, the pleading tone,   50

With which I sang another's love,
　　Interpreted my own!

She listen'd with a flitting blush,
　　With downcast eyes and modest grace.
And she forgave me, that I gaz'd　　　55
　　Too fondly on her face!

But when I told the cruel scorn,
　　That craz'd this bold and lovely Knight;
And how he roam'd the mountain woods,
　　Nor rested day or night;　　　60

And how he cross'd the Woodman's paths,
　　Thro' briars and swampy mosses beat;
How boughs rebounding scourg'd his limbs,
　　And low stubs gor'd his feet.

How sometimes from the savage den,　　　65
　　And sometimes from the darksome shade,
And sometimes starting up at once,
　　In green and sunny glade;

There came and look'd him in the face
　　An Angel beautiful and bright,　　　70
And how he knew it was a Fiend,
　　This mis'rable Knight!

And how, unknowing what he did,
　　He leapt amid a lawless band,
And sav'd from outrage worse than death　　　75
　　The Ladie of the Land.

And how she wept, and clasp'd his knees,
　　And how she tended him in vain,

And meekly strove to expiate
   The scorn that craz'd his brain;   80

And how she nurs'd him in a cave;
   And how his madness went away,
When on the yellow forest leaves
   A dying man he lay;

His dying words – but when I reach'd   85
   That tenderest strain of all the ditty,
My fault'ring voice and pausing harp
   Disturb'd her soul with pity.

All impulses of soul and sense
   Had thrill'd my guiltless Genevieve –   90
The music and the doleful tale,
   The rich and balmy eve;

And hopes and fears that kindle hope,
   An undistinguishable throng;
And gentle wishes long subdu'd,   95
   Subdu'd and cherish'd long.

She wept with pity and delight –
   She blush'd with love and maiden shame,
And like the murmurs of a dream,
   I heard her breathe my name.   100

I saw her bosom heave and swell,
   Heave and swell with inward sighs –
I could not choose but love to see
   Her gentle bosom rise.

Her wet cheek glow'd; she stept aside,   105
   As conscious of my look she stept;

[*184*]

Then suddenly, with tim'rous eye,
    She flew to me, and wept;

She half-inclos'd me with her arms –
    She press'd me with a meek embrace;   110
And, bending back her head, look'd up,
    And gaz'd upon my face.

'Twas partly love, and partly fear,
    And partly 'twas a bashful art,
That I might rather feel than see,   115
    The swelling of her heart.

I calm'd her fears, and she was calm,
    And told her love with virgin pride;
And so I won my Genevieve,
    My bright and beaut'ous bride.   120

And now once more a tale of woe,
    A woeful tale of love, I sing:
For thee, my Genevieve! it sighs,
    And trembles on the string.

When last I sang the cruel scorn   125
    That craz'd this bold and lonely Knight,
And how he roam'd the mountain woods,
    Nor rested day or night;

I promis'd thee a sister tale
    Of Man's perfidious cruelty: 130
Come, then, and hear what cruel wrong
    Befel the Dark Ladie.

The Mad Monk

I heard a voice from Etna's side;
    Where o'er a cavern's mouth
    That fronted to the south
A chesnut spread its umbrage wide:
A hermit or a monk the man might be;   5
    But him I could not see:
And thus the music flow'd along,
In melody most like to old Sicilian song:

'There was a time when earth, and sea, and skies,
    The bright green vale, and forest's dark recess,   10
With all things, lay before mine eyes
    In steady loveliness:
But now I feel, on earth's uneasy scene,
    Such sorrows as will never cease; –
    I only ask for peace;   15
If I must live to know that such a time has been!'
A silence then ensued:
    Till from the cavern came
    A voice; – it was the same!
And thus, in mournful tone, its dreary plaint renew'd: 20

'Last night, as o'er the sloping turf I trod,
    The smooth green turf, to me a vision gave
Beneath mine eyes, the sod –
    The roof of Rosa's grave!

My heart has need with dreams like these to strive,   25
    For, when I woke, beneath mine eyes I found
    The plot of mossy ground,
On which we oft have sat when Rosa was alive. –
Why must the rock, and margin of the flood,
    Why must the hills so many flow'rets bear,   30
Whose colours to a *murder'd* maiden's blood,
    Such sad resemblance wear? –

[*186*]

'*I struck the wound*, – this hand of mine!
For Oh, thou maid divine,
   I lov'd to agony!   35
The youth whom thou call'd'st thine
   Did never love like me!

'Is it the stormy clouds above
   That flash'd so red a gleam?
     On yonder downward trickling stream? –   40
'Tis not the blood of her I love. –
The sun torments me from his western bed,
   Oh, let him cease for ever to diffuse
   Those crimson spectre hues!
Oh, let me lie in peace, and be for ever dead!'   45

Here ceas'd the voice. In deep dismay,
Down thro' the forest I pursu'd my way.

A Letter to . . . . . .

Well! if the Bard was weatherwise, who made
The grand old Ballad of Sir Patrick Spence,
This Night, so tranquil now, will not go hence
Unrous'd by winds, that ply a busier trade
Than that, which moulds yon clouds in lazy flakes,   5
Or the dull sobbing Draft, that drones & rakes
Upon the Strings of this Eolian Lute,
   Which better far were mute.
For lo! the New Moon, winter-bright!
And overspread with phantom Light,   10
(With swimming phantom Light o'erspread
But rimm'd & circled with a silver Thread)
I see the Old Moon in her Lap, foretelling
The coming-on of Rain & squally Blast –

[*187*]

O! Sara! that the Gust ev'n now were swelling,   15
And the slant Night-shower driving loud & fast!

A Grief without a pang, void, dark, & drear,
A stifling, drowsy, unimpassion'd Grief
That finds no natural Outlet, no Relief
    In word, or sigh, or tear –   20
This, Sara! well thou know'st,
Is that sore Evil, which I dread the most,
And oft'nest suffer! In this heartless Mood,
To other thoughts by yonder Throstle woo'd,
That pipes within the Larch tree, not unseen,   25
(The Larch, which pushes out in tassels green
It's bundled Leafits) woo'd to mild Delights
By all the tender Sounds & gentle Sights
Of this sweet Primrose-month – & *vainly* woo'd
O dearest Sara! in this heartless Mood   30
All this long Eve, so balmy & serene,
Have I been gazing on the western Sky
And it's peculiar Tint of Yellow Green –
And still I gaze – & with how blank an eye!
And those thin Clouds above, in flakes & bars,   35
That give away their Motion to the Stars;
Those Stars, that glide behind them, or between,
Now sparkling, now bedimm'd, but always seen;
Yon crescent Moon, as fix'd as if it grew
In it's own cloudless, starless Lake of Blue –   40
A boat becalm'd! dear William's Sky Canoe!
– I see them all, so excellently fair!
    I see, not feel, how beautiful they are.

    My genial Spirits fail –
    And what can these avail   45
To lift the smoth'ring Weight from off my Breast?
    It were a vain Endeavor,
    Tho' I should gaze for ever
                    [*188*]

On that Green Light which lingers in the West!
I may not hope from outward Forms to win   50
The Passion & the Life whose Fountains are within!
These lifeless Shapes, around, below, Above,
    O what can they impart?
When even the gentle Thought, that thou, my Love!
    Art gazing now, like me,   55
    And see'st the Heaven, I see –
Sweet Thought it is – yet feebly stirs my Heart!

    Feebly! O feebly! – Yet
    (I well remember it)
In my first Dawn of Youth that Fancy stole   60
With many secret Yearnings on my Soul.
At eve, sky-gazing in 'ecstatic fit'
(Alas! for cloister'd in a city School
The Sky was all, I knew, of Beautiful)
At the barr'd window often did I sit,   65
And oft upon the leaded School-roof lay,
    And to myself would say –
There does not live the Man so stripp'd of good affections
As not to love to see a Maiden's quiet Eyes
Uprais'd, and linking on sweet Dreams by dim Connections 70
To Moon, or Evening Star, or glorious western Skies –
While yet a Boy, this Thought would so pursue me
That often it became a kind of Vision to me!

    Sweet Thought! and dear of old
    To Hearts of finer Mould!   75
Ten thousand times by Friends & Lovers blest!
    I spake with rash Despair,
    And ere I was aware,
The Weight was somewhat lifted from my Breast!
O Sara! in the weather-fended Wood,   80
Thy lov'd haunt! where the Stock-doves coo at Noon,
    I guess, that thou hast stood

And watch'd yon Crescent, & it's ghost-like Moon.
And yet, far rather in my present Mood
I would, that thou'dst been sitting all this while   85
Upon the sod-built Seat of Camomile –
And tho' thy Robin may have ceas'd to sing,
Yet needs for *my* sake must thou love to hear
The Bee-hive murmuring near,
That ever-busy & most quiet Thing   90
Which I have heard at Midnight murmuring.

    I feel my spirit moved –
    And wheresoe'er thou be,
    O Sister! O Beloved!
    Those dear mild Eyes, that see   95
    Even now the Heaven, *I* see –
There is a Prayer in them! It is for *me* –
And I, dear Sara – *I* am blessing *thee*!

It was as calm as this, that happy night
When Mary, thou, & I together were,   100
The low decaying Fire our only Light,
And listen'd to the Stillness of the Air!
O that affectionate & blameless Maid,
Dear Mary! on her Lap my head she lay'd –
    Her hand was on my Brow,   105
    Even as my own is now;
And on my Cheek I felt thy eye-lash play.
Such Joy I had, that I may truly say,
My Spirit was awe-stricken with the Excess
And trance-like Depth of it's brief Happiness.   110

Ah fair Remembrances, that so revive
The Heart, & fill it with a living Power,
Where were they, Sara? – or did I not strive
To win them to me? – on the fretting Hour
Then when I wrote thee that complaining Scroll   115
[*190*]

Which even to bodily Sickness bruis'd thy Soul!
And yet thou blam'st thyself alone! And yet
   Forbidd'st me all Regret!

And must I not regret, that I distress'd
Thee, best belov'd! who lovest me the best?   120
My better mind had fled, I know not whither,
For O! was this an absent Friend's Employ
To send from far both Pain & Sorrow thither
Where still his Blessings should have call'd down Joy!
I read thy guileless Letter o'er again –   125
I hear thee of thy blameless Self complain –
And only this I learn – & this, alas! I know –
That thou art weak & pale with Sickness, Grief & Pain –
   And *I – I* made thee so!

O for my own sake I regret perforce   130
Whatever turns thee, Sara! from the Course
Of calm Well-being & a Heart at rest!
When thou, & with thee those, whom thou lov'st best,
Shall dwell together in one happy Home,
One House, the dear *abiding* Home of All,   135
I too will crown me with a Coronal –
Nor shall this Heart in idle Wishes roam
   Morbidly soft!
No! let me trust, that I shall wear away
In no inglorious Toils the manly Day,   140
And only now & then, & not too oft,
Some dear & memorable Eve will bless
Dreaming of all your Loves & Quietness.
Be happy, & I need thee not in sight.
Peace in thy Heart, & Quiet in thy Dwelling,   145
Health in thy Limbs, & in thine Eyes the Light
Of Love, & Hope, & honorable Feeling –
Where e'er I am, I shall be well content!
Not near thee, haply shall be more content!

To all things I prefer the Permanent.   150
And better seems it for a heart, like mine,
Always to *know*, than sometimes to behold,
     Their Happiness & thine –
For Change doth trouble me with pangs untold!
To see thee, hear thee, feel thee – then to part   155
     Oh! – it weighs down the Heart!
To *visit* those, I love, as I love thee,
Mary, & William, & dear Dorothy,
It is but a temptation to repine –
The transientness is Poison in the Wine,   160
Eats out the pith of Joy, makes all Joy hollow,
All Pleasure a dim Dream of Pain to follow!
My own peculiar Lot, my house-hold Life
It is, & will remain, Indifference or Strife.
While *ye* are *well* & *happy*, 'twould but wrong you   165
If I should fondly yearn to be among you –
Wherefore, O wherefore! should I wish to be
A wither'd branch upon a blossoming Tree?

But (let me say it! for I vainly strive
To beat away the Thought) but if thou pin'd,   170
Whate'er the Cause, in body or in mind,
I were the miserablest Man alive
To know it & be absent! Thy Delights
Far off, or near, alike I may partake –
But O! to mourn for thee, & to forsake   175
All power, all hope of giving comfort to thee –
To know that thou art weak & worn with pain,
And not to hear thee, Sara! not to view thee –
     Not sit beside thy Bed,
     Not press thy aching Head,   180
     Not bring thee Health again –
     At least to hope, to try –
By this Voice, which thou lov'st, & by this earnest Eye –
Nay, wherefore did I let it haunt my Mind
                    [*192*]

The dark distressful Dream!   185
I turn from it, & listen to the Wind
Which long has rav'd unnotic'd! What a Scream
Of agony by Torture lengthen'd out
That Lute sent forth! O thou wild Storm without!
Jagg'd Rock, or mountain Pond, or blasted Tree,   190
Or Pine-grove, whither Woodman never clomb,
Or lonely House, long held the Witches' Home,
Methinks were fitter Instruments for Thee,
Mad Lutanist! that in this month of Showers,
Of dark brown Gardens, & of peeping Flowers,   195
Mak'st Devil's Yule, with worse than wintry Song
The Blossoms, Buds, and timorous Leaves among!
Thou Actor, perfect in all tragic Sounds!
Thou mighty Poet, even to frenzy bold!
    What tell'st thou now about?   200
'Tis of the Rushing of an Host in Rout –
And many Groans from men with smarting Wounds –
At once they groan with smart, and shudder with the Cold!
'Tis hush'd! there is a Trance of deepest Silence,
Again! but all that Sound, as of a rushing Crowd,   205
And Groans & tremulous Shudderings, all are over –
And it has other Sounds, and all less deep, less loud!
    A Tale of less Affright,
    And temper'd with Delight,
As William's Self had made the tender Lay –   210
    'Tis of a little Child
    Upon a heathy Wild,
Not far from home – but it has lost it's way –
And now moans low in utter grief & fear –
And now screams loud, & hopes to make it's Mother   215
    hear!

'Tis Midnight! and small Thoughts have I of Sleep –
Full seldom may my Friend such Vigils keep –
O breathe She softly in her gentle Sleep!

N   [193]

Cover her, gentle Sleep! with wings of Healing.
And be this Tempest but a Mountain Birth!   220
May all the Stars hang bright above her Dwelling,
Silent, as tho' they *watch'd* the sleeping Earth!
Healthful & light, my Darling! may'st thou rise
    With clear & cheerful Eyes –
And of the same good Tidings to me send!   225
    For, oh! beloved Friend!
I am not the buoyant Thing, I was of yore –
When like an own Child, I to Joy belong'd;
For others mourning oft, myself oft sorely wrong'd,
Yet bearing all things then, as if I nothing bore!   230

    Yes, dearest Sara! yes!
There *was* a time when tho' my path was rough,
The Joy within me dallied with Distress;
And all Misfortunes were but as the Stuff
Whence Fancy made me Dreams of Happiness: 235
For Hope grew round me, like the climbing Vine,
And Leaves & Fruitage, not my own, seem'd mine!
But now Ill Tidings bow me down to earth
Nor care I, that they rob me of my Mirth
    But oh! each Visitation   240
Suspends what Nature gave me at my Birth,
    My shaping Spirit of Imagination!

I speak not now of those habitual Ills
That wear out Life, when two unequal Minds
Meet in one House, & two discordant Wills –   245
    This leaves me, where it finds,
Past cure, & past Complaint – a fate austere
Too fix'd & hopeless to partake of Fear!

But thou, dear Sara! (dear indeed thou art,
My Comforter! A Heart within my Heart!)   250
Thou, & the Few, we love, tho' few ye be,
Make up a world of Hopes & Fears for me.

And if Affliction, or distemp'ring Pain,
Or wayward Chance befall you, I complain
Not that I mourn – O Friends, most dear! most true!   255
   Methinks to weep with you
Were better far than to rejoice alone –
But that my course domestic Life has known
No Habits of heart-nursing Sympathy,
No Griefs, but such as dull and deaden me,   260
No mutual mild Enjoyments of it's own,
No Hopes of it's own Vintage, None, O! none –
Whence when I mourn'd for you, my Heart might borrow
Fair forms & living Motions for it's Sorrow.
For not to think of what I needs must feel,   265
But to be still & patient all I can;
And haply by abstruse Research to steal
From my own Nature all the Natural Man –
This was my sole Resource, my wisest plan!
And that, which suits a part, infects the whole,   270
And now is almost grown the Temper of my Soul.

   My little Children are a Joy, a Love,
       A good Gift from above!
But what is Bliss, that still calls up a Woe,
       And makes it doubly keen   275
Compelling me to *feel*, as well as know,
What a most blessed Lot mine might have been.
Those little Angel Children (woe is me!)
There have been hours, when feeling how they bind
And pluck out the Wing-feathers of my Mind,   280
Turning my Error to Necessity,
I have half-wish'd, they never had been born!
That seldom! But sad Thoughts they always bring,
And like the Poet's Philomel, I sing
My Love-song, with my breast against a Thorn.   285

With no unthankful Spirit I confess,
This clinging Grief too, in it's turn, awakes
That Love, and Father's Joy; but O! it makes
The Love the greater, & the Joy far less.
These Mountains too, these Vales, these Woods, these
     Lakes,   290
Scenes full of Beauty & of Loftiness
Where all my Life I fondly hop'd to live –
I were sunk low indeed, did they *no* solace give;
But oft I seem to feel, & evermore I fear,
They are not to me now the Things, which once they   295
     were.

O Sara! we receive but what we give,
And in *our* Life alone does Nature live.
Our's is her Wedding Garment, our's her Shroud –
And would we aught behold of higher Worth
Than that inanimate cold World allow'd   300
To the poor loveless ever-anxious Crowd,
Ah! from the Soul itself must issue forth
A Light, a Glory, and a luminous Cloud
     Enveloping the Earth!
And from the Soul itself must there be sent   305
A sweet & potent Voice, of it's own Birth,
Of all sweet Sounds the Life & Element.

O pure of Heart! thou need'st not ask of me
What this strong music in the Soul may be,
     What, & wherein it doth exist,   310
This Light, this Glory, this fair luminous Mist,
This beautiful & beauty-making Power!
Joy, innocent Sara! Joy, that ne'er was given
Save to the Pure, & in their purest Hour,
Joy, Sara! is the Spirit & the Power,   315
That wedding Nature to us gives in Dower
     A new Earth & new Heaven

Undreamt of by the Sensual & the Proud!
Joy is that strong Voice, Joy that luminous Cloud –
　　We, we ourselves rejoice!　　　　　　　　　320
And thence flows all that charms or ear or sight,
All melodies the Echoes of that Voice,
All Colors a Suffusion of that Light.

Sister & Friend of my devoutest Choice!
Thou being innocent & full of love,　　　　　　325
And nested with the Darlings of thy Love,
And feeling in thy Soul, Heart, Lips, & Arms
Even what the conjugal & mother Dove
That borrows genial Warmth from those, she warms,
Feels in her thrill'd wings, blessedly outspread –　330
Thou free'd awhile from Cares & human Dread
By the Immenseness of the Good & Fair
　　Which thou see'st every where –
Thus, thus should'st thou rejoice!
To thee would all Things live from Pole to Pole,　335
Their Life the Eddying of thy living Soul –
O dear! O Innocent! O full of Love!
A very Friend! A Sister of my Choice –
O dear, as Light & Impulse from above,
Thus may'st thou ever, evermore rejoice!　　　340

Chamouny; the Hour Before Sunrise

A HYMN

Hast thou a charm to stay the morning star
In his steep course – so long he seems to pause
On thy bald awful head, O Chamouny!
The Arvè and Arveiron at thy base
Rave ceaselessly; but thou, dread mountain form,　5

Resist from forth thy silent sea of pines
How silently! Around thee, and above,
Deep is the sky, and black: transpicuous, deep,
An ebon mass! Methinks thou piercest it
As with a wedge! But when I look again,   10
It seems thy own calm home, thy crystal shrine,
Thy habitation from eternity.
O dread and silent form! I gaz'd upon thee,
Till thou, still present to my bodily eye,
Did'st vanish from my thought. Entranc'd in pray'r,   15
I worshipp'd the Invisible alone.
Yet thou, meantime, wast working on my soul,
E'en like some deep enchanting melody,
So sweet, we know not, we are list'ning to it.
But I awoke, and with a busier mind,   20
And active will self-conscious, offer now
Not, as before, involuntary pray'r
And passive adoration! –
                              Hand and voice,
Awake, awake! and thou, my heart, awake!
Awake ye rocks! Ye forest pines, awake!   25
Green fields, and icy cliffs! All join my hymn!
And thou, O silent mountain, sole and bare,
O blacker, than the darkness, all the night,
And visited, all night, by troops of stars,
Or when they climb the sky, or when they sink –   30
Companion of the morning star at dawn,
Thyself Earth's rosy star, and of the dawn
Co-herald! Wake, O wake, and utter praise!
Who sank thy sunless pillars deep in earth?
Who fill'd thy countenance with rosy light?   35
Who made thee father of perpetual streams?
And you, ye five wild torrents, fiercely glad,
Who call'd you forth from Night and utter Death?
From darkness let you loose, and icy dens,
Down those precipitous, black, jagged rocks   40

For ever shatter'd, and the same for ever!
Who gave you your invulnerable life,
Your strength, your speed, your fury, and your joy,
Unceasing thunder, and eternal foam!
And who commanded, and the silence came –   45
'Here shall the billows stiffen, and have rest?'

Ye ice-falls! ye that from yon dizzy heights
Adown enormous ravines steeply slope,
Torrents, methinks, that heard a mighty voice,
And stopp'd at once amid their maddest plunge!   50
Motionless torrents! silent cataracts!
Who made you glorious, as the gates of Heav'n,
Beneath the keen full moon? Who bade the sun
Clothe you with rainbows? Who with lovely flow'rs
Of living blue spread garlands at your feet?   55
God! God! The torrents like a shout of nations,
Utter! The ice-plain bursts, and answers God!
God, sing the meadow-streams with gladsome voice,
And pine groves with their soft, and soul-like sound,
The silent snow-mass, loos'ning, thunders God!   60
Ye dreadless flow'rs! that fringe th' eternal frost!
Ye wild goats, bounding by the eagle's nest!
Ye eagles, playmates of the mountain blast!
Ye lightnings, the dread arrows of the clouds!
Ye signs and wonders of the element,   65
Utter forth, God! and fill the hills with praise!

And thou, O silent Form, alone and bare,
Whom, as I lift again my head bow'd low
In adoration, I again behold,
And to thy summit upward from thy base   70
Sweep slowly with dim eyes suffus'd by tears,
Awake, thou mountain form! rise, like a cloud!
Rise, like a cloud of incense, from the earth!
Thou kingly spirit thron'd among the hills,

[199]

Thou dread ambassador from Earth to Heav'n –
Great hierarch, tell thou the silent sky,
And tell the stars, and tell the rising sun,
Earth with her thousand voices calls on God!

The Pains of Sleep

When on my bed my limbs I lay,
It hath not been my use to pray
With moving Lips or bended Knees;
But silently, by slow degrees,
My spirit I to Love compose,   5
In humble trust my eyelids close,
With reverential Resignation,
No Wish conceiv'd, no Thought exprest,
Only a *Sense* of Supplication,
A *Sense* o'er all my soul imprest   10
That I am weak, yet not unblest;
Since *round* me, *in* me, every where,
Eternal Strength and Goodness are! –

But yesternight I pray'd aloud
In Anguish and in Agony,   15
Awaking from the fiendish Crowd
Of Shapes and Thoughts that tortur'd me!
Desire with Loathing strangely mixt,
On wild or hateful Objects fixt;
Pangs of Revenge, the powerless Will,   20
Still baffled, and consuming still,
Sense of intolerable Wrong,
And men whom I despis'd made strong
Vain-glorious Threats, unmanly Vaunting,

Bad men my boasts and fury taunting   25
Rage, sensual Passion, mad'ning Brawl,
And Shame and Terror over all!
Deeds to be hid that were not hid,
Which, all confus'd I might not know,
Whether I suffer'd or I did: 30
For all was Horror, Guilt and Woe,
My own or others, still the same,
Life-stifling Fear, Soul-stifling Shame!

Thus two nights pass'd: the Night's Dismay
Sadden'd and stunn'd the boding Day.   35
I fear'd to sleep: Sleep seem'd to be
Disease's worst malignity.
The third night when my own loud Scream
Had freed me from the fiendish Dream,
O'ercome by Sufferings dark and wild,   40
I wept as I had been a Child –
And having thus by Tears subdued
My Trouble to a milder mood –
Such Punishments, I thought, were due
To Natures, deepliest stain'd with Sin,   45
Still to be stirring up anew
The self-created Hell within;
The Horror of their Crimes to view,
To know and loathe, yet wish and do!
With such let Fiends make mockery –   50
But I – Oh wherefore this on *me*?
Frail is my Soul, yea, strengthless wholly,
Unequal, restless, melancholy;
But free from Hate, and sensual Folly!
To live beloved is all I need,   55
And whom I love, I love indeed.

Phantom

All look and likeness caught from earth
All accident of kin and birth,
Had pass'd away. There was no trace
Of aught on that illumined face,
Uprais'd beneath the rifted stone   5
But of one spirit all her own; –
She, she herself, and only she,
Shone through her body visibly.

Psyche

The butterfly, the ancient Grecians made
The soul's fair emblem, and its only name –
But of the soul, escaped the slavish trade
Of mortal life! – For in this earthly frame
Ours is the reptile's lot, much toil, much blame,   5
Manifold motions making little speed,
And to deform and kill the things whereon we feed.

Human Life

If dead, we cease to be; if total gloom
    Swallow up life's brief flash for aye, we fare
As summer-gusts, of sudden birth and doom,
    Whose sound and motion not alone declare,
But are their whole of being! If the breath   5
    Be Life itself, and not its task and tent,
If even a soul like Milton's can know death;

O Man! thou vessel purposeless, unmeant,
Yet drone-hive strange of phantom purposes!
   Surplus of Nature's dread activity,   10
Which, as she gazed on some nigh-finished vase,
Retreating slow, with meditative pause,
   She formed with restless hands unconsciously.
Blank accident! nothing's anomaly!
   If rootless thus, thus substanceless thy state,   15
Go, weigh thy dreams, and be thy hopes, thy fears,
The counter-weights! – Thy laughter and thy tears
   Mean but themselves, each fittest to create
And to repay the other! Why rejoices
   Thy heart with hollow joy for hollow good?   20
   Why cowl thy face beneath the mourner's hood?
Why waste thy sighs, and thy lamenting voices,
   Image of Image, Ghost of Ghostly Elf,
That such a thing as thou feel'st warm or cold?
Yet what and whence thy gain, if thou withhold   25
   These costless shadows of thy shadowy self?
Be sad! be glad! be neither! seek, or shun!
Thou hast no reason why! Thou canst have none;
Thy being's being is contradiction.

On Donne's Poetry

With Donne, whose muse on dromedary trots,
Wreathe iron pokers into true-love knots;
Rhyme's sturdy cripple, fancy's maze and clue,
Wit's forge and fire-blast, meaning's press and screw.

Work Without Hope

All Nature seems at work. Slugs leave their lair –
The bees are stirring – birds are on the wing –
And Winter slumbering in the open air,
Wears on his smiling face a dream of Spring!
And I the while, the sole unbusy thing,   5
Nor honey make, nor pair, nor build, nor sing.

Yet well I ken the banks where amaranths blow,
Have traced the fount whence streams of nectar flow.
Bloom, O ye amaranths! bloom for whom ye may,
For me ye bloom not! Glide, rich streams, away!   10
With lips unbrightened, wreathless brow, I stroll:
And would you learn the spells that drowse my soul?
Work without Hope draws nectar in a sieve,
And Hope without an object cannot live.

Song

Though veiled in spires of myrtle-wreath,
Love is a sword which cuts its sheath,
And through the clefts itself has made,
We spy the flashes of the blade!

But through the clefts itself has made   5
We likewise see Love's flashing blade,
By rust consumed, or snapt in twain;
And only hilt and stump remain.

Epitaph

Stop, Christian passer-by! – Stop, child of God,
And read with gentle breast. Beneath this sod
A poet lies, or that which once seem'd he.
O, lift one thought in prayer for S.T.C.;
That he who many a year with toil of breath   5
Found death in life, may here find life in death!
Mercy for praise – to be forgiven for fame
He ask'd, and hoped, through Christ. Do thou the same!

Fragments

1

Let Eagle bid the Tortoise sunward soar –
As vainly Strength speaks to a broken Mind.

2

And my heart mantles in its own delight

3

                              I have experienced
The worst the world can wreak on me – the worst
That can make Life indifferent, yet disturb
With whisper'd discontent the dying prayer –
I have beheld the whole of all, wherein
My heart had any interest in this life
To be disrent and torn from off my Hopes
That nothing now is left. Why then live on?

That hostage that the world had in its keeping
Given by me as a pledge that I would live —
That hope of Her, say rather that pure Faith
In her fix'd Love, which held me to keep truce
With the tyranny of Life — is gone, ah! whither?
What boots it to reply? 'tis gone! and now
Well may I break this Pact, this league of Blood
That ties me to myself — and break I shall.

Textual Commentary

Coleridge was not always honest about his own poems. He was capable of deliberately deceiving both his friends and the public. He told Thomas Poole that *A Letter*, from which *Dejection: An Ode* was later extracted, had been written to him. On the other hand William Sotheby was assured that it had been written to Wordsworth. In fact it was a love-poem to Sara Hutchinson. The published version is addressed to none of these but to an unknown by the name of Edmund, and that was only the least of the many suppressions involved. Not much more than a third of the original poem was revealed to the public. They were left to understand the 'dejection' of the new title without the poetry that explained it as being caused by Coleridge's unhappy marriage, his love for Sara and his envy of Wordsworth. The remaining passages, removed from their proper context and arranged in a new order, lose much of their meaning. For instance Coleridge had originally described the guilty fear that his bitterness had made Sara ill as a 'dark distressful Dream'; but this phrase in the published version has to describe a natural storm which the poet is watching through his window. For an editor to apply the convention of the 'final version' in cases such as this would be pharasaical. At best the later poem could only be regarded as a separate work in its own right, at worst as the remnants of a vivisection. But the true poem is alive in the original text: as it was before it had to be hastily dissected in order to fulfill Coleridge's contract with the *Morning Post*. An equally clear, though less important, example is *The Raven*. This tells of a raven whose family died when their tree was felled for ship-building; the bird is later

[*207*]

delighted to watch the resulting ship sink, and to hear 'the last shriek of the perishing souls'. The appropriately callous conclusion is that 'Revenge was sweet'. Publishing it twenty years after its composition however, Coleridge added a cosy subtitle – *A Christmas Tale* – and a new ending:

> We must not think so; but forget and forgive,
> And what Heaven gives life to, we'll still let it live.

The poem was thus made to close telling lies about itself, replacing its own poetic justice with an alien justice which betrays the poetry. Coleridge admitted as much in a manuscript note on the new lines:

> Added thro' cowardly fear of the Goody! What a Hollow, where the Heart of Faith ought to be, does it not betray? this alarm concerning Christian Morality, that will not permit even a Raven to be a Raven, nor a Fox a Fox, but demands conventicular justice to be inflicted on their unchristian conduct, or at least an antidote to be annexed.

No editor should add his own hypocrisy to that which Coleridge confesses here. Coleridge revised his poems for a variety of reasons, and with very uneven results. Sometimes he simply wanted to pretend that he had not in his youth held the views which his early poetry expressed all too clearly. In 1807 he wrote to Miss Cruikshank saying that she had done him 'some little disservice' in borrowing 'the first edition' of his poems, and assuring her that his principles had been 'at all times, decidedly anti-jacobin, and anti-revolutionary'. He often needed money quickly, and was thus tempted to turn the beginning of an incomplete poem into what could pass as a self-contained unit. In this way the *Introduction to the Tale of the Dark Ladie* became *Love*. He seems to have thought that the products of his sometimes morbid imagination might offend the delicate sensibilities of contemporary taste. *The Pains of Sleep* and *Christabel* were accordingly doctored. The latter lost the climatic lines of the passage describing Genevieve's stripping to reveal that 'her bosom and half her side' were 'lean and old and foul of hue'. Hazlitt was probably exaggerating when he claimed that the omitted line 'was necessary to make common sense' of the entire poem. But without it the horror of that particular episode cannot be crystallized and one remembers Coleridge's own remark that 'Poetry, like schoolboys, by too frequent and severe correction may be cowed into dullness'. On the other hand *Frost at Midnight* raised no embarrassing issues, and the revisions Coleridge made to it over a period of thirty years seem to have been motivated only by a desire to make the poem's original statement more economic and powerful.

An editor in fact has to be eclectic in his choice of texts. Scholars who favour a consistent adherence to the 'final text' might argue that to be eclectic is to be subjective, and that the personal taste of an editor stands between the poems and the reader if the convention is abandoned. But the convention itself seems to me a rationale by which scholars abandon that commitment to enquiry and thought without which scholarship means nothing. There is no logic in assuming that an author at the end of his life is the person best placed to grasp the essence of a poem written decades earlier, and therefore the best judge of how that essence can most effectively be expressed. Coleridge particularly (who changed his mind about nearly every major attitude of his youth) was likely to be more out of sympathy with his early poetry than the modern reader. What had the old man of Highgate to do with the young radical who wrote *To a Young Ass*? This poem deserves to be printed with its bold scorn for 'The tumult of a scoundrel Monarch's Breast', and not with the tame line which in later editions replaced it: 'The aching of pale Fashion's vacant breast!' Such an evasively generalized last line cannot be a consistent end to the poem. This sort of choice does not involve the imposition of an individual's aesthetic taste. It merely requires that an editor allows a poem to be honestly itself – even if this involves dismantling some muffling dishonesties supplied by its own author.

o

The case of *The Ancient Mariner* is more complex. It was conceived as a collaborative venture with Wordsworth, and the mood on the famous walking tour was probably light-hearted enough to disguise from them the seriousness of the project. Wordsworth certainly claimed to have 'droll enough recollections' of it. So one would expect the 1798 version to later be given a little polishing for the most innocent of reasons. Its archaic spellings and self-consciously quaint diction were a concession to a merely modish contemporary taste (or perhaps merely a joke at the expense of that fashion) and they were rightly seen later as trivia which distracted from what was important about the poem, and cut. But much more sweeping omissions were made in the second edition. Coleridge would be revising under the shadow of Wordsworth's note which stressed the poem's 'defects' and claimed 'that many persons had been much displeased with it'. The decision to leave out five key stanzas may therefore have been neither Coleridge's alone nor considered (see notes to lines 530–551). It certainly distorted, rather than clarified, the poem. Coleridge's mood in 1800 anyway made it a peculiarly bad time to be tampering with his earlier poetry: in December of that year he claimed to 'have altogether abandoned the writing of verse being convinced that [he] never had the essentials of poetic Genius'. This kind of humility was of course never far from envy of Wordsworth whom he regarded at the time as 'a great, a true Poet' to be contrasted with himself who was 'only a kind of a Metaphysician'. It was not a frame of mind in which Coleridge would be very resilient about Wordsworth's complaint that *The Ancient Mariner*'s events 'having no necessary connection do not produce each other; and the imagery is somewhat too laboriously accumulated'. Coleridge had let the side down by failing to finish *Christabel* for the 1800 edition, and Wordsworth had had to produce *Michael* instead, so he would not be well-placed to protest. But a modern editor need not be so inhibited. The original conception had been that the five unpopular stanzas were obtrusively echoed by the matching set that followed. Together the passage established that red shadows invading the serenity of a moonlit scene could lead either to the corpses once again at their most threatening, or to the relief of rescue by friendly spirits who would be seen standing in the traditional pose of the conqueror above prone bodies rendered harmless again. The point of the carefully paralleled sequences is in fact precisely that events lack the kind of cheery logic which allows one to guess what they will produce. Moreover in this case the 'laboriously accumulated' imagery in which every detail echoes one in the parallel sequence is meant to be noticed. The omens are elaborate so that their ability to produce such contrary results can be seen as cruelly confusing. The crew after all have supposedly died because they had Wordsworth's simplistic faith in the way events produce each other. Once it was clear that good weather followed the killing of the albatross, they felt confident that it must have been a wise move. When they are becalmed and the mariner sees a ship, he assumes this event will produce rescue. Both deductions are proved bitterly false, and fate is determined not by the logic of cause and effect, but by a game of dice. There had to be a final statement of all this before the mariner (and the reader) could be allowed to land on the less obviously alarming coast of England. In the full poem this was provided in the parallel passages in which the same events produce now returned threat, and now rescue, and the endless nature of the cycle briefly evoked by the rescue too being only temporary:

> Then vanish'd all the lovely lights;
>   The bodies rose anew:
> With silent pace, each to his place,
>   Came back the ghastly crew.

The original readers, recently alerted to verbal parallels, would not have seen much finality in the fact that the ship then 'went down like lead'. They would recall that all had seemed well when earlier the albatross at last fell off 'and sank/like lead into the sea'. The agency in fact may change, but the agony will recur in one form or another. (It was precise of Coleridge in the errata of the 1800 text to change 'since then, at an uncertain hour./That agency returns' to 'That *agony* returns'.) The two parallel sequences are thus wholly interdependent; to omit one is to destroy the original point of the other.

The 1800 revisions are typical of a textual editor's problems. The omission of the archaisms is a clarification, the omission of the five stanzas a distortion. Such choices must be made, and the subsequent history of the poem gives one no more faith in the likelihood of revisions simply reflecting Coleridge's development as a poet. They are as likely to be symptoms of his decline as a man. The Malta trip of 1804 provided details of life at sea which appeared useful for subsequent editions. But the trip was motivated by the collapse of all that Coleridge held dear. His marriage was over; his friendship with the Words-worths impossibly confused by his love for Sara Hutchinson; his confidence as a poet destroyed. The notebooks show that the voyage encouraged him in his guilty isolation to draw parallels between his own situation and that of the Ancient Mariner. It would have been surprising if they had been very close, considering how different Coleridge's existence had been in the happy, productive time of the poem's composition. Inevitably the comparison involved perversion of the truth about both his poem and his life. Sadly it encouraged him to try and adapt his poem to the changing image he had of himself as he grew older. When he managed to convince himself that he was surrounded by the comforting angels of an orthodoxly Christian universe, he had to try and convince his readers that the mariner was similarly provided. The true poem was too strong to admit more than a marginal invasion by such aliens, but this has been sufficient to lead most critics away from the poem.

We cannot tell when the major revisions for *Sibylline Leaves* – including the angels of the marginalia – were made. But the note-books show Coleridge working on the poem in 1807. One of the reasons for change was depressingly mundane.

He had to publish a new edition of his poems because he needed cash and he believed that a better price could be gained, if he could argue that old poems previously published in *Lyrical Ballads* had been substantially revised. He feared that a 'defect of novelty' in view of *The Ancient Mariner*'s 'having past thro'' several editions in the L.B.' might weaken the appeal of the Volume. In 1815 he was still trying to find a publisher, and assured Byron whose aid he was seeking, that the poems previously published in the *Lyrical Ballads* had been 'corrected throughout, with very considerable alterations and additions, some indeed almost re-written'. In 1816 he found his publishers and protested to them that £150 was not an exorbitant price for works which had been 'corrected with all the force of my maturest judgement'. He soon decided however, even though the financial motive was now gone, that the judgements had not been mature enough. He revised as he read the proofs and was still not satisfied. Indeed he tried to pass off so many last-minute revisions as responses to printer's errors that Gutch was glad to have kept the corrected sheets, and thus to be able to prove that the errata Coleridge was demanding were the result of his changing his mind, and not of Gutch's misreading of his corrections. Ill, and desperately busy with other work, Coleridge moaned as he revised that it was 'useless to pluck single thorns from a Thorn-bush'. It was nearly ten years since he had first tried to revise his poems for this edition, and he had given up in 1807 because of the difficulty of finishing 'two poems, four fifths of which had been written years ago' – 'these are two that I cannot with propriety place anywhere but the beginning of the volume', he complains elsewhere. Assuming that the insoluble *Christabel* was one of them, the other one is likely to have been *The Ancient Mariner* which had been put at the beginning of *Lyrical Ballads*. If so, many of the revisions may date from 1807 and his talk of 'finishing' (rather than revising) and of 'four-fifths' would suggest a major abandonment of the original poem. Alternatively they could be as late as the rushed items he forced on to the printers

[215]

after returning the corrected proofs. Neither hypothesis justifies any automatic faith that Coleridge was simply bringing his 'maturest judgement' to bear on the problem of how best to express his original conception. Two revisions we know were made so late that they had to go into the errata. The skeletons of leaves, which helped the hermit to find in his own environment parallels to the nightmare world represented by the returning ship, become for the first time 'brown'. This is merely an attempt to improve on visual description, and makes no differences to the passage's real import which is that the mariner is hardly home and dry if he returns to a land where the wolf eats the she-wolf's young. We therefore let Coleridge's correction stand. But the other revision in the errata is more serious. It is the omission of the deliberately grotesque stanza in which the wind whistles through Death's eye-sockets and fleshless jaw. In moving his poem towards a Christian moral Coleridge could not wholly suppress such a central fact of the plot as the sacrifice of the entire crew, except the supposedly guilty member. But he could attempt to tone down Death into something less alarming than the poem insists on. The hideous form of Death is appropriate to the savage world in which it was allowed to prey according to the random throw of dice. But clearly in a Christian poem Death which would have to be the gateway to heaven cannot be so ugly. The suppression of this stanza seems to me a supression of something which contributes to the poem's central impact, and I have therefore restored it.

The most serious attempt to distract the reader from the poem in the *Sibylline Leaves* version is of course the addition in the margin of the ageing Coleridge's own interpretation of his poem. Partly just a feeble literary joke, this must have always been intended to confuse the unwary as indeed it continues to do. Whether Coleridge was optimistic enough to hope that the marginalia would be regarded as much a part of the poem proper as they now are is debatable. But the marginalia are by their very nature perverting. They are a third-person, and thus by implication objectively true, account of a story whose essence is that it is a first-person narrative. Its full title, its narrative framework of the hypnotized listener, its disturbing vividness, all stress that it is at once event and account. The poem breaks through simplistic distinctions between 'subjective feeling' and 'objective reality'. It concentrates by its very form on the fact that the mariner is condemned to recurring moments of 'total recall' of which this is but a single example, condemned to experience again all that he felt alone on the wide, wide sea. The marginalia turn the speaker into a specimen. Worse, they lie. It is clearly not true, nor ever could be, that 'the curse is finally expiated' and the very real creature that the mariners fed on biscuit-worms cannot become 'a pious bird of good omen' without being ludicrous. To tell the reader in the margin that it is a good omen, when the succeeding stanzas demonstrate how impossible it is until too late to tell whether it is of good or bad omen, is to make nonsense of the poem at its very core. Coleridge claimed that Walter Scott's handling of superstition put the writer in a damagingly superior position to his story: 'that discrepance between the Narrator and the Narrative chills and deadens the Sympathy.' The narrator in the marginalia puts a similarly cold distance between the reader's sympathy and the story as experienced by the mariner.

An editor must clearly prevent an author from telling lies in the margin about the meaning of an early work. But an editor must allow an author to improve on its expression. The Malta trip allowed Coleridge to observe details – 'The steers-man's face by his lamp gleamed white' – which were useful to the evocation of an eerie sea voyage regardless of its moral implications. Such details appearing for the first time in the same text as that which introduced the marginalia force one to be eclectic. The choices are not always easy, but to evade them would be to concur in deceit. The old Coleridge's primary concern may have been his own respectability, but an editor's responsibility is to the poem. Where Coleridge in dealing with details of expression brought the reader closer to the poem

[215]

a revision is allowed to stand. But where it is clear that Coleridge's concern was with views he had not held at the time of composition, and that his intention was to distract the reader from the poet's import, a revision is discarded. The reader has a right to the true poem, and an editor has a duty to present it. Even its own author must not be allowed to conceal it any longer, and it must finally be allowed, like its own pawing horse let go, to cross that discrepance between narrator and narrative. Coleridge said that 'the Poet must always be in perfect sympathy with the Subject of the Narrative, and tell his tale with "a most believing mind"'. We have tried to establish the best text to fulfill those requirements.

Notes

Page 101: TO THE AUTHOR OF 'THE ROBBERS': This was probably written in 1795 when Coleridge's admiration for Schiller was such that he planned to translate the complete works into English. The tone of *The Robbers* (which was first produced in 1782) is best shown in Coleridge's own words, written on the night that he first read it: 'I had read chill and trembling until I came to the part where the Moor fires a pistol over the Robbers who are asleep – I could read no more. . . . Who is this Schiller? This convulser of the Heart? Did he write his Tragedy amid the yelling of Fiends? . . . Upon my soul, I write to you because I am frightened – I had better go to Bed. Why have we ever called Milton sublime? That Count de Moor – horrible Wielder of heart-withering Virtues – ! Satan is scarcely qualified to attend his Execution as Gallows Chaplain.'

lines 2–4: Coleridge means 'If I had written your play'.

line 6: mortal: Coleridge commented: 'It is strange that in the Sonnet to Schiller I wish to die – *die* that nothing may stamp me *mortal* – this *Bull* never struck me till Charles Lloyd mentioned it – the Sense is evident enough – but the word is ridiculously ambiguous.'

line 9: sublimity: Compare Coleridge's later view (1822): 'Schiller has the material Sublime; to produce an effect, he sets you a whole town on fire, and throws infants with their mothers into the flames, or locks up a father in an old tower. But Shakespeare drops a handkerchief, and the same or greater effects follow.'

Page 101: MONOLOGUE TO A YOUNG JACK ASS IN JESUS PIECE: Written in 1794 when Coleridge was preaching 'pantisocracy' – 'a scheme of emigration on the principles of an abolition of individual property.' With Southey and others he was planning to set up an ideal community on the banks of the Susquehannah river in North America. Coleridge himself described the poem later as 'a ludicro-splenetic Copy of Verses, with the diction purposely appropriate', but at the time the poem's basic idea would not have been intrinsically comic. In 1794 he commented on Job 5:23 ('For thou shalt be in league with the stones of the field; and the beasts of the field shall be at peace with thee') that 'The good man' was 'in league with all nature'. The original blend of sincere social protest with humorous hyperbole in the treatment of his own solution can only be regained by a return to the original manuscript version. This we print. In the published version Coleridge suppressed lines 28–34 (presumably because they seemed likely to undermine the cause he was then supporting) and the last line which was too dangerously 'republican'.

Page 103: THE EOLIAN HARP: Written in 1795, the year of his marriage to Sara Fricker who is addressed in the poem. Later versions insert the following passage before line 18:

> *O! the one Life within us and abroad,*
> *Which meets all motion and becomes its soul,*
> *A light in sound, a sound-like power in light,*
> *Rhythm in all thought, and joyance every where –*

This was first added as errata in the *Sibylline Leaves* of 1817, and, though it is impressive enough to recall the comparable passage in *A Letter* (lines 315–323), it does not suit the poem to which it was attached. The addition makes Sara inconsistently reject a passionate and serious belief, an earnest product of that 'Faith that inly *feels*'. Originally Sara's 'mild reproof' interrupted Coleridge's almost flippant handling of intellectual theories: 'many idle flitting Phantasies' of an 'indolent and passive Mind'. We print the 1803 version which allows the poem's conclusion to be at least logical. It also clears the poem of the naive allegorization of Nature (Miltonic comments on flowers – 'Meet emblems they of Innocence and Love!' – and on the peaceful star – 'such should Wisdom be').

line 49: Coleridge's own foot-note reads 'L'athée n'est point a mes yeux un faux esprit; je puis vivre avec lui aussi bien et mieux qu'avec le devot, car il raisonne davantage, mais il lui manque un sens, et mon ame ne se fond point entièrement avec la sienne: il est froid au spectacle le plus ravissant, et il cherche un syllogisme lorsque je rends un action de grace. 'Appel a l'impartiale postérité', par la Citoyenne Roland, troisième partie, p. 67.' Mme. Roland was a Girondist whose friends were known to Wordsworth when he was in revolutionary France, and Dorothy Wordsworth was reading the book in 1796.

Page 104: REFLECTIONS ON ENTERING INTO ACTIVE LIFE: The two concluding paragraphs of this poem have been omitted since they add nothing to its chief interest which is in lines 24–40. Written in 1795 before anything comparable in Wordsworth's poetry, they describe the peculiar experience which was to become the basis of much of his best verse: a moment of mystical intensity, based on the beauty of the landscape, and supported by virtually pantheist ideas. The text is that of the first published version (1796). Later editions made the pantheism more tentative so that 'the whole World' only 'Seem'd imag'd' in the present landscape, in contrast to the original's 'was imag'd'. They also made a moral exemplum of the Bristol businessman whose 'thirst for idle gold' was replaced by 'wiser feelings' as he considered Coleridge's cottage. The original version was sub-titled 'A Poem which affects not to be Poetry'. Coleridge was consciously attempting a more relaxed, and apparently spontaneous, style in this kind of work than that which readers were likely to associate with the word 'Poetry'. He had difficulty however in finding a suitable term for the genre. He used 'Effusion' at first (the title for instance of the 1797 version of what had originally been called a 'monologue' to the young ass and of the 1796 version of the E.H.). Later sub-titles described *The Nightingale* as a 'Conversational' (1798), or 'Conversation' poem (1817). The three greatest poems of this kind however – *Frost at Midnight, This Lime-Tree Bower My Prison,* and *A Letter* – are given no such sub-titles; and when Wordsworth in describing his feelings about *Tintern Abbey* used the formula Coleridge had evolved, he wisely avoided the problem of classification.

Page 106: RELIGIOUS MUSINGS: Written 1794–6. The war between Britain and France had begun in 1794 and this, coupled with the slave-trade, is used to express Coleridge's disillusionment with conventional Christianity. Against it is set a faith in an imminent God 'one omnipresent Mind' in whom all men can know themselves 'Parts and proportions of one wondrous whole'. It is interesting that Coleridge (before he could be under any influence from Wordsworth) was already claiming that an awareness of God as 'Nature's essence, mind, and energy' 'fraternises man' and 'constitutes/Our charities and bearings'.

line 53: Fiends of Superstition: In a note to the 1797 text Coleridge said: 'if the attributing of sublime properties to things or persons, which those things or persons neither do or can possess, be Superstition; then Avarice and Ambition are Superstitions'. Coleridge sees these 'superstitions' as causing war and the slave-trade (the 'more hideous Trade' of line 58).

line 71: Thee to defend, meek Galilaean: Coleridge in this passage is of course attacking the established church for sanctioning war and oppression as necessary for the defence of Christ.

Page 110: THE DESTINY OF NATIONS: The poem's confused struggle with the idea of spirits 'weaving human fates' and teaching mankind

through 'obscure fears' has its obvious relevance to *The Ancient Mariner*.
It ends indeed with a fragment immediately suggestive of the Mariner's
'land of ice and snow':

> *And first a landscape rose*
> *More wild and waste and desolate than where*
> *The white bear, drifting on a field of ice,*
> *Howls to her sundered cubs with piteous rage*
> *And savage agony.*

This was originally presented as the kind of alarming vision imposed on
humanity by spirits 'headstrong, or with petition'd might from God'. The
first alternative suggests that Coleridge may not have been as confident as
he claims (in line 47) that the spirits can be relied upon to 'evolve the
process of eternal good'. Perhaps the Polar Spirit of *The Ancient Mariner*
was one of the 'rebellious' spirits who seize power 'o'er dark realms'
(line 48). Certainly the defence of terrifying legends in the subsequent
passage should be read by anyone interested in *The Ancient Mariner*.

Written in 1795–6, the poem is largely made up of lines Coleridge
contributed to Southey's *Joan of Arc*, and of his own unpublished poem
on the same subject.

Page 113: THIS LIME-TREE BOWER MY PRISON: The text is that of the
letter sent to Southey, dated 17th July 1797. The later published versions
tone down the views implied in the climax, omitting the description of
Nature as 'a living thing/That acts upon the mind', and suggesting that
God was revealed as much in spite of the 'hues' as because of them. In the
final version they 'veil' the Almighty Spirit, rather than 'clothe' him and a
'yet' is interposed before 'he makes/Spirits perceive his presence'.
Coleridge's own account of the poem's origins in his accompanying letter
to Southey is considerably less dramatic than that implied in the second
line of the poem:

> dear Sara accidentally emptied a skillet of boiling milk on my foot,
> which confined me from all walks longer than a furlong. While
> Wordsworth, his Sister, & C. Lamb were out one evening, sitting in
> the arbour of T. Pool's garden which communicates with mine, I
> wrote these lines.

line 4: whom I may never meet again: the suggestion is hyperbolic certainly,
but not outrageously so. The Wordsworths (on a visit from Racedown)
had not yet decided to take Alfoxden and so become Coleridge's neigh-
bours. At this stage Coleridge can still choose to ascribe to Lamb the
experience of Nature which forms the poem's climax. This is not dictated

solely by the consideration that Lamb has been 'In the great City pent' and is therefore more likely to benefit from the prescription than Wordsworth. It could well be a fairly random choice since Wordsworth had not yet written the poetry which makes us regard the experience described as peculiarly 'Wordsworthian'.

line 5: springy: 'elastic, I mean' (S.T.C.'s note).

line 9: plumy ferns: 'The ferns, that grow in moist places, grow five or six together & form a complete Prince of Wales Feather – i.e. plumy' (S.T.C.'s note).

lines 20–26: 'You remember I am a Berkleian' (S.T.C.'s note). George Berkeley (after whom Coleridge's second son was named in 1798) lived from 1685 to 1753. His philosophy asserted 'that all the choir of heaven and furniture of earth, in a word all those bodies which compose the mighty frame of the world have not any subsistence without a mind; that their *being* is to be perceived or known.' But though he believed of material things that 'their esse is percipi', he did not claim that they were simply created by the human mind. There was 'an omnipresent Mind, which knows and comprehends all things, and exhibits them to our view in such a manner, and according to such rules, as he himself hath ordained, and are by us termed the laws of nature'. It was Berkeley's insistence on the spiritual activity of the universe, rather than those of his views which anticipate Hume's, which seems to have attracted Coleridge at this time. 'Withersoever we direct our view,' Berkeley had written, 'we do at all times see manifest tokens of the Divinity: everything we see, hear, feel, or otherwise perceive by Sense, being a sign or effect of the power of God, as in our perception of those very motions which are produced by men.' However, Coleridge's reference to Berkeley as an influence should not be taken as exclusive. His explanation of such moments of emotion seems to have involved more pantheism and materialism than would have been possible in Berkeley's idealism. But the intellectual justifications which lie behind the claims made for the experience are anyway less important than the intensity of feeling itself. It is this, attached to a particular moment of insight into landscape, which makes the passage important in the history of English poetry. It is this, rather than the obviously similar style, which makes it clear that poems like *Tintern Abbey* (written a year later) owe a great debt to Coleridge.

lines 48–55: Compare *A Letter, lines* 95–98.

Page 115: THE FOSTER-MOTHER'S TALE: Like *The Dungeon* (which immediately follows it here) this is an extract from Coleridge's tragedy, *Osorio.* Commissioned by the dramatist Sheridan, the play was written in 1797, but not performed until 1813 when it ran for twenty nights at Drury

Lane. Coleridge's own description of the play – made when he was still writing it – was 'romantic & wild & somewhat terrible'. The text here is that of 1800 in which Coleridge cut sixteen lines of irrelevant (and bad) dialogue from the beginning, and Maria's comment that the story was 'Such as would lull a listening child to sleep/His rosy face besoil'd with unwiped tears'. The latter is clearly inappropriate to a tale whose hero is meant to be a stimulating ideal rather than a pathetic failure. Coleridge twice in his letters describes his beloved son Hartley as like the hero of this poem, once to clarify Hartley's 'hatred of confinement', and once to gloss the child's account of his own preferences: 'I thought how I love the sweet Birds, & the Flowers, & Derwent & Thinking; & how I hate Reading, & being wise, & being Good.'

Page 117: THE DUNGEON: See beginning of note above. The last ten lines of this poem have sometimes been pressed into service as a summary of popular interpretations of *The Ancient Mariner*. Even taking this passage out of context it is hard to see how its atmosphere could be very reminiscent of the later poem. 'Nature' of 'soft influences' and 'sunny hues' seems to be unfairly disguised in the land of ice and snow from a hero whom there is anyway no reason to think of as an 'angry spirit' when he kills the albatross. It would be equally fair to use *The Dungeon* as evidence that Coleridge was unlikely to approve a divine penal code as harsh as that under which the mariner is supposed to suffer; that he would expect the mariner's every 'pore and natural outlet' to be 'shrivell'd up' by extreme terror and pain, just as the convict's is 'By Ignorance and parching Poverty'; that the mariner's punishment too would ensure merely that his 'energies roll back upon his heart,/And stagnate and corrupt'; that 'friendless solitude, groaning and tears,/And savage faces' would leave him too 'Circled with evil, till his very soul/Unmoulds its essence, hopelessly deform'd/By sights of ever more deformity!'

Page 119: THE RIME OF THE ANCIENT MARINER
Title: In the second edition of 1800 Coleridge added to the title the words: 'A Poet's Reverie'. They were not reprinted after 1805, and were presumably motivated by the same kind of defensiveness as motivated the Preface to *Kubla Khan* (see page 248). The original title rightly warns the reader that this is to be very much the mariner's own story. Coleridge wrote a number of poems at this time in which a narrative framework allowed a character to tell the story. Comparison makes one wonder how far the reader is asked to credit the mariner's account as objectively true. *The Three Graves* (not in this selection), for instance, is openly concerned less with the verifiable facts of the universe than with what that universe

would seem like to a human mind under particular strain. Coleridge writes in the Preface:

> I was not led to choose this story from any partiality to tragic, much less to monstrous events . . . but from finding in it a striking proof of the possible effect on the imagination, from an idea violently and suddenly impressed on it. . . . I conceived the design of shewing that instances of this kind are not peculiar to savage or barbarous tribes, and of illustrating the mode in which the mind is affected in these cases, and the progress and symptoms of the morbid action on the fancy from the beginning.

The poem's heroine is solemnly cursed by her mother, and soon becomes convinced that she is tormented by 'daemons' and 'imps of hell'. Her husband also suffers; he has guilty dreams of murder from which he awakes crying for God's forgiveness. Since the fatal curse is made on the day the young couple are to be married, *The Three Graves*, like *The Ancient Mariner*, exploits the incongruity of a nightmare juxtaposed with wedding celebrations. The poems were both originally conceived as collaborative ventures for Wordsworth and Coleridge to write together, were begun at about the same time and imitate the style of the traditional ballad. Could the mariner's vengeful universe – like that of *The Three Graves* – be composed merely of the 'symptoms of the morbid action on the fancy', a portrait of what the universe will seem like to a man obsessed with a terrifying curse? He has seen all his ship-mates curse him and perish, and is left alone amongst the dead. He would be likely to explain his lone survival not in terms of random factors like stronger constitution, but by assumption of guilt. He is a religious man – and a medieval, superstitiously religious man at that – and there is only one way of explaining the terrible distinction made between himself and his friends which leaves the universe ordered: only one thing which he has recently done, and they haven't: killed an albatross. The rationale by which the mariner sees patterns of justice in the midst of horror is never patronized by the poem. He may – in his simple, medieval superstitions – be expressing a 'religious' version of the truth as profound as the 'psychological' one discussed in the Preface of *The Three Graves*. He may indeed be a man committed to the cyclical process of redemption. But his view may also be that of a mind 'hopelessly deform'd by sights of ever more deformity': like the hero of *The Dungeon* (page 117) he suffers the pain of 'uncomforted and friendless solitude', and we need not assume that Coleridge thinks of this as making him an utterly reliable witness to more than his own experience. The trite moral at the end is certainly at some level Coleridge's, but its language (and thus its limitations) are to some extent the mariner's: the words of a man who has to find a way of staying sane in spite of his experiences on a ship of the dead. The active universe is partly the product of Coleridge's own pantheist beliefs, but the choice of agents is determined by the mariner's imagination which is Roman Catholic, medieval, and – once he has seen his colleagues curse him as they die – guilt-ridden. He has an urgent and recurring need to define this experience so that he can live with the memory. The moral may be evidence that in his own terms he is succeeding. The passing from land to land is less reassuring. Such combinations seem less confusing if one remembers that the poem is not called 'the Testament of S.T.C.' but *The Rime of the Ancient Mariner*.

Argument: As in the first edition of 1798. The emphasis is on the story, however mysterious that is promised to be. In 1800 Coleridge made this more tendentiously moralistic by adding the words: 'how the Ancient Mariner cruelly, and in contempt of the laws of hospitality, killed a Sea-bird; and how he was followed by many and strange Judgements; and in what manner he came back to his own Country.' The laws of hospitality are obviously a long way from the specifically christian code to which Coleridge tried to accommodate the poem towards the end of his life; and the judgements being described as 'strange' has a nice ambiguity. But the addition is still a distracting attempt to tell the reader what to look for in the poem before he starts. According to Wordsworth the Albatross was not originally the central factor:

> in the course of this walk was planned the Poem of the Ancient Mariner, founded on a dream, as Mr. Coleridge said, of his friend, Mr. Cruik-shank. Much the greatest part of the story was Mr. Coleridge's invention; but certain parts I myself suggested, for example, some crime was to be committed which should bring upon the Old Navigator, as Coleridge afterwards delighted to call him, the spectral persecution, as a consequence of that crime, and his own wanderings. I had been reading in Shelvock's Voyages a day or two before that while doubling Cape Horn they frequently saw Albatrosses in that latitude, the largest sort of sea-fowl, some extending their wings 12 or 13 feet. 'Suppose,' said I, 'you represent him as having killed one of these birds on entering the South Sea, and that the tutelary Spirits of those regions take upon them to avenge the crime.' The incident was thought fit for the purpose and adopted accordingly. (Fenwick notes)

The 'spectral persecution' seems to have been decided on before the 'incident' which was to provoke it; it is even hinted that he may be punished not only for that but enigmatically enough for 'his own wanderings'.

[224]

lines 1–4: The poem starts abruptly. A listener is chosen by a hero who is described in the briefest terms. Wordsworth was to complain about this lack of detail in his apologetic note to the 1800 edition: 'the principal person has no distinct character, either in his profession of Mariner, or as a human being who having been long under the control of supernatural impressions might be supposed himself to partake of something supernatural.' The reply made by Lamb in a letter to Wordsworth is sufficient answer to this charge: 'I totally differ from your idea that the Mariner should have had a character and a profession. This is a beauty in *Gulliver's Travels*, where the mind is kept in a placid state of little wonderments; but the Ancient Mariner undergoes such trials as overwhelm and bury all individuality or memory of what he was – like the state of a man in a bad dream, one terrible peculiarity of which is, that all consciousness of personality is gone. Your other observation is, I think as well, a little unfounded: the Mariner from being conversant in supernatural events, *has* acquired a supernatural and strange cast of phrase, eye, appearance, etc. which frighten the wedding guest.' Lamb of course was talking about the poem as a whole: initially the wedding-guest (like the reader) sees the Mariner as almost humorously harmless, a 'greybeard loon'. This false sense of security, established by the setting of a wedding, at once points up the subsequent horror by contrast and protects it from the charge of melodramatically ignoring the mundane side of life.

lines 9–16: Printed as in the original version of 1798. Later versions suppressed this uncouth humour so typical of the traditional ballad, and so appropriate to the casual atmosphere that the Mariner has to destroy. It was replaced by a literary version which makes the stanza virtually superfluous: 'He holds him with his skinny hand,/'There was a ship, 'quoth he./'Hold off! unhand me, grey-beard Loon!'/Eftsoons his hand dropt he.'

lines 25–28: Neither here, nor elsewhere, are we told what the purpose of the voyage was. Perhaps the omission is simply to make the story more excitingly enigmatic. Perhaps Coleridge thought it would be difficult to discuss the ship's plans without mentioning the captain who would be responsible for their direction; and a captain would certainly be an embarrassment to a sea-story whose hero is to be an ordinary seaman, condemned by the unanimous vote of his equals rather than by the judgement of a single superior. Perhaps Coleridge merely wanted to leave room for as many implications as an unspecified voyage can have. The potential symbolism of exploration and slave-trading can exist side by side with the more general associations of sea-travel: life as a journey, the extremes of human experience as distant lands and so on. It should certainly be noticed that the one thing we are told is that disaster was not feared. They set out 'merrily' to the cheers of the spectators.

lines 45–48: We print the original 1798 version of this stanza, in preference to the final version in which the storm is personified as a 'tyrannous' bird of prey who 'struck with his o'ertaking wings,/And chased us south along'. The revision may originally have been conceived simply as clearing out the parodies of the old ballad style – 'the old words and the strangeness of it' which Wordsworth complained in a letter to his printer had prevented *Lyrical Ballads* selling well. But it damages the cumulative force of the story by which the Mariner describes each stage of his voyage in the language appropriate to his feelings at that time: the storm – like all the forces of nature – seemed to the Mariner at the outset easy to understand. Only later in the story has he the experience by which he can see it as the hound of heaven described in this revision.

line 69: The Albatross is not described as actually having the value of 'a Christian soul'. The Mariner merely says that the bird appears as such a relief in this desolate landscape that the sailors behaved as if it had been a human being. 'A Christian soul' is almost certainly used in the archaic sense appropriate to the time (the voyage apparently antedates Magellan's sailing round the South of America in 1520: see lines 109–110). It was a lightly used idiom meaning little more than 'a man and a brother'.

line 71: Printed as in the original version of 1798. Coleridge later wished to make the Albatross less mundane, so evaded this indignity by the revision: 'It ate the food it ne'er had eat.' Revising the poem as a respectable Christian gentleman, Coleridge wished to make the Albatross less real and more symbolic. Originally it had been very definitely a bird – whether to stress Coleridge's pantheist faith in the value of all living things, or to emphasize the apparent triviality of the 'crime' for which he is so savagely punished. In 1817, Coleridge felt bound to suppress lines like this so that the Albatross could appear as an image of orthodox Christian values. Christian critics have thus been able to represent 'the pious bird of good omen' as representative of Christ, divine grace and so on. Thus exalted far beyond the sordid realms of ornithology, the Albatross could hardly be shown as eating worms without becoming blasphemous.

lines 75–82: 1817 gloss: 'And lo! the Albatross proveth a bird of good omen, and followeth the ship as it returned northward through fog and floating ice.' Again the ageing Coleridge's paraphrase implies a tendentious interpretation. The Albatross here seems to bring good luck since its arrival coincides with a good wind. But at line 101 its death happens to precede the clearing of the fog so that the bird then seems to the sailors to represent bad luck. This is a misinterpretation for which they are supposedly punished with death; yet it is based on the same logic used by the gloss to lines 75–82.

lines 83–86: 1817 gloss: 'The ancient Mariner inhospitably killeth the pious bird of good omen.' At this crucial point the Mariner is a great deal less informative than the later commentary suggests. Perhaps he can hardly bear to tell the fact itself, and this is why he tells us nothing about his motives at the time, or his immediate reactions. Or perhaps he simply did not have any motive, or any strong feelings then about having done it, and tells each episode in a style appropriate to his state of mind at that time. Coleridge musing on the action of some sailors he saw on his Malta trip who kept shooting at a hawk wrote 'O strange Lust of Murder in Man! – It is not cruelty/it is mere non-feeling from non-thinking.' Doubtless Coleridge would have believed at the time of composition that the casual killing of animals was wrong because of the insensitivity involved. But he never became a vegetarian, and perhaps the Mariner saw the bird as a way of relieving a tedious diet. The ship has had no opportunity of revictualling (see lines 47–8) and we know the biscuits were wormy. There is certainly the suggestion that it was intended to make some use of the bird's body since it is not thrown overboard. It is still available days later when the sailors decide to hang it around the Mariner's neck. Certainly Coleridge cannot have thought his readers would see the killing of a bird as a crime until he added the new Argument of 1800. To say that the Mariner himself is led to believe that he is guilty does not provide an answer, but merely beg a question: Is the Mariner led by the forces of divine love to see retrospectively his action in a true light; or is he tortured by a series of disasters into a state of Neurotic Guilt – the surrender to sick fantasy so well described by Coleridge in the *Pains of Sleep* (page 200)?

lines 87–90: Printed as in the original version. The second edition tried to refine the Mariner's appropriately simple diction and homely similes into a more elegantly literary style: the sun 'now rose' rather than 'came up' and was 'Still hid in mist' rather than 'Broad as a weft'.

line 101: Printed as in the first edition. A reviewer complained at 'God's own head', and Coleridge substituted 'an Angel's head' in the first revision. In 1817, when he was resolved to introduce actual angels into the poem, the simile was an embarrassment and Coleridge suppressed it.

lines 123–126: The 1817 gloss claims here that 'the albatross begins to be avenged' but the poem gives no such information to the reader. The ship, as far as we can yet tell, is becalmed by natural weather conditions. Twenty lines later we are told that the crew now see the lack of wind as a judgement on the Mariner for killing the Albatross, but even then we need not agree with them. Their superstitions are now established as self-contradictory, and there is no evidence that the Mariner himself is immediately persuaded that they are right. Only after a series of dramatic events including the death of the crew, the Albatross falling from the Mariner's neck as he prays, and the mysterious movement of the ship, does he hear voices connecting the disasters of the voyage with the death of the Albatross. The chronology of the Mariner's own account is ignored by the 1817 marginalia which often anticipate, and thus pervert, the poem's carefully timed revelations.

line 135: At first only some of the sailors believe in a vengeful spirit following them from the place where the Albatross was killed. For evidence they have only their nightmares which could be regarded as intrinsically subjective. But as the terrible thirst described in the next stanza grows, the need to explain their agony presumably spreads to the entire crew until at line 144 'old and young' are willing to find a scapegoat.

lines 137–138: To be understood as the reported speech of the sailors. Compare lines 95–96 where the following lines make it clear that this is what is intended.

lines 135–138: 1817 gloss: 'A Spirit had followed them; one of the invisible inhabitants of this planet, neither departed souls nor angels; concerning whom the learned Jew, Josephus, and the Platonic Constantinopolitan, Michael Psellus, may be consulted. They are very numerous, and there is no climate or element without one or more.' Coleridge's embarrassment about the Polar Spirit is evident in this self-conscious joke at the pedantry of early editors. In 1817 Coleridge's moralism insists that the Polar Spirit like all the agents of punishment should have a more than subjective reality, but his religious orthodoxy requires that the Spirit should be comparatively unimportant: the fancies of a discarded pantheism had to be seen as less significant than Christian angels. The gloss to lines 431–436, while claiming that the Polar Spirit is definitely more than the hallucination of a terrified sailor, reassures the orthodox that it still has to act 'in obedience to the angelic troop'. But the poem at that point still makes it clear that the Polar Spirit is offended at the killing of his pet. He acts to revenge a personal affront, not to punish a sin.

lines 163–164: As in the original version. Later editions obscured the contrast between the Mariner's heroic act of will and the helplessness of his fellows: 'Through utter drought all dumb *we* stood!/I bit my arm.' The irony that the man whom they so unjustly ostracized is willing to bleed for their rescue should not be forgotten in the larger irony that his heroism leads only to their deaths.

lines 166–170: The Mariner's first thought when rescue is in sight is not his own relief but that of his friends, and the implied expectation that he will be accepted by them again: 'they (not "we") for joy did grin.'

line 187: The emphasis on 'her' here and in line 189 is curious. Perhaps it means that the Mariner knows this ship of old and speaks with the horror of growing recognition. Certainly the generalized statement later that Life-in-Death 'thicks man's blood with cold' implies that he has met, or at least heard of, her on other occasions. Alternatively there may be the suggestion that the Mariner – made delirious by thirst – feels uncertain as to whether the sails and ribs belong to his own ship or another. He is looking into the sun and seems to get no assistance from his fellows in decyphering what he sees. Their joy was caused not because they saw it themselves but because they heard him call out that there was a sail; and he alone reports its apparent movements (lines 171–174). It is one of the many moments in the poem where one cannot tell how subjective the mariner's vision is meant to be.

lines 194–199: This stanza is supplied from a manuscript revision Coleridge made in the margin of a *Lyrical Ballads*, 1798. By 1800 when he first had an opportunity to include it in the printed text Wordsworth's protests about the 'strangeness' of the poem damaging the edition as a whole presumably prevented Coleridge from adding to this consciously grotesque episode. The stanza reinforces the association between the 'skeleton ship' and the plankless hulks of slaving vessels.

lines 200–204: As in the edition of 1800. The description of death was not cut out until the edition of 1817. The more conventionally moral universe of the later editions is meant to be consistent with a Christian optimism: the unqualified horror of death would hardly have been appropriate. Coleridge had anyway come to think of 'Gothic horror' as vulgar.

line 213: To be able to whistle for a wind was of course a much-valued power among sailors. Here the forces of nature (as represented by the wind) are under the control of Life-in-Death who decides men's fates by the most arbitrary means possible. If Coleridge is really describing the Mariner's discovery of a pantheist universe in which all nature has one life of love it is strange that the winds, the moon, sun, and stars seem to behave with an almost callous indifference to the Mariner's fortunes.

lines 214–217: As in the original version. The stanza was omitted in 1817.

lines 218–247: The editors disagree as to which is the preferable version of this passage, and it seemed best to offer both to the reader so that he could decide for himself.

The textual history of the passage is roughly this:

(a) The earlier editions up to and including that of 1805 have only one stanza at this point:

> *With never a whisper in the Sea*
> *Off darts the Spectre-ship;*
> *While clombe above the Eastern bar*

> *The horned Moon, with one bright Star*
> *Almost between the tips.*

(b) There is an entry in Coleridge's note-book clearly designed as an elaboration of (a):

> *With never a whisper on the main*
> *Off shot the spectre ship:*
> *And stifled words & groans of pain*
> *Mix'd on each murmuring lip*
> *And we look'd round, & we look'd up*
> *And Fear at our hearts as at a Cup*
> *The Life-blood seem'd to sip*
> *The Sky was dull & dark the Night,*
> *The Helmsman's Face by his lamp gleam'd bright,*
> *From the Sails the Dews did drip*
> *Till clomb above the Eastern Bar*
> *The horned moon, with one bright Star*
> *Within its nether Tip.*
> *One after one, by the stardogg'd moon, &c –*

This entry was probably made in 1806. There are no divisions to indicate where one stanza would end and another begin.

(c) The next edition of the poem to be published after the composition of the note-book elaboration appeared in 1817. The text of that edition at the relevant point reads:

> *The Sun's rim dips; the stars rush out:*
> *At one stride comes the dark;*
> *With far-heard whisper, o'er the sea,*
> *Off shot the spectre-bark.*
>
> *We listened and looked sideways up!*
> *Fear at my heart, as at a cup,*
> *My life-blood seemed to sip!*
> *The stars were dim, and thick the night,*
> *The steersman's face by his lamp gleamed white;*
> *From the sails the dews did drip –*
> *Till clomb above the eastern bar*
> *The horned Moon, with one bright star*
> *Within the nether tip.*

This text which seems to me to be the correct one is printed on page 129. Opposite it will be found the version preferred by Professor Empson. This inserts into the 1817 text (a) the first four lines of the note-book

[230]

entry (b), adapting the first line for consistency, and presenting the four lines in the format of a separate stanza. Professor Empson's arguments for the inclusion of these lines can be found on page 51 of his Introduction. My reasons for following the 1817 published text here are given below.

What was Coleridge's intention in expanding the 1805 text at this point? The original stanza (a) makes two points: that the death-ship departed; and that night had now fallen: and it makes them in that order. The moon and star are the first reference to the passing of time since we were in the later afternoon with the sun low in the sky behind the death-ship. Appropriately the ominous departure of the death-ship is associated with night-fall. But in 1805 this had hardly been stressed. In the note-book revision Coleridge tries to extract more drama from this association (the sky being now dull and dark, the helmsman isolated in the lamp-light, the rising moon being a culmination of the process of dusk: 'Till clomb above . . .' replacing 'While clomb above . . .'). But the expansion involves more than the indirect drama of dusk. Coleridge seeks to describe directly the fear. Against the sinister silence of the departing ship he sets the incoherent complaints of the terrified crew, and he suggests their sense of panic in the fine idea of the blood being drained from the heart.

These two associated ideas – the dusk and fear – seem to be what he wished to expand. And when he came to polish the expansion for publication in the 1817 edition (c) he seems to have decided that the dramatic sequence of night-fall should be exploited still further. The sudden tropical dusk could fall directly with the departure of the ship: the death-ship being the last visible object at any distance before the ocean was suddenly and alarmingly hidden. The very speed of dusk could be made to seem frighteningly decisive, as if Nature had immediately written confirmation of the sentences decided upon: 'The Sun's rim dips; the stars rush out:/At one stride comes the dark.' This is but one of three significant improvements made by the published text, and it seems to me a master-stroke. The economically suggested personification of Night ('At one stride') leaves it still a very real night but comparable to a living creature in its apparent decisiveness. The sun's dipping motion vaguely suggests the collapse of something reassuring.

The second improvement is a change in the use of sound. In (b) the ship had been silent in contrast to the mumbling men. But as Coleridge tried to fit the expanded passage back into the poem as a whole, he decided to reverse this – wisely I think. 'Groans of pain' – however much stifled – had been a rather obvious way of evoking human suffering. He seems to have decided to suggest it instead by that strange hypersensitivity to auditory and visual stimuli that often accompanies terror. So in (c) the sailors are plunged into a horrified and horrifying silence. Their senses are exceptionally alert; where they cannot understand, they strain to at least hear and see. The ship now makes a sinisterly gentle whispering sound as it leaves them, and this sound is made more terrible by their awed and attentive silence. In a way that is paradoxical but wholly convincing they strain to hear the last 'far-heard' sound of the ship that horrifies them. So the uneconomical 'And we look'd round, and we look'd up' of (b) is replaced by 'We listened and looked sideways up' – which is at once a more precise and larger statement. Their enemy the ship has already been established as noisy ('The game is done! I've won! I've won!'/ Quoth she, and whistles thrice'). By contrast the sailors, abandoned in the silence of the sea, cannot even attempt to express their feelings in words. Coleridge's use of sound and silence here seems to have been deliberate because the 1817 text presents for the first time a further reinforcement to the pattern in a revision to a line in the next stanza. In the 1805 edition he had stated only once that the sailors were silent as they died. Now in the 1817 text he repeats it: 'One after one by the horned Moon/(Listen, O Stranger! to me!')' (1805) becomes in 1817 'One after one, by the star-dogged Moon,/Too quick for groan or sigh'.

Coleridge's third alteration of the note-book sketch is specifying the direct description of feeling so that it applies to the Mariner himself. The shocked attentiveness ('We listened and looked sideways up') can be common to all. But the fear – though by clear implication it must be shared – is described as the Mariner's own. This seems to me only logical. The sensation of fear is brilliantly captured by the image of the heart being drained of its normal steady rhythm of blood: the kind of image which could only be based on personal recollection. Technically the Mariner can only vouch for a feeling so precisely defined as being his own. It is too powerful and too personal to be a generalization. So 'And Fear at our hearts as at a Cup/The Life-blood seem'd to sip' is changed to 'Fear at *my* heart, as at a cup, *My* life-blood seem'd to sip'. This is anyway much neater since the metaphor is implicitly singular (*a* cup) and had had to serve as description of something going on in plural hearts. I think Coleridge had realized that the expansion sketched out in 1806 was more significant than he had at first supposed; realized on considering his poem as a whole that these additions were introducing into the story the earliest direct reference to anyone's feelings. The crew have earlier been observed by the Mariner to do things that imply feeling ('What evil looks/Had I from old and young'), but he had never tried to explicitly describe their sensations of hatred or fear. And of course he had not described his own; his silence on that is one of the most striking things about the early part of the poem. Now the note-book additions broke this pattern and Coleridge working for the 1817 edition is perhaps conscious of an important choice.

He decides that the new departure should only be a revelation by the Mariner, that his knowledge of the crew's feelings will remain limited to the observation & implicit deductions used earlier. The Mariner is to that extent to remain isolated even here. The crew's inability to express their feelings has after all already been stressed ('Then while through drought all dumb they stood/I bit my arm and suck'd the blood/And cried, A sail, a sail!') and will be again: 'The body and I pulled at one rope,/But he said nought to me'. The Mariner's fear was one experienced in isolation: he is isolated both by his actual superiority to them (his ability to shed his own blood so as to call for rescue) and by the inferior status they allocate him ('the Albatross/About my neck was hung'). Throughout the poem he only tells us what he himself sees, or at least thinks he sees. Nowhere else does he claim intuitive insight into the hearts of his colleagues. Nowhere else after the Albatross has been hung round his neck do they attempt to speak. It is their last bitter communication with him, and a cruelly nonverbal one.

Finally, Coleridge may have decided to cut the note-book lines (about the crew's pain) simply because he had to. Granted the new idea he rightly thought was too good not to use ('The Sun's rim dips; the stars rush out: At one stride comes the dark') his rhyme-scheme no longer allowed them. The ship has to become a 'bark' to rhyme with 'dark' and thus cannot introduce the rhyme for 'murmuring lip'. But why then did he not think of making up a separate stanza by repetition as in the version on page 128 of this edition? Because the context is one of sudden decisive action (Off *shot* the spectre-bark; At one stride comes the dark) and the poem is consistent in using repetition only for continuing actions or static situations. All moments of action are described in the kind of rapid verse to which roomy repetition is wholly antithetical:

> *I shot the Albatross.*
>
> *Instead of the cross, the Albatross*
> *About my neck was hung.*
>
> *When that strange shape drove suddenly*
> *Betwixt us and the Sun.*
>
> *I bit my arm, and sucked the blood*
>
> *The Albatross fell off, and sank*
> *Like lead into the sea.*
>
> *They groaned, they stirred, they all uprose,*
>
> *Then like a pawing horse let go,*
> *She made a sudden bound:*

> *It flung the blood into my head,*
> *And I fell down in a swound.*
>
> *I took the oars;*

Moments of continuing or repeated action or moments of stasis in the poem's story are on the other hand often supported by repetition. The surly accusations of the crew are obviously repeated endlessly:

> *For all averred, I had killed the bird*
> *That made the breeze to blow.*
> *Ah wretch! said they, the bird to slay,*
> *That made the breeze to blow!*

and the appropriateness of repetition to the horrible monotony of the becalming is obvious:

> *Day after day, day after day,*
> *We stuck, nor breath nor motion;*
> *As idle as a painted ship*
> *Upon a painted ocean.*
>
> *Water, water, every where,*
> *And all the boards did shrink;*
> *Water, water, every where,*
> *Nor any drop to drink.*
>
> *A weary time! a weary time!*

The initial sighting of the ship of death leads to a continuing act of observation. The approach of what seems to be a rescue is rightly felt to be maddeningly slow:

> *At first it seemed a little speck,*
> *And then it seemed a mist;*
> *It moved and moved, and took at last*
> *A certain shape, I wist.*
>
> *A speck, a mist, a shape, I wist!*
> *And still it neared and neared:*

Clearly this is technically an event, but it is felt by the impatient mariner to have the tantalizing steadiness of a permanent situation and so repetition is used. Similarly the two hundred deaths happening in sequence obviously demands the language of repetition given it by the 1817 revision:

> *One after one, by the star-dogged Moon,*
> *Too quick for groan or sigh,*
> *Each turned his face with a ghastly pang,*
> *And cursed me with his eye.*

> *Four times fifty living men,*
> *(And I heard nor sigh nor groan)*
> *With heavy thump, a lifeless lump,*
> *They dropped down one by one.*

The appropriateness of the repetitions in the description of the Mariner endlessly unable to die on the ship of the dead is obvious; as is that in the final moral where the Mariner presumably hopes he is telling permanent truths of continuing relevance. But repetition of an action as sudden and decisive as the departure of the death-ship as the rapid dusk descends and makes all invisible seems to be wholly inconsistent with the poem's method.

line 259: The reference to the cross-bow (with which he shot the Albatross) shows that the Mariner is reminded by the death of his shipmates of the last death he has seen, that of the bird. It may be that the 'heavy thump' with which they fall recalls the sound made by the dead Albatross landing on the deck. He must now begin to believe the first of the two superstitions the crew made up about albatrosses. The loneliness imposed when the crew felt justified in hating him is now reinforced by guilt.

line 270: As 1798. Changed in 1817 to 'never a saint took . . .', to avoid blasphemy no doubt. Yet this is the edition which made the Mariner's 'horrible penance' the deliberate choice of heaven.

lines 272–273: The 1817 gloss ('He despiseth the creatures of the calm,') distracts the reader from the real horror of the stanza, which can only marginally be a moral one. His attitude to the creatures of the sea is merely a side-effect of his attitude to the dead men. He is mystified by his own survival, and horrified by their wasted beauty. They blamed him for the ship being becalmed, and he thinks that he – however unwittingly – summoned Death to them with his cry of 'A sail, a sail'. The stanza describes the thoughts he had alone amongst the corpses – the thoughts that explain how he became obsessed with the idea that they died cursing him.

line 274: 1798: This was reduced in 1817 to 'a thousand thousand'. Perhaps the smaller number was intended to imply that they were larger creatures than say, plankton. The Mariner would then have less excuse for failing to observe their individual beauty. It is possible that these 'slimy things' are the same species that the mariner saw 'crawl with legs/Upon the slimy sea' (lines 129–30). But if so they cannot be the 'water-snakes' of line 309 which clearly do not have legs. Either the Mariner's experience is so subjective that he sees legs which are not there, or the creatures he blesses are simply a different species from those which revolt him. Either interpretation helps to explain why his gesture of love is followed by only a temporary relief from suffering.

lines 284–288: The emphasis on the eye recalls how earlier thirst 'glazed each weary eye' when the whole crew was alive and prepares us for the recurring concern with 'the curse in a dead man's eye'. But the poem contains more references to sight that can be explained by the surface plot. The words 'eye', 'eyes' or 'eye-balls' occur twenty times. Nearly all the poem's characters are explicitly presented as beings who see: the 'glittering eye' the mariner has gained from his experience is matched by the 'great bright eye' of the ocean looking at the moon. The hermit 'raised his eyes' to pray while the Pilot's boy's 'eyes went to and fro'. To the Pilot himself the ship has 'a fiendish look'. Death is made the final negation because one only sees in him 'the holes of his eyes'. The sun seems to 'peer' at the Mariner. The verb 'to see' is used eleven times, and 'to look' appears as often even though the poem also makes use of 'to watch' and 'to behold'. The mariner's style constantly emphasizes that he can only relate events as they appeared to him. He says 'I looked' (4 times), 'I saw' (4 times), 'I heard' (6 times), 'I watch'd' (twice). This could be argued to increase the credibility of the story by reminding the reader that it is an eye-witness account. But its effect often seems to be to suggest that the account is not necessarily an objective one, that he can only tell what 'seemed there to be'. One feels little distinction between the Mariner's saying 'I saw', and his more openly subjective phrases such as 'I thought', 'I ween' and even 'I dreamt'.

lines 293–294: Possibly the Mariner remembers some superstition that not even God can resist a human curse at full strength. Or perhaps he is merely inventing a superstition, because the dying hatred of his mates is more important to him than *any* theology.

lines 299–302: 1817 gloss: 'In his loneliness and fixedness he yearneth towards the journeying Moon, and the stars that still sojourn, yet still move onward; and everywhere the blue sky belongs to them, and is their appointed rest, and their native country and their own natural homes, which they enter unannounced, as lords that are certainly expected and yet there is a silent joy at their arrival.' The beauty of this prose is often acknowledged but it has been used to support very different interpretations of the poem. Clearly the Mariner regards relationship with a mixture of tenderness and envy as lonely people do. But do these stars move in accordance with the same natural laws that support human love? Do they represent a harmony which the mariner has offended? Or does their serenity merely emphasize the injustice of the Mariner's suffering just as the moon's cool beams 'bemock' the unnaturally burning sea?

lines 308–312: 1817 gloss: 'By the light of the Moon he beholdeth God's creatures of the great calm.' The great calm of course is very much in the eye of the beholder – the Mariner focuses his eyes on the water-snakes.

But presumably the creepy-crawlies with legs, and the 'charméd water' which 'burnt alway/A still and awful red' are also still visible. He saw the 'slimy things' which revolted him when there was nothing else to see but the 'rotting deck' where 'the dead men lay'. He sees the water-snakes after he has been calmed by the beauty of the night sky.

lines 324–327: 1817 gloss: 'The spell begins to break.' Doubtless encouraged by this gloss, critics have tried to argue that the Mariner is saved from this moment on. He has learnt to love the universe again. He is thus forgiven and allowed to go home. But the fall of the Albatross into the sea is but one of a number of moments at which the Mariner and the reader are given false hope. Early in the story, both are doubtless a little rattled by the crew's inventing the superstition of the albatross being a bird of good fortune; so, when it turns out that good weather follows its killing, there is relief. But then they are becalmed. There is hope again when a ship is seen apparently coming to their rescue; but it turns out to be an agent of death. The release from the Albatross is clearly intended to gull the readers again into thinking the universe is after all merciful. But the corpses of the men who hung it about his neck are soon to rise up and torment him with other accusations.

lines 349–353: These sights must be the *aurora,* well known to be found only in polar regions. Moreover he wakes up with his throat cold so the ship must have travelled round the Cape of Good Hope. Coleridge seems to have been content to leave the nature of the journey home mysterious and potentially magical, but Africa is a large obstacle. Here as in the journey from the Equator to England Coleridge has the mariner unconscious to justify the lack of information.

lines 363–4: Printed as in *Lyrical Ballads,* 1798. In 1800 Coleridge reversed the statement and wrote: 'The loud wind never reached the ship,/Yet now the ship moved on!' In the first version the spirits which animate the dead men are not in any religious sense 'heavenly'. They are spirits of nature, perhaps specifically spirits of the wind, but certainly not too dignified to be delivered by a stormy gust. Also this wind arrives with the lightning, and Coleridge knew from Galvani that the electrical forces visible in lightning are regularly at work in the human body. The frogs' legs that all twitched at Galvani when they were hung up drying for his dinner, on metal hooks, had fascinated Europe when his conclusions were published in 1791 (English translation 1793). Whatever the exact nature of the spirits in the first edition they seem to be morally ambiguous so that they may as well arrive on a mysterious wind as by any other means. In 1800 Coleridge seems to have been afraid that the corpses coming to life was being misinterpreted as a simple ghost story. He therefore added in lines 383–87 making it clear that ' 'Twas not those souls, that fled in pain,/Which to their corses came again'. He then went on (because he needed a rhyme for 'Wedding-Guest' in the new stanza?) to say that far from being ghosts they were 'a troop of spirits blest'. Perhaps it now seemed indelicate to say that these were landed on the ship by a wind which 'roar'd/And dropp'd down like a stone!'

The 1817 gloss to the additional stanza elaborates on the hint so casually made in 1800: 'But not by the souls of the men, nor by daemons of earth or middle air, but by a blessed troop of angelic spirits, sent down by the invocation of the guardian saint.' This was serious perversion of the original intention. When in 1800 he had called the spirits 'blest', he was putting them no higher than he had placed himself when in his delirium he had thought he was 'a blessèd ghost' (line 344). Later at line 403 he says they sang like angels which would make no sense as a compliment if they had actually been angels.

lines 381–2: As in the original edition of 1798, omitted in all subsequent editions.

lines 390–404: This idyllic passage makes one almost forget that the singers have the appearance of the 'ghastly crew'. It lulls the reader into yet another phase of false security to be exploded when he is later told that 'The pang, the curse, with which they died,/Had never passed away'.

lines 411–426: As in the first edition. The passage was omitted from later versions – perhaps because it emphasized just how personal a portrait of the universe is being given. We are reminded again of the framework. There is a suggestion that the Wedding-guest is held not so much by the credibility of the tale, as by the transformation which the teller has obviously suffered ('For that, which comes out of thine eye, doth make/ My body and soul to be still'). Finally the Mariner himself provides further evidence that his being left alone amongst the dead has disorientated his most basic assumptions. Now that no-one can see him (the corpses are not looking) he questions his own existence, and thinks he must be 'as thin as air'. He is about to hear voices telling him that he is being justly punished for a major crime in killing the Albatross. There is no doubt that the Mariner is now reduced to a state in which he is prepared to believe them. But there is no need for the reader to agree with this any more than with the suggestion that the Mariner was temporarily 'as thin as air'.

lines 431–436: 1817 gloss: 'The lonesome Spirit from the south-pole carries on the ship as far as the Line, in obedience to the angelic troop, but still requireth vengeance.' There is of course no such suggestion of hierarchy within the poem. The various forces of torment interact without any implication of an overlord who could act as a court of appeal.

line 449: The Mariner hears the voices while he is still unconscious, but is he in a mediumistic trance or a nightmare?

line 461: In view of what the voice says, that it is as 'soft as honey-dew' only gives added horror to the tormentor. An insinuating imitation of tenderness traditionally bodes ill for someone in a ballad.

lines 480–487: Why will the ship go slow once the Mariner wakes up? Perhaps his constitution can stand the strain of such speed only while he is in a trance. The general point is clear – the movement of the ship is now dependent on the state of the mariner's mind. He awakes from a coma to find himself almost home. He would recognize from the climate (the 'gentle weather') that he had travelled a great distance from the Equator where he was last awake. As is common with people recovering from lengthy comas, he finds it difficult to believe he has been unconscious for so long: supernaturally fast travel is a more credible alternative. The fact that the ship may soon move more slowly seems a paradoxical explanation of why the voices must hurry. Perhaps we are meant to deduce that when the ship slows down the final struggle for the Mariner's soul will begin, and they want to be in at the climax – perhaps to aid the rescue. But it seems easier to see the voices as aspects of the Mariner's guilt-ridden mind, articulating his unconscious thoughts: these could reasonably include the fear that were he to regain full consciousness, he would only find himself becalmed again.

lines 492–495: As the curse returns, and the Mariner is once again unable to pray, we are reminded how false was the hope offered when he found himself able to pray and the Albatross fell off (324–327). Such cruel fluctuations may be the creations of neurotic guilt, or of vicious forces in the universe. They can hardly be the work of a divine justice, or the result of special help from angels.

lines 496–9: 1817 gloss: 'The curse is finally expiated.' This is of course nonsense. The corpses have yet to make their most terrifying appearance.

lines 506–517: As the ship nears home, the mariner sees it as propelled by less bizarre forces. But the sense of guilt remains. Surrounded by the corpses of the men he thinks he has killed, he observes bitterly that the wind can only be felt by him. But the wind that takes him home to safety also ferries the dead.

lines 530–551: As in the original edition of 1798, suppressed in all subsequent editions. Once restored they constitute damning evidence of the extent to which the 1817 marginalia were telling lies about the poem. The four stanzas describing the corpses at their most cruelly terrifying are carefully matched with the four following which relate how the mariner was once again given relief. The spirits of punishment and of forgiveness are clearly shown as being initially indistinguishable. They come out of an ironically peaceful bay in the guise of red shadows, and the verbal parallelism is deliberately obtrusive. The forces of the universe are so indecypherable that the same occurrences can be omens either of threatening horror, or of blessed relief and rescue. The echoing of one passage by the other must be deliberate. Lines 531–2, for instance, are identical with lines 557–8. The first stanza of each episode stresses the serenity of the scene in the moonlight. The second in both cases says that the bay is white in the light of the moon before red, shadowy shapes emerge from it. The third stanzas, though both starting with the same line, diverge in preparation for the significant contrast of the fourth. Here the Mariner turning his eyes back to the deck sees in one case the corpses come to life in a threatening posture, and in the other the same corpses prone: 'lifeless' with rescuing spirits standing above the defeated in the traditional stance of the conqueror. The sinisterly raised arms burning like the torches in the one are matched by the consolingly waved hands in the other. The reader is in fact likely to commit the same sin in interpreting the initial stages of each episode as that for which the crew were punished with death: culpable equivocation when presented with an omen (the slaying of the Albatross in their case). They at first get it wrong because subsequent weather-conditions mislead them. They are guessing the implications of the omen by reference to what they see happening after it; and that is all that the reader can do at the end in deciding which red shadows mean trouble, and which mean assistance. Either the rulers of this universe are deliberately ambiguous, in spite of their savage punishment of those who guess wrong. Or the Mariner is so transformed by his experience that he is now able to see in his environment threat or mercy depending on his mood. In either case the game of chance played for his soul can now be seen to be the perfect metaphor for his situation. The same dice are thrown always, and yet are capable of either arbitrary result. It could be argued that the bodies are not burnt to frighten the Mariner but to eliminate the risk of their being later adopted by evil spirits. In this case friendly spirits would be doing a job analogous to driving a stake through the heart of a body used by a vampire. But the poetry does not make it sound like a reassuring hygiene job. The 'stony eye-balls' which 'glitter'd on/In the red and smoky light' are too alarming. They remind one of lines 488–491 where 'All fixed on me their stony eyes,/That in the Moon did glitter'. There one had little sense that the corpses were merely packaging for friendly spirits and would be hygienically treated to avoid later misuse. They were in fact explicitly the 'dead men' and 'For a charnel-dungeon fitter'. There seems in fact to be no end to their disturbing duality until they are sunk at the bottom of the sea; even then of course the Mariner has to go on with the knowledge that at any 'uncertain hour' he may find himself being punished by the return of 'that agony'.

lines 580–585: As in original 1798 text, omitted from all subsequent editions. It carries on the fluctuation of the parallel passages showing that the bodies are only temporarily incapacitated by the seraph-band.

lines 609–619: The Hermit's ability to find analogies in his own environment for the damage which the ship displays suggests that England is only *less obviously* frightening than the land of ice and snow. The owl cheering on the wolf who is eating his own cubs is the only bird in the poem apart from the Albatross. If it is the Hermit who finally teaches the Mariner to love all birds and beasts one assumes he did not emphasize the examples Coleridge chose to use.

line 631: It is difficult to know who in the poem's mythology is responsible for the sinking of the ship. Possibly some Spirit of the Harbour is refusing to have the Polar Spirit's dirty washing thrown in at his front door. Perhaps friendly spirits (such as the two Voices?) are trying to finally release the Mariner. Perhaps the avenging spirits are merely discarding a piece of equipment which will not be useful to them now that the Mariner is home; here they will be using the subtler methods of compelling him to remember and imposing the obsessional need to explain.

line 646: For the second time, the Mariner's self-possession in a moment of crisis is contrasted with the helplessness of those around him. Small craft are liable to be drawn into the suction of a sinking ship; he is the only one with the will and energy to resist the danger positively. The official rescue squad is in almost comical disarray: the Pilot unconscious, his assistant hysterical, the Hermit obliviously praying. 'I took the oars' has the same heroic decisiveness as 'I bit my arm, I sucked the blood,/And cried, A sail! a sail!'. Wordsworth complained in his treacherous 1800 note that the Mariner 'does not act, but is continually acted upon'. As well as performing these two heroic actions, the mariner is the only man on board who acts against the Albatross.

line 655: The Hermit is near to collapse, which makes it unlikely that he is intended to represent an ideal harmony with the forces that sank the ship.

lines 668–9: The hypnotic powers of the Mariner, derived from a unique experience, are reminiscent of the arrogant claims made at the end of *Kubla Khan* (page 177). Both poems can be seen as celebrations of the romantic artist: a man who has known the extremes of experience (whether by drinking the milk of paradise, or being alone on a wide, wide sea); and of whom conventional society should beware.

lines 679–682: The Mariner's emphasis here on his loneliness should be borne in mind as he goes on to say how sweet he finds the idea of old men, and babes and loving friends joining together in worship. One of the

Q

attractions of church for him may be vicarious pleasure in a social life he is condemned never to share. Bizarre in appearance, journeying from land to land, obsessed with the memory of how he seemed to kill his ship-mates, the Mariner clearly has no family life himself. Indeed the nature of his experience is such that when it is narrated the listener turns away from the wedding: the symbol of conventional society's cohesion. The syntax is such that it is possible to interpret lines 683–691 as saying not that the Mariner does go to church with the goodly company, but merely that he wishes he could. *lines 692–699:* The moral does not summarize the poem's implications. A God who loves all creatures would hardly let an entire ship's crew die on the throw of a dice. Why should he dress his own representatives in almost the same uniforms as those worn by the Devil's party? Why should he create a species in which the adult males eat their young? If the Mariner has now learnt to love all creatures why is he only shown blessing exceptionally attractive water-snakes, and not, for instance, the creepy-crawlies whose legs so revolted him, or that sadistic owl? Is Coleridge simply evading here the implications of his poem? Perhaps we should regard these words as very much the Mariner's. It must be sad enough to remember what his experiences actually taught him while he is reliving them in his compulsive telling of the 'ghastly tale'. As soon as he finishes it, he experiences again that sense of liberation he had when he completed his account to the Hermit; and then perhaps he is able to forget its meaning. At such times he would retreat into the most consolingly contradictory faith. Certainly the moral of Christian optimism has little effect on the listener within the poem. The Wedding-Guest – in spite of being finally assured that the world was ruled by a just and loving God – was a sadder, as well as a wiser, man next day. Was it sorrow at dis-covering in the Mariner's tale evidence that the world was ruled by alien and arbitrary forces? Or was it merely pity for the Mariner as a man so battered by a series of wholly coincidental events that he had been reduced to a living death through his sense of guilt?

THE GLOSSES – l. 1: An ancient Mariner meeteth three Gallants bidden to a wedding feast, and detaineth one. l. 17: The Wedding-Guest is spellbound by the eye of the old sea-faring man, and constrained to hear his tale. l. 29: The Mariner tells how the ship sailed southward with a good wind and fair weather, till it reached the line. l. 37: The Wedding-Guest heareth the bridal music; but the Mariner continueth his tale. l. 45: The ship driven by a storm towards the south pole. l. 59: The land of ice, and of fear-ful sounds where no living thing was to be seen. l. 67: Till a great sea-bird, called the Albatross, came through the snow-fog, and was received with great joy and hospitality. l. 75: And lo! the Albatross proveth a bird of good omen, and followeth the ship as it returned northward through fog and floating ice. l. 83: The ancient Mariner in-hospitably killeth the pious bird of good omen. l. 95: His shipmates cry out against the ancient Mariner, for killing the bird of good luck. l. 101: But when the fog cleared off, they justify the same, and thus make themselves accomplices in the crime. l. 107: The fair breeze continues; the ship enters the Pacific Ocean, and sails northward, even till it reaches the Line. l. 113: The ship hath been suddenly becalmed. l. 123: And the Albatross begins to be avenged! l. 135: A Spirit had followed them; one of the invisible inhabitants of this planet, neither departed souls nor angels; concerning whom the learned Jew Josephus, and the Platonic Constantinopolitan, Michael Psellus, may be consulted. They are very numerous, and there is no climate or element without one or more. l. 143: The shipmates, in their sore distress, would fain throw the whole guilt on the ancient Mariner: in sign whereof they hang the dead sea-bird round his neck. l. 151: The ancient Mariner beholdeth a sign in the element afar off. l. 161: At its nearer approach it seemeth him to be a ship; and at a dear ransom he freeth his speech from the bonds of thirst. l. 168: A flash of joy; l. 171: And horror follows. For can it be a ship that comes onward without wind or tide? l. 181: It seemeth him but the skeleton of a ship. l. 189: And its ribs are seen as bars on the face of the setting Sun. The Spectre-Woman and her Deathmate, and no other on board the skeleton ship. l. 205: Like vessel, like crew! l. 210: Death and Life-in-Death have diced for the ship's crew, and she (the latter) winneth the ancient Mariner. l. 232: At the rising of the Moon, l. 248: One after another, l. 252: His shipmates drop down dead. l. 256: But Life-in-Death begins her work on the ancient Mariner. l. 260: The Wedding-Guest feareth that a Spirit is talking to him; l. 266: But the ancient Mariner assureth him of his bodily life, and proceedeth to relate his horrible penance. l. 273: He despiseth the creatures of the calm. l. 276: And envieth that they should live, and so many lie dead. l. 289: But the curse liveth for him in the eye of the dead men. l. 299: In his loneliness and fixedness he yearneth towards the journeying Moon, and the stars that still sojourn, yet still move onward; and everywhere the blue sky belongs to them, and is their appointed rest, and their native country and their own natural homes, which they enter un-announced, as lords that are certainly expected and yet there is a silent joy at their arrival. l. 308: By the light of the Moon he beholdeth God's creatures of the great calm. l. 318: Their beauty and their happiness. l. 321: He blesseth them in his heart. l. 324: The spell begins to break. l. 333: By grace of the holy Mother, the ancient Mariner is refreshed with rain. l. 345: He heareth sounds and seeth strange sights and commotions in the sky and the element. l. 364: The bodies of the ship's crew are inspired and the ship moves on; l. 385: But not by the souls of the men, nor by daemons of earth or middle air, but by a blessed troop of angelic spirits, sent down by the invocation of the guardian saint. l. 431: The lonesome spirit from the south-pole carries on the ship as far as the Line, in obedience to the angelic troop, but still requireth vengeance. l. 447: The Polar Spirit's fellow-daemons, the invisible in-habitants of the element, take part in his wrong; and two of them relate, one to the other, that penance long and heavy for the ancient Mariner hath been accorded to the Polar Spirit, who returneth southward. l. 476: The Mariner hath been cast into a trance; for the angelic power causeth the vessel to drive northward faster than human life could endure. l. 484: The supernatural motion is retarded; the Mariner awakes, and his penance begins anew. l. 496: The curse is finally expiated. l. 518: And the ancient Mariner beholdeth his native country. l. 558: The angelic spirits leave the dead bodies, l. 560: And appear in their own forms of light. l. 596: The Hermit of the wood. l. 609: Approacheth the ship with wonder. l. 628: The ship suddenly sinketh. l. 633: The ancient Mariner is saved in the Pilot's boat. l. 656: The ancient Mariner earnestly entreateth the Hermit to shrieve him; and the penance of life falls on him. l. 665: And ever and anon throughout his future life an agony constraineth him to travel from land to land; l. 692: And to teach by his own example, love and reverence to all things that God made and loveth.

Page 146: CHRISTABEL: Coleridge gave his friends many different explanations of his failure to complete this poem. He was no more consistent when summarizing how the story was to have been carried on. According to Gillman, Christabel was to have been shown suffering for her lover who was 'exposed to various temptations in a foreign land', but eventually defeating 'the power of evil represented in the person of Geraldine'. Elsewhere Gillman gives a fuller account claiming that the evil spirit was simply disguised as Geraldine, and when forced to discard this pretence appears as Christabel's lover instead. The impostor then begins 'a courtship most distressing to Christabel, who feels – she knows not why – great disgust for her once favoured knight'. But, according to this account, Christabel was to be actually at the altar about to marry the evil spirit, before being rescued from the delusion by the arrival of the real lover. Coleridge's son Derwent, on the other hand, though agreeing that the 'sufferings of Christabel were to have been represented as vicarious, endured for her "lover far away"', gives a very different account of the role planned for Geraldine. She was not meant to be a 'witch or goblin, or malignant being of any kind, but a spirit, executing her appointed task with the best good will'. The ambiguity of Geraldine in that part of the poem that was written was – as it still is – the central difficulty in any attempt to discover what Coleridge intended. In 1819 he was even having to protest 'that Hazlitt from pure malignity has spread about the Report that Geraldine was a Man in disguise'; but the unexplained horror with which Geraldine's going to bed with Christabel is described makes the suggestion understandable. Coleridge himself said that Part Two had been written with two lines by Crashaw very much in mind; 'Since 'tis not to be had at home,/She'll travel to a martyrdom' but the implications of this allusion remain ambiguous. It has been used by modern critics to justify interpretations in which Christabel as the central figure suffers martyrdom for the sake of her lover; but she after all *is* 'at home' and it is *Geraldine* who has had to travel. However it is arguable that the dualism inherent in Coleridge's portrayal of Geraldine creates a usefully disturbing ambiguity rather than simply clumsy inconsistency, and attempts to resolve it may be unprofitable; they certainly seem unlikely to succeed. The version printed here is that of the manuscript at Dove Cottage Library. It retains two vital lines of the climax to Part One (ll. 237, 239) which were cut out when Coleridge published the poem sixteen years after writing it. Their omission, though doubtless making the poem less indelicate for contemporary readers, conceals from the reader a central piece of information on which the rest of the passage depends. Since *Christabel* was written between 1797 and 1800, its treatment of demonology may well be relevant to discussion of *The Ancient Mariner*. In 1800 Coleridge noted down Josephus' definition of demons – 'the spirits of wicked men which enter the living and kill them unless aid is forthcoming.' We can't tell whether Coleridge was interested in this because of *The Ancient Mariner* (then being revised for its second publication), or because of his attempts at that time to complete *Christabel*. Geraldine, whose skin is 'lean and old and foul of hue' sometimes recalls Life-In-Death whose 'skin was as white as leprosy', but more often she seems to be like the evil spirits that usurp the bodies of the crew. If she is a spirit masquerading as a human being, she seems to be up against opposition using similar methods, a 'guardian spirit,' Christabel's mother who seems able to appear to both Geraldine and Christabel (ll. 193–197, 304–306). There are even moments – such as Geraldine's bemoaning 'The mark of my shame, the seal of my sorrow' – when in her mysterious agony of guilt she reminds one of the mariner himself. But perhaps it is her very ambiguity, her capacity to at one moment appear as the loving agent of those 'who live in the upper sky', at another to seem a 'vision foul of fear and pain' which most recalls the world of *The Ancient Mariner*. When Coleridge published *Christabel* in 1816 he added to the end of the poem the lines given below. They were written about his son Hartley and have so little to do with *Christabel* that Coleridge had to reverse his account of Sir Leoline's emotions to avoid obvious self-contradiction. Sir Leoline's fatherly feelings which in the original had reinforced his anger 'And did *not* work confusion there' had to be changed in the published version so that they 'did *but* work confusion there'. It seems that Coleridge felt compelled to at least produce a superficial pattern in that portion of the poem he had managed to write; the first part had a conclusion, and this little poem written in 1801 could be used at the end of the second part to make the poem's essentially fragmentary nature less obvious. The 1816 volume only contained two other poems and one of these was the admitted 'Fragment' of *Kubla Khan* ... so Coleridge's reaching for the following lines is understandable:

> *A little child, a limber elf,*
> *Singing, dancing to itself,*
> *A fairy thing with red round cheeks,*
> *That always finds, and never seeks,*
> *Makes such a vision to the sight*
> *As fills a father's eyes with light;*
> *And pleasures flow in so thick and fast*
> *Upon his heart, that he at last*
> *Must needs express his love's excess*
> *With words of unmeant bitterness.*

Perhaps 'tis pretty to force together
Thoughts so all unlike each other;
To mutter and mock a broken charm,
To dally with wrong that does no harm.
Perhaps 'tis tender too and pretty
At each wild word to feel within
A sweet recoil of love and pity.
And what, if in a world of sin
(O sorrow and shame should this be true!)
Such giddiness of heart and brain
Comes seldom save from rage and pain,
So talks as it's most used to do.

Page 168: FROST AT MIDNIGHT: The text is that of the final version. None of the revisions made after its composition in 1798 seem motivated by anything other than Coleridge's concern to express most economically the original mood of serene meditation. The two major revisions are simply omissions of distractingly lengthy expansion of thoughts sufficiently stated in the final, shortened version. In its earlier published form the poem had continued after the last line with:

Like those, my babe! which ere tomorrow's warmth
Have capp'd their sharp keen points with pendulous drops,
Will catch thine eye, and with their novelty
Suspend thy little soul; then make thee shout,
And stretch and flutter from thy mother's arms
As though wouldst fly for very eagerness.

These lines seem to add nothing but verbiage; clarify neither Coleridge's love for Hartley nor his faith in Nature as an educational force; more seriously they weaken – by closing with the child's excitement rather than the peacefulness of the moon – a poem whose chief achievement is the evocation of a mood.

line 15: Only that film: 'In all parts of the kingdom these films are called *Strangers* and supposed to portend the arrival of some absent friend' (Coleridge's own note).

lines 51–3: Compare *This Lime-Tree Bower My Prison*, lines 11–15.

Page 170: FEARS IN SOLITUDE: Coleridge himself had extracts of this poem reprinted in 1809 in an attempt to prove that his early writings did not have 'the least bias to Irreligion, Immorality, or Jacobinism'. In spite of Coleridge's careful selection of passages, it failed to convince his readers even at the time. Southey wrote to Danvers when the extracts were published: 'If he was not a Jacobine, in the common acceptation of the name, I wonder who the Devil was.' The selection printed here gives a fairer indication of the poem as a whole than does Coleridge's which, of course, implies a more straight-forwardly patriotic and generally orthodox piece. Appropriately enough Coleridge altered the title of the poem when he so selectively published it again to 'Fears *Of* Solitude'. Elsewhere he calls the original poem 'a sort of middle thing between Poetry and Oratory', and we have selected extracts mainly to typify the views it expresses.

Page 174: THE NIGHTINGALE: Coleridge sent this poem to Wordsworth in 1798 with the following lines of introduction:

> *In stale blank verse a subject stale*
> *I send per post my Nightingale;*
> *And like an honest bard, dear Wordsworth,*
> *You'll tell me what you think my Bird's worth.*

> *My opinion's briefly this –*
> *His bill he opens not amiss;*
> *And when he has sung a stave or so,*
> *His breast and some small space below,*
> *So throbs & swells, that you might swear*
> *No vulgar music's working there.*
> *So far, so good; but then 'od rot him!*
> *There's something falls off at his bottom.*
> *Yet sure no wonder it should breed,*
> *That my Bird's Tail's a tail indeed*
> *And makes its own inglorious harmony*
> *Aeolio crepitu, non carmine.*

line 40: the poem is, of course, addressed to William and Dorothy Wordsworth.
line 50: The castle has been identified as Enmore Castle, near Nether Stowey, owned by Lord Egmont. His agent, John Cruikshank was credited with inspiring *The Ancient Mariner*, by reporting to Coleridge a 'strange dream' in which he 'fancied he saw a skeleton ship with figures in it', and the 'gentle Maid' of line 69 seems to have been Cruikshank's sister, Ellen.
line 91: My dear babe: Hartley Coleridge (born 19th September 1796) who appears in *Frost at Midnight,* and a poem later appended to *Christabel* (see notes to *Christabel*). The anecdote here is a versification of an entry

Coleridge made in his note-book: 'Hartley fell down & hurt himself – I caught him up crying & screaming – & ran out of doors with him. The Moon caught his eye – he ceased crying immediately – & his eyes & the tears in them, how they glittered in the Moonlight!'

Page 177: KUBLA KHAN: Coleridge's own account of the poem's origin is as follows:

> In the summer of the year 1797, the Author, then in ill health, had retired to a lonely farm-house between Porlock and Linton, on the Exmoor confines of Somerset and Devonshire. In consequence of a slight indisposition, an anodyne had been prescribed, from the effects of which he fell asleep in his chair at the moment that he was reading the following sentence, or words of the same substance, in 'Purchas's Pilgrimage': 'Here the Khan Kubla commanded a palace to be built, and a stately garden thereunto. And thus ten miles of fertile ground were inclosed with a wall'. The Author continued for about three hours in a profound sleep at least of the external senses, during which time he has the most vivid confidence, that he could not have composed less than two to three hundred lines; if that indeed can be called composition in which all the images rose up before him as *things*, with a parallel production of the correspondent expressions, without any sensation or consciousness of effort. On awakening he appeared to himself to have a distinct recollection of the whole, and taking his pen, ink, and paper, instantly and eagerly wrote down the lines that are here preserved. At this moment he was unfortunately called out by a person on business from Porlock, and detained by him above an hour, and on his return to his room, found, to his no small surprise and mortification, that though he still retained some vague and dim recollection of the general purport of the vision, yet, with the exception of some eight or ten scattered lines, and images, all the rest had passed away like the images on the surface of a stream into which a stone has been cast, but, alas! without the after restoration of the latter!

This account dates from 1816. It was designed as an apology for 'A Fragment' which Coleridge felt had to be offered as a 'psychological curiosity' rather than because of 'any supposed *poetic* merits'. Critics have therefore felt free to mistrust it. There has been controversy about the date of *Kubla Khan*, the extent of the influence of opium if any, and the significance of Coleridge's misquotation from *Purchas his Pilgrimage*: the passage in fact reads 'In Xamdu did Cublai Can build a stately Palace, encompassing sixteene miles of plaine ground with a wall, wherein are fertile Meddowes, pleasant Springs, delightfull Streames, and all sorts of beasts of chase and game, and in the middest thereof a sumptuous house of pleasure.' Is Coleridge's Kubla supposed to be an ideal creator, or a self-indulgent tyrant who is culpably insensitive to the forces represented by the sacred river? Does the damsel with the dulcimer represent a worthier alternative, or merely the imaginative means by which the poet can imitate an admirable Kubla? And how should we read 'Could I revive within me/ Her symphony and song': does it imply a resignation to failure, or a qualified optimism? One possibility is that Coleridge vaguely had Napoleon in mind when writing the poem. Coleridge associated Napoleon's worst ambitions with the savagery traditionally ascribed by the 18th Century Englishman to the East. Napoleon's behaviour would have been more comprehensible if he had been brought up 'in the untamed plains of Tartary'; he was attempting to transform 'the nations of Europe into the unreasoning hordes of a Babylonian or Tartar Empire'. When Napoleon invaded Egypt and claimed to have become a Mahommedan, 'the Saviour of the East' as Coleridge ironically called him, was clearly comparable to earlier threats to Europe posed by Moslem invaders. Coleridge described him as a 'Mad realizer of Mad Dreams' but was at first ambivalent about the grandeur of his plans. In one curious entry in his note-book he sees Napoleon's ambition to lay out the world anew as comparable to the creativity of both the poet, and the gardener – 'Poet Bonaparte – Layer of a World-garden'. This obviously brings one close to the role of Kubla Khan; perhaps Coleridge's discomfort about the poem and his dismissal of its ability to mean anything very coherent can be explained by his being vaguely aware of this connexion. To claim for the poet as dangerously revolutionary a role, as that occupied in the European imagination by the Mongol invaders was one thing; to associate it with the very recent threat of Napoleon would have been too much.

line 1: Khan: Coleridge almost certainly pronounced this as it was often spelt in his time, 'Can'.

line 3: Alph: Various suggestions have been made as to the name's implications: including the Nile, the Alpheus of Greek mythology (which flowed underground before emerging as the fountain Arethusa), and the initial letter of the Greek Alphabet, Alpha, with its suggestion of the origin of language.

lines 30–1: the space between these sections is reinstated from the manuscript.

line 41: Mount Abora: Possibly Mount Amara whose summit according to Peter Heyleyn's *Cosmographie* (1652) was enclosed by a high wall. Inside it there were gardens and places where 'the younger sons of the *Emperour* are continually inclosed, to avoid sedition: they enjoy whatever is fit for delight or *Princely* education'. It contained 'such ravishing

[249]

pleasures of all sorts, that some have taken (but mistaken) it for the place of *Paradise*'.

Page 179: LINES COMPOSED IN A CONCERT-ROOM: The version given here is that of first publication (1799, also the year of composition), but with the final couplet omitted. When published in the *Morning Post* this version ended with the unaccountably incomplete lines 'Leaving un . . . . . undebas'd/A . . . . . . world made worthy of its God'. Coleridge apparently never found satisfactory words to fill the blanks, and in all later editions cut out the last eighteen lines of the poem. These three omitted stanzas are essential to the poem's meaning, but clearly the last of them seriously damages its effect by ending so lamely. The best compromise seems to be to allow the poem to continue to the revolutionary thoughts which are its proper conclusion, and to omit only the last two incomplete lines. Coleridge's decision to suppress the other sixteen lines as well in 1817 was clearly motivated by ideological embarrassment.

Page 181: INTRODUCTION TO THE TALE OF THE DARK LADIE: The version of first publication in 1799. The pretence Coleridge later made that this was not the beginning of an incomplete poem, but a poem in its own right called *Love* led him to suppress the opening four stanzas and the last three. Lines 101–104 were also suppressed, though in this case the motivation is presumably Bowdlerization.

Page 186: THE MAD MONK: Written in 1800, this is clearly the stylistic source of Wordsworth's *Immortality Ode* of 1802.

It is also an example of Coleridge's interest in the way that distressed minds see reflexions of their own guilt and fear in the environment around them. Coleridge wrote that *The Three Graves* of 1798 (like the *Ancient Mariner* written in collaboration with Wordsworth) was designed to show 'the possible effect on the imagination from an idea violently and suddenly impressed on it . . . the progress and the symptoms of the morbid action on the fancy from the beginning'. *The Mad Monk* is clearly based on a similar idea, and therefore may have its relevance to *The Ancient Mariner* which it resembles in its use of a narrative framework, and the tone of its ending. *The Ancient Mariner* could be seen as a dramatic monologue – as concerned with the way a man in extreme suffering sees the universe, as with the objective nature of the universe itself.

Page 187: A LETTER TO . . . . . .: Written on 4th April 1802 to Sara Hutchinson. Her sister, Mary, was to marry Wordsworth, and her life to be more and more bound up with that of William and Dorothy. Coleridge by contrast was trapped in a bitterly unhappy marriage, guilty about his beloved children and frustrated in his illicit love for Sara, whom he saw as only likely to be made miserable by further contact with him. He was physically ill, convinced of his inadequacy as a writer, jealously aware of Wordsworth's continuing success both as poet and man, and confused as to what was cause, and what effect, in the vicious circle of his miseries. Most of this revealingly autobiographical poem was never published by Coleridge. The remainder, reordered so as to alter its implications, was published as *Dejection: An Ode*.

line 86: the seat was built as an act of friendship by Coleridge and the Wordsworths in 1800.

line 284: Philomel: The Nightingale – perhaps a sad reference to Coleridge's poem and the times of easy friendship and shared creativity with the Wordsworths.

Page 197: CHAMOUNY; THE HOUR BEFORE SUNRISE: The poem was in fact inspired by a landscape much closer to home than the Alps. Coleridge wrote in a letter to Sotheby in September 1802: 'Nature has her proper interest; & he will know what it is, who believes & feels, that every Thing has a Life of it's own, & that we are all *one Life*. A Poet's *Heart & Intellect* should be *combined, intimately* combined & *unified*, with the great appearances in Nature – & not merely held in solution & loose mixture with them, in the shape of formal Similes. . . . That this is deep in our Nature, I felt when I was on Sca' fell – . I involuntarily poured forth a Hymn in the manner of the *Psalms*, tho' afterwards I thought the Ideas &c disproportionate to our humble mountains – & accidentally lighting on a short Note in some Swiss Poems, concerning the Vale of Chamouny, & it's Mountain, I transferred myself thither, in the Spirit, & adapted my former feelings to these grander external objects.' A letter of 25th August gives a more detailed account of the experience on Sca Fell and at Lodore: 'What a sight it is to look down on such a Cataract! – the wheels, that circumvolve in it – the leaping up & plunging forward of that infinity of Pearls & Glass Bulbs – the continual *change* of the *Matter*, the perpetual *Sameness* of the *Form* – it is an awful Image & Shadow of God & the World.' 'Lodore is the Precipitation of the fallen Angels from Heaven, Flight & Confusion, & Distraction, but all harmonised into one majestic Thing by the genius of Milton, who describes it. . . . I have seen nothing equal to it in the Prints & Sketches of the Scotch & Swiss Cataracts.' In trying to adapt the inspiration of the Lake District to the more modish setting of the Alps Coleridge did himself some poetic disservice. In his own manuscript note to a revised line in a later text he confesses 'I had written a much finer Line when Sca' Fell was in my Thoughts'. We print the first available text complete with that 'finer line' (line 28) from the *Morning Post* of 11th September 1802.

Page 200: THE PAINS OF SLEEP: The text is that of the earliest known draft; it was sent to Southey in a letter of 11th September 1803. The version that Coleridge published in 1816 aspires to a restraint and dignity quite alien to the poem. Lines 52–4, for instance, were cut presumably because they caught all too perfectly a tone of whining self-pity and throughout the published version Coleridge polishes away the rawness with which he had revealed his guilt-obsessed nightmares. More detailed accounts in the Note-books suggest that the female Life-in-Death figure which haunts so much of the poetry was only too familiar to Coleridge in his own dreams:

'I was followed up & down by a frightful pale woman, who, I thought, wanted to kiss me, & had the property of giving a shameful disease by breathing in the face . . . & again I dreamt that a figure of a woman of a gigantic Height, dim & indefinite & smokelike appeared – & that I was forced to run up toward it.'
(October 1802)

'Awoke after long struggles & with faint screaming from persecuting Dream . . . struggling up against an unknown impediment, some woman on the other side about to relieve me.'
(November 1803)

'Bad dreams out rushes a university Harlot, who insists on my going with her / offer her a shilling – seem to get away a moment / when she overtakes me again / I am not to go to another while she is "biting" – these were her words / – this will not satisfy her . . . the Harlot in white with her open Bosom . . . in an after Dream / a little weak contemptible wretch offering his services, & I (as before afraid to refuse them) literally & distinctly remembered a former dream, in which I had suffered most severely, this wretch leaping on me & grasping my Scrotum.'
(December 1803)

It has recently been argued that this nightmare woman was the product of opium which Coleridge was taking in increasing amounts in 1803. But she appears in the poetry as early as 1791. In *Honour,* for instance Coleridge is seduced by Pleasure:

> *Around my neck she throws her fair white arms,*
> *I meet her loves, and madden at her charms.*

[252]

However, Geraldine-like, she turns out to be 'a hideous hag' and offers only 'Disease and loathing and remorse'. In *Happiness* written in the same year 'Luxury' is personified in remarkably similar terms and certainly by 1800 the nightmare woman is well-documented in the Note-books: 'a most frightful dream of a Woman whose features were blended with darkness catching hold of my right eye & attempting to pull it out – I caught hold of her arm fast – a horrid feel – Wordsworth cried out aloud to me hearing my scream – heard his cry & thought it cruel he did not come. . . . When I awoke my right eyelid swelled' (November 1800). The relevance of such nightmares to the guilt-obsessed ancient mariner is obvious.

Page 202: PSYCHE: 'Psyche means both Butterfly and Soul' (Coleridge's own note).

Page 204: SONG: Compare Byron's *So, We'll Go No More A Roving* (1817):

> So, we'll go no more a roving
>   So late into the night,
> Though the heart be still as loving,
>   And the moon be still as bright.
>
> For the sword outwears its sheath,
>   And the soul wears out the breast,
> And the heart must pause to breathe,
>   And love itself have rest.
>
> Though the night was made for loving,
>   And the day returns too soon,
> Yet we'll go no more a roving
>   By the light of the moon.

Index of First Lines

(*Note*: * indicates the first lines of extracts from longer poems which are not necessarily the opening lines of the poems themselves.)